The Teachings of
Denver C. Snuffer, Jr.

Volume 6:
2019

Reader's Edition

Reader's Edition ISBN 979-8-501108-41-7
Hardcover Edition ISBN 978-1-951168-71-1

Published in the United States by
Restoration Archive LLC

The Restoration Archive website address: www.restorationarchives.com

Table of Contents

Preface 5

Editor's Notes 13

Problems in Restoration History 15

Appendix to Eight Essays..29

Book of Mormon as a Covenant 39

Signs Follow Faith 63

Response from the Lord on Acceptance of Scriptures.........95

Celebrating the Family of Joseph and Emma Smith 97

Civilization..119

Temple Conference Q&A Session......................................177

The Second Annual Joseph Smith Restoration Conference 197

Love Others as Yourself...211

Authority, Keys, and Kingdom 229

The Book of Mormon Holds the Covenant Pattern for the Full
Restoration 249

Keeping the Covenant Conference Q&A Session 287

Appendix: Personal Revelation..307

Preface

If Christ's prophecy is true, Gentiles must at some point reject the fullness of the gospel. They must become extraordinarily lifted up in the pride of their hearts. How might this have already been accomplished? Does the claim they are the "only true church" and only they will be saved (while all others will be damned) fit the charge? The Lord foretold of gentile pride that will be *above all nations and above all the people of the whole earth* (3 Nephi 7:5 RE). There is evidence to suggest this has happened and is happening.

Mormon warned the Gentiles about polluting the holy church of God by loving wealth more than the suffering and needy (see Mormon 4:5 RE). If Mormon has given us the correct interpretation, the Gentiles have lifted themselves up in pride and love money and substance in a way that pollutes their church and offends God. This should awaken us. It is time for us to face our awful situation. Nothing can be done to improve this bleak outlook until our failures are acknowledged.

The Book of Mormon also predicts that, despite their failure, some few Gentiles could yet become covenant people and be numbered with Israel. Christ gave a sign to watch for as evidence the covenants made with the Father were about to be fulfilled. The sign was that at some point following the gentile rejection of the fullness, some few Gentiles would accept a covenant. When they accept the covenant, they become numbered with the remnant. These covenant Gentiles, numbered with the remnant, will build the last days' Zion.

> *The gentiles, if they will not harden their hearts, that they may repent, and come unto me, and be baptized in my name, and know of the true points of my doctrine, that they may be numbered among my people, O house of Israel — and when these things come to pass, that thy seed shall begin to know these things, it shall be a sign unto them that they may know that the work of the Father hath already commenced unto the fulfilling of the covenant which he hath made unto the people who are of the house of Israel. And when that day shall come, it shall come to pass that kings shall shut their mouths, for that which had not been*

told them shall they see, and that which they had not heard shall
they consider. (3 Nephi 9:11 RE)

This promised sign happened on September 3, 2017 in Boise, Idaho when the Lord renewed a covenant with the Gentiles. Some of the Gentiles are now numbered among the Lord's people as part of the House of Israel. They have the right, if they continue faithfully, to establish Zion. To do so, the lusts, strife, and contentions that doomed the Gentiles in Joseph Smith's day must be avoided.

The history of the Restoration is incomplete and still being written. Its conclusion will be years in the future, and there is tremendous work left to complete. Until everything returns and God has gathered again in one all of His revelations, restored the patriarchal religion taught from the time of Adam until Abraham, established Zion, and opened the veil between Heaven and Earth so that God, men, and angels again mingle with one another, the Restoration is not finished.

When the Earth is full of the knowledge of God as the seas are filled with water, the Restoration will be completed. At that future time, no one will need to say to another, "Know the Lord," because everyone will know Him.

Until then, there is a great task remaining. If you do not realize the work remains undone, then you do not believe the Book of Mormon.

All of us need to awaken and arise from the deep slumber that has overtaken the Restoration. We have been misled. We have fallen from the truth. We have rejected the fullness. And we must repent and return—or, as the Book of Mormon warns, "awake and arise" from this awful situation.

Study the depths of the Scriptures, and you'll find yourself in company with angels who will come help you to understand what is in them— and in particular, above all, study the Book of Mormon. The Book of Mormon is a giant Urim and Thummim. Used in the correct way, you'll find yourself in the company of angels who are helping to tutor you—in a conversation—as you look into an understanding of what's written in the Scriptures. But it follows an order. It follows a pattern.

The Book of Mormon explains a mature form of faith in God: resilient in the face of difficulty, enduring in the day of trouble, comforting in the moment of affliction. The faith of the Book of Mormon writers is not superficial, conditional, and weak. It bears up under trial; it is proven in troubles; it accompanies during afflictions. What if trials, afflictions, and troubles are not really negative? What if they are gifts provided as an opportunity to prove us therewith so that we and God may show what is in our heart?

We want a faith that will respond like Google. We don't want God to prepare a banquet; we want fast-food and a short-order cook and someone that will slap something on our plate fast, fast, fast! And the Book of Mormon is saying, "Slow down. Diligence isn't quick. Patience isn't fast."

Patience. Patience and diligence. Diligence and patience (see Alma 16:29-30 RE).

There is a great deal left to be done. And there is no one seriously entertaining the possibility of constructing a city of holiness, a city of peace, a people that are fruit "worthy to be laid up against the harvest." No one has made the effort until now. And while you may look at us and say, "You've done a crude job; you've done a rudimentary job; it needs improvement," then help us improve it! Stop sitting back and throwing rocks! This is a time to gather, not to disperse.

If you'll look at the words of the covenant that was offered in September of 2017, what you'll find is that Christ wants us—like the Book of Mormon explains—to be meek, to be humble, and to be easily entreated.   And therefore, entreat one another to honor God, and recognize that all of us aspire to be equal, whether you're at the top or at the root of the allegorical tree. The aspiration is the same: to be equal.

God's covenant is for and about people: His people. It is not possible for **an individual** to keep the covenant. Everybody rises together, or everybody fails together. The covenant can only be kept as a community. Individuals acting alone can never accomplish what is required of the group.

The prophecies of God's last-days' work and the fulfillment of God's covenants with the Fathers are not merely for individual salvation. The covenants are about "people" or a divinely organized community. Righteous individuals (isolated and scattered throughout the world) are incapable of vindicating the promises God made to the Fathers. There must be people gathered together and living the correct pattern before the Lord returns.

The Lord has every intention of keeping His promise to Enoch. There will be those who are gathered. There must be people gathered to a place, a holy city that meets the description and fulfills the promises God made. The people must gird up their loins or, in other words, must be living the godly religion that declares things as they really are —a religion founded on truth. Truth requires us to know things as they were, as they are, and as they are to come. Many past things that are hidden from the world must be revealed. God's people must know ancient truths so their hearts can turn to the Fathers. But it will be to covenant people, not individuals, to whom this outpouring will be given. A covenant body will belong in a New Jerusalem. The City of Enoch will "meet **them** there," and then they and the Lord "will receive **them** into our bosom." This is something more than individual salvation. Those involved will be individually saved, but the community itself must exist as something greater than individuals. There must be a "body" or "bride" for the Bridegroom to embrace.

The Lord is equal to the challenge He has set by covenant with the Fathers. He will establish a new civilization. It will be founded on the fullness of His gospel. Lost truths will be restored. The path of righteousness will be returned.

Society is broken. Everywhere we see corrupt cultures based on corrupt laws, corrupt religions, corrupt values, and ultimately, corrupt thought. Beginning again requires re-civilizing people. To be free from corruption requires a change in thinking. If the Lord is to accomplish this, there will need to be a new temple at the center of that new civilization.

The first temples were the center of life, government, education, culture, and art. This was handed down from the first generations. The temple was the foundation before and will need to be the foundation again. When there has been an apostasy, temple-building has been part of restoring. A new civilization will only become possible through teachings learned in the future House of God. The necessary ordinances can only be restored in that setting. There you will receive an uncorrupted restoration of the original faith taught from the time of Adam until Abraham.

It is not enough to avoid outright evil. We have to be good. Being "good" means to be separate from the world, united in charity toward each other, and to have united hearts. If we are to be ready when the wedding party arrives, we must follow the Lord's commandments to us. They are for our good. He wants us to awaken and arise from an awful slumber.

The last-days' Zion and her people were planned, foretold, and chosen thousands of years ago to live on Earth when righteousness would come down out of Heaven. They will be here when truth is sent forth out of the Earth to bear testimony of Christ. And like a flood, righteousness and truth will sweep the Earth. Any who have witnessed a flood know that floodwaters carry a great deal of debris, dirt, and detritus. Today there is a flood of information, recordings, and teaching sweeping the Earth. Righteousness is sweeping the Earth, while floodwaters are disturbing the whole world. The flood overflowing the world today includes the promised righteousness and truth, but it requires the Lord's elect to distinguish between the filth, folly, and foolishness to find freedom from sin through Christ, who is the foundation of righteousness and truth.

We will never be Zion if we do not repent. All of us must repent, turn to face God with full purpose of heart, acting no hypocrisy, or we will not establish godly peace among us.

The Answer to the Prayer for Covenant and the Covenant are the beginning blueprint. That blueprint teaches the need to be better people. Following it is more challenging than reciting it. No one can learn what is required without doing it. Working together is the only way a society can grow together. Failing to do the hard work outlined in the covenant is failing to prepare for Zion.

If we do keep the Covenant, God's work will continue and will include the fullness previously offered to the Gentiles and rejected by them. The fullness can only be returned through a temple accepted by God as His House. He must return to restore that which has been lost. But ungodly people cannot build an acceptable house for God. Only those who keep the covenant together can establish a new civilization, with God's holy House at its center.

When the Gentiles repent and they return, then they're numbered back —just like the descendants of the Nephites. When they are awakened and repent and are taught the truth and return unto God, **all** become one house, one fold, one people.

> And I will remember the covenant which I have made with my people, and I have covenanted with them that I would gather them together in mine own due time, that I would give unto them again the land of their fathers for their inheritance… (3 Nephi 9:8 RE)

So, it should begin to emerge into your view that covenanting, remembering, repenting, returning, and accepting what God has to offer is the component in the last days that distinguishes whether or not the Gentiles are **redeemed**, whether or not they are to be **gathered**, whether or not they are to be **recognized** in the own due time of the Lord as His, to be protected and to be preserved against the harvest. It's not enough merely to have genealogical connection back to some remnant of Father Abraham.

It was always the design that the Gentiles should be gathered in—or that what is, in all likelihood, an unsavory, bitter-fruit-producing branch of the original tree should be taken and gathered back to the original root and gather nourishment from that original root, that they may come in and be numbered among the house of Israel. It's always been the intention of the Lord to restore the Gentiles and to make them the means through which the last-days' work would become accomplished.

There are numerous other passages in the Book of Mormon that speak to the same thing. The Book of Mormon is a forerunner—a harbinger —that was intended to say to the people who receive it: There are covenants that go back to the very beginning, to the original Fathers. Those covenants got renewed/they got restored/they got continued in the person of Abraham (who received all that had been there originally) coming out of apostasy and being adopted back into that line of Patriarchs. That original covenant material provoked the creation of the Book of Mormon, and it is one of the major testimonies that is given to us by the Book of Mormon about the work that God intends to do in the last days.

You can believe in the Bible; you can accept Jesus as your Savior; you can be (in the words of the Evangelical community) "born again." You can be (in the words of Latter-day Saints) someone whose "calling and election is made sure." But the work of God, at this point, is not merely about individual salvation; it is the work of fulfilling the covenants that were made with the Fathers. It is the work of restoring again that original gospel (of which the law given to Moses pointed forward to but did not comprehend).

You will always be free to choose, but the work of the covenants that the Book of Mormon foretell are to be accomplished through the reclaiming (by repentance and returning to Him) of Gentiles that will, ultimately, reach out to (and include) restoring the Lamanites/restoring the Jews to a knowledge of the works of the Father, that—**that**—is what is on the mind of God today. **That** is the purpose of the covenant that was given unto us in Boise just a few years ago. **That** is what fulfilling the covenant ultimately requires that **we** labor to achieve.

That effort began in earnest with the reclaiming of the Scriptures and the presenting of those to the Lord for His acceptance—and the marvelous news that God accepted them as adequate for His purpose for us and the commitment that He would labor with us to go forward (see "Response from the Lord on Acceptance of Scriptures," April 6, 2019, included in this volume).

Anyone can join the party. Anyone can come into this work. Anyone can remain a Catholic or a Presbyterian or a Latter-day Saint if they choose to do so. It doesn't matter. Those things are more like civic clubs. I don't care if you're a Rotarian or a Kiwanis Club member— means about the same thing as belonging to any of those church organizations. Associate with whoever you like to associate with, but you **must** accept baptism. You **must** accept the Book of Mormon. It **is** a **covenant**. The covenant must be accepted, and you **must** help labor alongside those who seek to return Zion.

There **is** a process that **is** underway. There are things we have to do. I believe when the command is given to build a temple that we're going to have to act with alacrity if we are going to be able to fulfill the covenants and the obligations that have been promised by God and handed to us to do.

But don't expect the world to get better, and don't expect organized religions to get better. Hopefully there will be more and more who come to take refuge among a band of believers who have no hierarchy, office, position, who have only ourselves to fellowship with informally, gathering at one another's homes, and occasionally renting facilities to meet in larger groups.

Each of us have the obligation to spread the truth and the knowledge that the Scriptures (that we now have) more accurately recover. We have to go back to what was given to us through Joseph Smith as the foundation in order to qualify to be able to move forward. The objective is clear: Rise up to occupy that high place where Zion is to be built. The battle rages all around. All must charge forward to engage the battle and hasten to the sound of that conflict. There must be success where others have failed.

April 11, 2021
Denver C. Snuffer, Jr.
Sandy, Utah

Editor's Notes

During 2017-2019, Denver embarked on a series of lectures for Christian audiences around the world, including live addresses in California, Texas, Georgia, Idaho, Alabama, and three in Utah. These lectures (some with Q&A sessions), together with a large body of video messages, papers, and blog posts, as well as other content (some of which is still underway as of this date), are scheduled to be compiled into a separate volume (or series, depending upon length) to be published after Denver indicates that the message he is delivering to the Christians has been completed. Therefore, those lectures are not included in this volume.

In January of 2021, while this volume was undergoing preparation for publication, the transcript of a lecture entitled "Personal Revelation," which was originally delivered October 16, 2008, became available. Denver subsequently expanded the transcript into a paper for inclusion in the Restoration Archive and for public release. That paper has therefore been added as an appendix to this volume.

Problems in Restoration History

Published on www.denversnuffer.com
January 1, 2019

Reconstructing a complete and accurate history for the Restoration using available records is challenging if not outright impossible. Although there have been many histories written attempting to provide an accurate account, serious problems remain in understanding the Restoration. There are two separate challenges. First, it is difficult to describe an accurate record of events. That is followed by the greater difficulty to decide how to interpret the events. History requires understanding how and why events are to be understood in an overall pattern. Determining that pattern is more challenging than sorting out the record.

Restoration history begins with Joseph Smith. He was a controversial figure, and people who met him became noteworthy because of their association with him. Assuming they had something to say regarding their relationship with him, their opinions about him became important to historians. Opinions based on personal experience with someone noteworthy are considered important, even if their contact was passing and colored by their prejudices, limitations, or ignorance. Hence, there are many contemporaneous opinions about Joseph Smith used by historians to reconstruct events.

Those unkindly disposed toward him took the opportunity to speak poorly about him. Any event that reflected badly (or any negative embellishment of an event) became part of the record. The earliest adverse account was by Doctor Philastus Hurlbut, who made it his mission to gather impugning affidavits about Joseph Smith. Eber D. Howe published that collection in the anti-Mormon book *Mormonism Unvailed.* There were also four derisive pamphlets antagonistic to Joseph Smith and the religion he was founding published in 1838. A flood of other unfavorable histories soon followed. Historians who want to portray Joseph in a negative light have a wealth of information from such sources with which to compose a contrary interpretation.

Followers and believers in Joseph's claims were disposed to tell—and oftentimes embellish—anything that held him in a positive light. Doting admirers wrote a great deal of laudatory material. Historians who want to portray Joseph in a heroic light also have a wealth of information from these sources with which to compose a positive interpretation.

Should the history of the Restoration be composed relying only on Joseph's critics? Should it be written relying only on Joseph's admirers? Until recently, most of the histories written of the Restoration chose one or the other. Recent histories attempt to walk a middle path and allow both sides to contribute to the story. However, both sides are prone to exaggeration and overstatement. Mixing them together is not much better than leaving them apart. Sorting through the contradictions has made for interesting storytelling, but it does not give an accurate history.

After the first challenge is addressed by deciding what facts to trust, the second problem is how to interpret the facts. Is there a theme? Is there an overall narrative that accounts for the facts, smoothing them into a consistent tale that makes sense?

Assembling events into a sensible story is influenced by what kind of historian tells the tale. For example, the Annales school of historical materialism categorizes events into major trends over long periods of time. Demographic changes, economic crises, even geography are used to explain why events happened. Cultural historians look at anthropological and linguistic themes to develop their account of history. Psychohistorians attempt to uncover the inner motivations of individuals to explain why things happened. They attempt to use social sciences to determine the emotional origin behind events. There are dozens of different schools of historical thought. How each retells these events is based on framing the experiences to fit their view of how history should be told. Writing history is explaining how to interpret events.

People do not live interpreted lives. They pass through a sequence of adventures, sometimes wildly disconnected from any overall theme, day-by-day, inside common experiences. Even if you are in the place at the time something happens because all the world is at war with one another, and you have been brought to the battlefield by one of the great opposing powers, your day will begin by waking up and eating breakfast. President Roosevelt and Adolph Hitler are not part of your daily experience. Even Eisenhower, as Supreme Commander of the Allied Forces, is so distant from an infantryman as to hardly be noticed in daily life. If you ask the infantryman to tell his story about what happened on June 6, 1944, he will tell you of the violence, noise, injuries, and death he witnessed on 175 yards of a 3.6-mile-long beach code-named "Omaha." Life is experienced in a microcosm. History is told as if each microcosm fit into a narrative having sweep and breadth and height to give meaning and message for the microcosm.

During the leading edge of the attack, one Navy sailor who piloted a landing craft filled with Army Infantrymen to Omaha Beach was so frightened by the conflagration he sailed toward that he dropped the ramp too soon, exposing the troops aboard to incoming fire. The Infantrymen on his boat—including my father—jumped into the English Channel weighed down by approximately 80 pounds of gear and munitions. Because they had not yet reached the beach, my father and his companions faced drowning as the first threat in the battle. Years later he reflected, "If I had known the Navy pilot was a coward, I would have shot him, commandeered the boat, and drove it ashore to save my friends. Everyone shorter than me drowned before they had a chance to fight."

What my father saw, heard, and felt that day was deeply personal and extremely local. His life that day (and every day thereafter) was experienced moment-to-moment with no overarching theme or school of interpretation guiding it. He lived it; it was his. And when he died after 86 years of those experiences, he took them all with him.

How should his story be told? Hiding behind tank traps on the shoreline was necessary to survive the incoming machine-gun and mortar fire. It was common sense. But after these men had been surrounded for a time by deafening death and dismemberment [and] pitiful cries from the dead and dying, paralyzing desperation turned to outrage and anger. That supreme moral indignation propelled first a few and then a wave of men from behind the safety of the tank traps, mortar divots, and fallen comrades to charge their protected enemy above. These men hazarded their lives to end this outrage. The value of lives of their slaughtered friends deserved respect. It was because of their losses that they charged forward to stop this unmerciful hail of death.

Were there geopolitical issues involved? Not for my father and his companions on that morning. Was military history being written? Of course, but that was nothing to those men. They gave it no thought. A violent and merciless enemy behind concrete and atop a bluff overlooking the beach needed to be destroyed. Every instant these predators remained capable of inflicting death was an insult to the memory of slain friends. More friends would die in coming moments if those in the bunkers overhead were not destroyed.

Great moments, even the greatest of moments, are experienced only by individuals inside a very small sphere. This is true of the Restoration. The great narratives that have been written about the Restoration tell us nothing about what happened. Historians always interpret and massage an account no one experienced, no one lived, no one understood as it happened. Historians provide interpretations. They cannot tell us what individuals understood when they were writing letters or diaries. They cannot explain how personal conversations were interpreted or how difficult events were framed in the lives of those who experienced them. Historians of the Restoration can never explain what individuals understood and experienced who wrote the letters and diaries, who had the personal conversations, who lived through the difficult events. We are all denied access to the daily thoughts of those now long deceased. We do not know, and those involved cannot tell us.

Perhaps it does not matter which school of history is used in retelling the story of the Restoration. Maybe all of them will invariably be wrong. That seems to be what Nephi predicted. Nephi condemns using our carefully studied historical techniques rather than inspiration from God:

> *They shall contend one with another, and their priests shall contend one with another, and they shall teach with their learning, and deny the holy ghost which giveth utterance. And they deny the power of God, the Holy One of Israel. And they say unto the people, Hearken unto us and hear ye our precept...there shall be many which shall teach after this manner false, and vain, and foolish doctrines, and shall be puffed up in their hearts, and shall seek*

*deep to hide their counsels from the Lord. And their works shall be
in the dark, and the blood of the saints shall cry from the ground
against them.* (2 Nephi 12:1 RE)

Restoration history has been more or less composed using the "learning
of men" or recognized historical interpretive forms. If teaching with
man's learning will cause us to accept false, vain, and foolish ideas, then
it is a mistake. True history should be informed by God's viewpoint.
Do people believe the Scriptures? I could not find a history written by
someone who trusted Scripture to provide the interpretation.

I wrote a history of the Restoration. In it, instead of interpreting
events from existing records, I used the Scriptures to give the
interpretation. The book assumes the prophecies found in the Book of
Mormon and the revelations of Joseph Smith give to us the correct
interpretation. Using the prophecies as the framework, I looked for
support in the known events to see if the events met the predicted
narrative. There is abundant proof. It is sobering.

For example, Christ prophesied the Gentiles would reject the fullness
of the gospel. He attributed the prophecy to His Father. The prophecy
is unequivocal and does not speak about gentile rejection as merely
possible or uncertain but declares it as an inevitable event to certainly
occur:

> *At that day when the gentiles shall sin against my gospel, and shall
> reject the fullness of my gospel, and shall be lifted up in the pride of
> their hearts above all nations and above all the people of the whole
> earth, and shall be filled with all manner of lyings, and of deceits,
> and of mischiefs, and all manner of hypocrisy, and murders, and
> priestcrafts, and whoredoms, and of secret abominations, and if
> they shall do all these things, and shall reject the fullness of my
> gospel, Behold, saith the Father, I will bring the fullness of my
> gospel from among them.* (3 Nephi 7:5 RE)

The question then is what would that have looked like? Was there
anything in the events from 1820 to 1844 to suggest the Gentiles did
reject the fullness of Christ's gospel? Joseph Smith was driven out of
Kirtland. In Missouri, the betrayal by church leaders (including the
three witnesses and several apostles) resulted in his imprisonment.

There is a detailed account of this treachery by the Mormons in a book about Joseph.

If Christ's prophecy is true, Gentiles must at some point reject the fullness of the gospel. They must become extraordinarily lifted up in the pride of their hearts. How might this have already been accomplished? Does the claim they are the "only true church" and only they will be saved (while all others will be damned) fit the charge? The Lord foretold of gentile pride that will be *above all nations and above all the people of the whole earth* (Ibid.). There is evidence to suggest this has happened and is happening.

As for lying and deceiving, the LDS Church appears to have adopted dishonesty as a policy to deal with troubling historical issues. The institution's history of deceit is not difficult to uncover. Because of this historic lack of honesty, the LDS Historian's Office is now publishing essays on church history to address this lack of candor. The essays attempt to explain First Vision Accounts; Plural Marriage in Kirtland and Nauvoo; Race and the Priesthood; Book of Mormon Translation; Translation and Historicity of the Book of Abraham; Joseph Smith's Teachings about Priesthood, Temple, and Women; and others. The LDS Church recently published a new version of the Restoration history using heterodox sources for the first time.

An example of some historical hypocrisy is evident in looking at the part the Mormons played in alienating their neighbors in Missouri and Illinois. The Missourians were rough, but Mormons were equally terrible neighbors. It was the July 4th "Salt Sermon" given by Sidney Rigdon that first threatened to "exterminate" the Missourians. However, when Mormons retell the events, they express outrage and contempt over Governor Lilburn Boggs' Extermination Order as if he originated the idea of "extermination." Even when Mormons were the aggressors, they portray themselves as victims and all others as their unjust persecutors. Sometimes Missourians were scared by threats from the Mormons. Sometimes Mormons shot first. Sometimes Mormons raided and burned farms first.

These are not happy things. There is no celebrating the gentile rejection of the fullness. But it is more harmful to ignore that rejection than to acknowledge it. There can be no attempt to fix the failure until there is an admission that it has happened. The fullness was rejected. Mormonism lapsed into apostasy.

Mormon warned the Gentiles about polluting the holy church of God by loving wealth more than the suffering and needy:

> *O ye wicked, and perverse, and stiffnecked people, why have you built up churches unto yourselves to get gain? Why have ye transfigured the holy word of God that ye might bring damnation upon your souls? Behold, look ye unto the revelations of God, for behold, the time cometh at that day when all these things must be fulfilled. Behold, the Lord hath shewn unto me great and marvelous things concerning that which must shortly come at that day when these things shall come forth among you. Behold, I speak unto you as if ye were present, and yet ye are not. But behold, Jesus Christ hath shewn you unto me, and I know your doing, and I know that ye do walk in the pride of your hearts. And there are none, save a few only, who do not lift themselves up in the pride of their hearts, unto the wearing of very fine apparel, unto envying, and strifes, and malice, and persecutions, and all manner of iniquity. And your churches, yea, even every one, have become polluted because of the pride of your hearts. For behold, ye do love money, and your substance, and your fine apparel, and the adorning of your churches, more than ye love the poor and the needy, the sick and the afflicted. O ye pollutions, ye hypocrites, ye teachers who sell yourselves for that which will canker, why have ye polluted the holy church of God? Why are ye ashamed to take upon you the name of Christ? Why do ye not think that greater is the value of an endless happiness than that misery which never dies? Because of the praise of the world? Why do ye adorn yourselves with that which hath no life, and yet suffer the hungry, and the needy, and the naked, and the sick, and the afflicted to pass by you and notice them not?* (Mormon 4:5 RE)

There is proof this has happened among the Gentiles who believe the Book of Mormon. The LDS church-owned *Deseret News* helped advance a program to discourage the public from noticing and contributing to beggars. Billboards in Salt Lake proclaimed:

- "Support panhandlers, and you support drug trafficking."
- "Support panhandlers, and you support crime."
- "Support panhandlers, and you support alcoholism."

LDS church-owned KSL did an expose titled, *Business of Begging: The real stories behind Utah panhandling,* in which every story they reported showed the panhandlers were engaged in fraud and criminality. There is compelling evidence—or at least some reason—to conclude the Gentiles, in their pride, suffer the needy and hungry to pass by unnoticed.

In addition to advocating that people suffer the hungry and needy to pass by unnoticed, the LDS Church has also accumulated great wealth. The Salt Lake television station, KUTV, reported that at the end of 2017, the LDS Church had stock investments totaling $32,769,914,000.00. The LDS Church invested in excess of $2 billion in a shopping mall across from Temple Square in Salt Lake City. In November 2013, the LDS Church purchased 382,834 acres in the Florida panhandle for $565,000,000. The *Christian Science Monitor* reported this purchase (added to the previous holdings—which include Deseret Ranches near Orlando, Florida) made the LDS Church the largest landowner in Florida.

The LDS Church does not make its financial information public. The total value of its land, banking, printing, radio, television, universities, and other non-religious holdings likely dwarf the total value of its extensive chapel, temple, and church administration properties. Consider for a moment the present value of the LDS Church against the words of Mormon that *ye do love money, and your substance, and your fine apparel, and the adorning of your churches, more than ye love the poor and the needy, the sick and the afflicted* (Ibid.). There is compelling proof (or at least some reason) to conclude that "the holy church of God" has been polluted by the Gentiles. Why not at least consider the possibility that prophecy has been fulfilled?

If Mormon has given us the correct interpretation, the Gentiles have lifted themselves up in pride and love money and substance in a way that pollutes their church and offends God. This should awaken people. It is time to face an awful situation. Nothing can be done to improve this bleak outlook until the failures are acknowledged.

In a January 1841 revelation, the Gentiles were commanded to build a temple. God offered to visit that temple and restore again the fullness. However, God's offer was conditional, and the required temple was to be built within "sufficient time" to meet His command:

> *But I command you, all you my saints, to build a house unto me, and I grant unto you a sufficient time to build a house unto me, and during this time your baptisms shall be acceptable unto me. But behold, at the end of this appointment, your baptisms for your dead shall not be acceptable unto me. And if you do not these things, at the end of the appointment, you shall be rejected as a church, with your dead, says the Lord your God. For verily I say unto you that after you have had sufficient time to build a house unto me, wherein the ordinance of baptizing for the dead belongs, and for which the same was instituted from before the foundation of the world, your baptisms for your dead cannot be acceptable unto me, for therein are the keys of the Holy Priesthood ordained that you may receive honor and glory.* (T&C 141:11)

The revelation does not explain how long the "appointment" would last. It did not set a limit on "sufficient time" for the command to be accomplished. But the Lord does make it very clear that if the commandment was not obeyed, the Gentiles faced the risk of being rejected as a church with their kindred dead. Accordingly, this revelation set a requirement that put the Gentiles in peril.

Although there was no set time, there was a sign given. The sign would make it possible to determine whether the time expired and the Gentiles were rejected. Here is the sign:

> *If you labor with all your mights, I will consecrate that spot that it shall be made holy. And if my people will hearken unto my voice and unto the voice of my servants whom I have appointed to lead my people, behold, verily I say unto you, They shall not be moved out of their place. And it shall come to pass that if you build a house unto my name and do not do the things that I say, I will not perform the oath which I make unto you, neither fulfill the promises which you expect at my hands, says the Lord. For instead of blessings, you, by your own works, bring cursings, wrath, indignation, and judgments upon your own heads, by your follies*

> *and by all your abominations which you practice before me, says the Lord.* (T&C 141:13)

The "appointment" that granted "sufficient time" would either be accomplished or the Gentiles would be rejected. The sign of accomplishing the commandment would be: "They shall not be moved out of their place." This could either mean the "servants…appointed to lead" (Joseph and Hyrum) would not be moved out of their place, or it could refer to the Gentiles that would not be moved out of Nauvoo. Either meaning was fulfilled by the sign of gentile rejection. Joseph and Hyrum were slain three-and-a-half years later on June 27, 1844. At that time, the Nauvoo Temple had only been completed up to the second floor. So, the servants were removed. Then in the winter of 1846, the Gentiles were forcibly evicted from Nauvoo under threat of attack. Both the Lord's chosen servants and the proud Nauvoo Gentiles themselves were moved out of their place. Either way, the events comport with the promised sign and testify that God rejected the Gentiles.

The second part of the sign foretold what would happen thereafter. Instead of securing the blessings God offered them, the Gentiles would inherit "cursings, wrath, indignation, and judgments upon [their] own heads, by [their] follies and by all [their] abominations." The history of the gentile suffering in their westward exile to live on a salt flat is well documented. Nauvoo was located beside the largest river in North America. The Gentiles relocated to a desert where they struggled for generations to survive.

Like Mormon, Nephi also foretold of the gentile failure to receive and obey when given the opportunity. He identified it as a problem caused by gentile leadership:

> *Yea, they have all gone out of the way, they have become corrupted; because of pride, and because of false teachers, and false doctrine, their churches have become corrupted, and their churches are lifted up; because of pride, they are puffed up. They rob the poor because of their fine sanctuaries; they rob the poor because of their fine clothing, and they persecute the meek and the poor in heart because in their pride they are puffed up. They wear stiff necks and high heads, yea, and because of pride, and wickedness, and*

abominations, and whoredoms, they have all gone astray, save it be a few who are the humble followers of Christ. Nevertheless, they are led, that in many instances they do err because they are taught by the precepts of men. (2 Nephi 12:2 RE)

This description by Nephi, though slightly different, contains the same message as Mormon's. Corrupt leaders who teach false doctrine would lead the Gentiles. As though they already had all truth that would save them, they would urge and condone pride in their religion. Again the theme of robbing the poor by aggregating religious wealth describes the gentile rejection of the truth. Nephi states bluntly, "They have all gone astray." There is no true church but only prideful false ones that proclaim corrupt and false doctrine. "All" have "gone astray"—except only some "few who are the humble followers of Christ." It was to those I dedicated the first book I wrote.

Although the Gentiles were destined to reject the fullness, they nevertheless kept the Book of Mormon in print for over a century-and-a-half. The Book of Mormon contains the guidance necessary to recover the fullness. And the Book of Mormon also predicts that, despite their failure, some few Gentiles could yet become covenant people.

Christ gave a sign to watch for as evidence the covenants made with the Father were about to be fulfilled. At some point following the gentile rejection of the fullness, some few Gentiles would accept a covenant. When they accept the covenant, they become numbered with the remnant. These covenant Gentiles, numbered with the remnant, will build the last days Zion.

The gentiles, if they will not harden their hearts, that they may repent, and come unto me, and be baptized in my name, and know of the true points of my doctrine, that they may be numbered among my people, O house of Israel — and when these things come to pass, that thy seed shall begin to know these things, it shall be a sign unto them that they may know that the work of the Father hath already commenced unto the fulfilling of the covenant which he hath made unto the people who are of the house of Israel. And when that day shall come, it shall come to pass that kings shall shut their mouths, for that which had not been told them shall they see, and that which they had not heard shall they consider. (3 Nephi 9:11 RE)

This happened on September 3, 2017 in Boise, Idaho when the Lord renewed a covenant with the Gentiles. Some of the Gentiles are now numbered among the Lord's people as part of the House of Israel. They have the right, if they continue faithfully, to establish Zion. To do so, the lusts, strife, and contentions that doomed the Gentiles in Joseph Smith's day must be avoided.

No single individual ever experienced the history of the Restoration. After the church historian left the faith and absconded with the records he had maintained, Joseph Smith wrote down his recollection of events in 1838. Joseph could only tell what he knew. Thereafter, histories have been written by weaving together excerpts from here and there, never attempting to see if the results mirrored the story Scripture foretold. Even excerpts from here and there are not the full pictures. Mark Twain observed:

> What a wee little part of a person's life are his acts and his words! His real life is led in his head and is known to none but himself. All day long, and every day, the mill of his brain is grinding, and his thoughts, not those other things, are his history. His acts and his words are merely the visible, thin crust of his world, with its scattered snow summits and its vacant wastes of water—and they are so trifling a part of his bulk! A mere skin enveloping it. The mass of him is hidden—it and its volcanic fires that toss and boil, and never rest, night nor day. These are his life, and they are not written, and cannot be written. Every day would make a whole book of eighty thousand words—three hundred and sixty-five books a year. Biographies are but the clothes and buttons of the man—the biography of the man himself cannot be written.

There are many histories of D-Day. The codename for that invasion was "Operation Overlord." The plan was intended to spread soldiers across sites on the shores of Normandy (codenamed Utah, Sword, Gold, Juno, and Omaha beaches). The hope was for some or all to break through the shoreline defenses and establish an Allied base of operations to invade Europe.

My father rarely spoke of Omaha Beach. He never used his role in D-Day as a credential. For him it was just an experience, not something to boast about. Most of those who met him after WWII were unaware of his experience. He did not want it to define him.

My mother said for a long time after the war he would have a recurring nightmare. He dreamt he was in a foxhole that was overrun by Nazis. When he tried to shoot the soldier in front of him, his gun fell apart. His enemy took advantage of his defenselessness and bayonetted my father, at which point he would awaken in a jump, sometimes letting out a yell. After some years, the nightmares ended.

My father was reluctant to talk about the war. When we could coax something from him, it would be a sentence, not a paragraph. He mentioned on one occasion the English Channel looked that morning as if it "was made of GI blood."

I was with him the night before he died. It was the first time he raised the subject of that battle. He said it puzzled him why his life had been spared when so many of his friends had died that morning. I gave him no answer but know that without his survival, I would not have been born. He was as healthy and well on the morning of June 7th as he had been before wading ashore on June 6th. Although his mind was perplexed by the kindness of providence watching over him and heaven allowing others to be injured or slaughtered that day, he lived gratefully and fully for nearly a half-century. His history was not written. In all the accounts that have explained D-Day, none of them can be complete if they do not address why providence spared some and took others. Of course, that is an answer only God can provide.

God has not written histories for most of this world's events. But God did give an account of the Restoration in Scripture. That account was composed as prophecy, foretelling how the Gentiles would first fail, and later some few would covenant with Him and be numbered with Israel.

The history of the Restoration is incomplete and still being written. Its conclusion will be years in the future, and there is tremendous work left to complete. Until everything returns and God has gathered again in one all of His revelations, restored the religion taught to Adam in the beginning, established Zion, and opened the veil between Heaven and Earth so that God, men, and angels again mingle with one another, the Restoration is not finished.

When the Earth is full of the knowledge of God as the seas are filled with water, the Restoration will be completed. At that future time, no one will need to say to another, "know the Lord," because everyone will know Him.

Until then, there is a great task remaining. If you do not realize the work remains undone, then you do not believe the Book of Mormon.

There is no reason to think us specially favored by God. But there is good reason to think us challenged by God to do much more than has been done by the Gentiles. There is every reason to fear failure because of the prior gentile failures. Even while a great and wealthy gentile church proclaims that it is the Lord's and it is the only true church and it cannot lead any astray, all need to awaken and arise from the deep slumber that has overtaken the Restoration. We have been misled. We have fallen from the truth. We have rejected the fullness. And we must repent and return—or, as the Book of Mormon warns, "awake and arise" from this awful situation.

There have been many casualties. We may miss those who are taken in by the many false claims exploding all around us. But the objective is clear: Rise up to occupy that raised bluff where Zion is to be built. The battle rages all around. All must charge forward to engage the battle and hasten to the sound of that conflict. There must be success where others have failed.

Appendix to Eight Essays

Published on www.denversnuffer.com
January 1, 2019

The most often discussed issue in Mormon history is polygamy. It is in the center of on-going controversy and continues to be publicly debated. A library of conflicting material has been written to imagine how it started. Therefore, polygamy is a useful topic to illustrate the challenge of reconstructing accurate history.

Mormons who followed Brigham Young were told that Joseph Smith introduced polygamy and intended to have it continue. Splinter groups from followers of Young likewise attribute its introduction and necessity to Joseph Smith. The RLDS rejected this idea. They trusted Smith's widow, Emma Smith, who denied that Joseph ever practiced polygamy. The renamed Community of Christ has (in recent years) begun to concede the point polygamy was Joseph Smith's creation.

Three documents are in this Appendix. They involve determining what events should be used for retelling history. These were written by eye-witnesses who lived through the events described in the letters and were composed in 1853, 1859, and 1879. The first two were written by William Marks, the stake president of Nauvoo at the time Joseph and Hyrum were killed. Both of his letters address polygamy. Both show Joseph Smith was opposed to the practice and intended to eliminate it in Nauvoo. These two letters raise as many questions as they answer but clearly show Joseph Smith was intent on eliminating polygamy or plural wives.

The third letter is by William B. Smith, one of the Church's twelve apostles and the brother of Joseph and Hyrum. He explains in his letter to Joseph's son what William understood caused the death of his father and uncle. William Smith believed there was a conspiracy among leaders in Nauvoo to kill Joseph and Hyrum. He also accuses Brigham Young, John Taylor, and Willard Richards of teaching secretly abominable doctrines involving the "plural wives system."

Even though the Nauvoo events and Carthage killings happened in the 1840s, we do not yet have an undisputed truth to tell. There are too many economic and ecclesiastical interests threatened by one story or the other. These three documents allow readers to reflect on how they should influence understanding events.

Should these sources be trusted? Did the stake president have a good opportunity to observe and report? Did he have any motivation to lie about the events? Did the brother and church apostle have a good opportunity to observe and report? Did he have any motivation to lie about the events? Should his suspicions be trusted? Does his description of those leading the LDS Church as "reveling in the spoils of the Church robbed from the innocent and unsuspecting saints" betray any jealousy or envy of their wealth and power? Or does it instead justify his conclusion that ambitious men benefitted by killing his brothers?

As a thought experiment, consider these three letters as reliable, and ask yourself: Do they change the way you understand the Restoration? If so, in what way do they change your understanding? Then consider them as unreliable, and ask yourself: Why should they be ignored? Are there any parts that should be considered, even if their overall message is unreliable? Does that change your understanding of the Restoration? If so, in what way do they change your understanding? Are they consistent with Scripture and prophecy?

Every document, letter, newspaper article, journal entry, and note that has been written by any of the eye-witnesses need to go through that same sifting. Almost all of the restoration histories were written by advocates without disclosing how they sifted their sources. They may not even have a criteria to test reliability. If they start with a premise in mind, they may cull through material to support their premise, ignoring and dismissing all contrary proof. This is how I wrote *Passing the Heavenly Gift*: I started with the premise that prophecy foretold what would happen. Then I looked to see if there was proof consistent with prophecy. That may not be what an impartial historian would do, but I believe it is the only likely way to find the truth.

—o0o—

Epistle of Wm. Marks, Chief Evangelical Teacher in the School of Faith, to all the Traveling Teachers, Quorums and Classes of said School, in Jehovah's Presbytery of Zion, Greeting:

Beloved Brethren:

Having been chosen and ordained chief Evangelical Teacher of the Schools of Faith in Jehovah's Presbytery of Zion, it becomes my duty, to say something by way of encouragement, and also by way of instruction to those who are placed under my care, and supervision, and first, by way of encouragement let me state what I know in reference to the work in which we are engaged, in order to do this I must of necessity refer to my experience in the church. I was a member of the church some ten years before the death of Joseph and Hyrum Smith. I was appointed President of the Stake in Kirtland, Ohio in 1837, and continued in that office at Kirtland until the fall of 1838, when I was called by Revelation to Far West, Mo.; but before I arrived there, the Saints were ordered to leave the State; and when the Stake was organized at Nauvoo in the fall of 1839, I was appointed President thereof and continued in that office up to the death of Joseph the prophet. I always believed the work was of Divine origin, and that Joseph Smith was called of God to establish the church among the Gentiles.

During my administration in the church I saw and heard of many things that was practiced and taught that I did not believe to be of God; but I continued to do and teach such principles as were plainly revealed, as the law of the church, for I thought that pure and holy principles only would have a tendency to benefit mankind. Therefore, when the doctrine of polygamy was introduced into the church as a principle of exaltation, I took a decided stand against it; which stand rendered me quite unpopular with many of the leading ones of the church. I was also witness of the introduction (secretly) of a kingly form of government in which Joseph suffered himself to be ordained a king, to reign over the house of Israel forever; which I could not conceive to be in accordance with the laws of the church, but I did not oppose this move, thinking it none of my business.

Joseph, however, became convinced before his death that he had done wrong; for about three weeks before his death, I met him one morning in the street, and he said to me, "Brother Marks, I have something to communicate to you, we retired to a by-place, and set down together, when he said: "We are a ruined people." I asked, how so? He said:

"This doctrine of polygamy, or Spiritual-wife system, that has been taught and practiced among us, will prove our destruction and overthrow. I have been deceived," said he, "in reference to its practice; it is wrong; it is a curse to mankind, and we shall have to leave the United States soon, unless it can be put down and its practice stopped in the church. Now," said he, "Brother Marks, you have not received this doctrine, and how glad I am. I want you to go into the high council and I will have charges preferred against all who practice this doctrine, and I want you to try them by the laws of the church, and cut them off, if they will not repent and cease the practice of this doctrine; and" said he, "I will go into the stand and preach against it, with all my might, and in this way we may rid the church of this damnable heresy."

But before this plan could be put into execution, the mob began to gather and our attention necessarily, was directed to them.

I again met Joseph when he was about to start for Carthage. He said to me, "Bro. Marks, I have become convinced since I last saw you, that it is my duty to go to Carthage, and deliver myself up as a lamb to the slaughter."

I mentioned the circumstances of these conversations with Joseph to many of the brethren, immediately after his death, but the only effect it had was to raise a report that Brother Marks was about to apostatize; and my statement of the conversation in reference to the practice of polygamy was pronounced false by the Twelve and disbelieved; but I now testify that the above statements are verily true and correct.

When I found that there was no chance to rid the church of that abominable sin, as I viewed it, I made my arrangements to leave Nauvoo, and I did so firmly believing that the plans and designs of the great Jehovah in inspiring Joseph to bring forth the book of Mormon would yet be carried out in his own time, and in his own way. Well brethren I have lived to see the foundation, and the platform laid, the principles revealed, and the order given whereby the great work of the Father, can, and will be accomplished. There is no doubt resting on my mind in reference to this work of Baneemy being the work of God, for I am fully convinced that it is the work it purports to be, the work of the Father, spoken of in the book of Mormon to prepare the way for the restoration of his covenants to the house of Israel. Now all who are convinced of this fact ought to move forward and take a decided stand to labor for Jehovah and the benefit of mankind.

I intend from this time henceforth to labor in the cause, and give my influence and substance to speed the work. Now, I call upon you my brethren, one and all, who have been ordained and set apart to teach, and gather up the remnant seed of the church, to use all diligence and perseverance to gather them up to the place of preparation, (which place will be made known through the Harbinger and Organ, in the sub-committee's report) that we may be prepared, and receive the necessary instructions, to bear the kingdom to Israel.

It is necessary that all should bear in mind that the school of works in its first department will be opened at the next Solemn Assembly; and all should be prepared to send up an offering of sufficient magnitude to entitle them to receive a large blessing. The present impoverished condition of the Lord's treasury and the urgent necessity of obtaining a printing Press, and the removing of the Chief teacher to the place of gathering, and other contingent expenses, appeal forcibly to us to bring a large offering to the next Solemn Assembly to meet the present requirements of the work. A printing Press, we must have, and Brother Thompson must be removed, which will require means to accomplish and all should have the privilege of contributing their gift oblations, for the accomplishment of so desirable an object.

The gathering should be taught and all who have means to remove and to sustain themselves through the winter should be to the place of gathering this fall, so as to get the necessary instructions, for the work hereafter to be assigned to them. I expect to be at the Solemn Assembly in August and to go from thence to the place of gathering, there to remain during the winter, and I want the Chiefs of the different Quorums of Traveling Teachers to report to me as often as once in a month, that I may know of their whereabouts and what they are doing that I may communicate to them such information as they need in reference to their mission, and that of their Quorums.

Signed, Wm. MARKS
St. Louis, June 15, 1853.

—oOo—

OPPOSITION TO POLYGAMY,
BY THE PROPHET JOSEPH.

BROTHER Sheen-

I feel desirous to communicate through your periodical, a few suggestions made manifest to me by the Spirit of God, in relation to the Church of Jesus Christ of Latter Day Saints. About the first of June, 1844, (situated as I was at that time, being the Presiding Elder of the Stake at Nauvoo, and by appointment the Presiding Officer of the High Council) I had a very good opportunity to know the affairs of the Church, and my convictions at that time were, that the Church in a great measure had departed from the pure principles and doctrines of Jesus Christ. I felt much troubled in mind about the condition of the Church. I prayed earnestly to my Heavenly Father to show me something in regard to it, when I was wrapt in vision, and it was shown me by the Spirit, that the top or branches had overcome the root, in sin and wickedness, and the only way to cleanse and purify it was, to disorganize it, and in due time, the Lord would reorganize it again. There were many other things suggested to my mind, but the lapse of time has erased them from my memory. A few days after this occurrence I met with Brother Joseph. He said that he wanted to converse with me on the affairs of the Church, and we retired by ourselves. I will give his words verbatim, for they are indelibly stamped upon my mind. He said he had desired for a long time to have a talk with me on the subject. of polygamy. He said it eventually would prove the overthrow of the Church, and we should soon he obliged lie leave the United States, unless it could be speedily put down. He was satisfied that it was a cursed doctrine, and that there must be every exertion made to put it down. He said that he would go before the congregation and proclaim against it, and I must go the High Council, and he would prefer charges against those in transgression, and I must sever them from the Church, unless they made ample satisfaction. There was much more said, but this was the substance. The mob commenced to gather about Carthage in a few days after, therefore there was nothing done concerning it. After the Prophet's death I made mention of this conversation to several hoping and believing that it would have a good effect, but to my great disappointment, it was soon rumored about that Brother Marks was about to apostatize, and that all that he said about the conversation with the Prophet was a tissue of lies. From that time I was satisfied that the Church would be disorganized, and the death of the Prophet and Patriarch tended to confirm me in that opinion. From that time I was looking for a reorganization of the Church and Kingdom of God. I feel thankful that I have lived to again behold the day, when the basis of the Church is the revelations of Jesus Christ, which is the only sure foundation to build upon. I feel to invite all my brethren to become identified with us, for the Lord is truly in our midst.

—o0o—

THE DEATH OF THE TWO MARTYRS.

Joseph; Dear Nephew: — Several times I have taken pen to write you on the subject of this caption, the death of the two Martyrs, and the principal causes that led to their death. But the causes have been so misunderstood and I have felt so diffident about writing the facts in the case as I understand them, that I have refrained from the task, for fear that the circumstances I have to name might throw a [black] influence upon the character of the man whom we all esteem as the prophet of God; and the longer I have put this matter off the more and more I have felt it impressed upon my mind that I should write. The history and the circumstances connected with the death of your father, and your Uncle Hyrum, are events that transpired, for the greater part while I was residing in Philadelphia in 1842-3-4, having charge of the Church in the east. But the links in the chain of circumstances that I am about to relate were occurrences that took place while I was on a visit to Nauvoo, for the purpose of attending the April Conference in 1844.

After attending the Conference held by the Church at that time, and also several of the political caucuses to nominate candidates for President of the United States, and business matters of this sort having been disposed of, (in which Lyman Wight, Brigham Young, John Taylor, Willard Richards, and H. C. Kimball were the principal speakers), I began to arrange matters to return to my family who were, as I have before stated, residing in the City of Philadelphia; and on the morning previous to my leaving Nauvoo, I called on your father and took breakfast with him. While seated at the table a conversation was had participated in by your mother, concerning some things that she had learned in the discharge of her mission among the Saints as one of a committee appointed by the Female Relief Society, to visit the Saints and look after the interest of the poor of Church; to enquire after their occupation and financial prospect for food and means of support. In relating her report she said that some complaint had been made to her by females whom she had visited, that John Taylor, Willard Richards, and Brigham Young had been teaching some doctrines among the Saints privately that was going to ruin the Church, unless there was a stop put to it, as it was contrary to the law and rules governing the Church. Your father remarked that he would attend to the matter as soon as he got through with his troubles with the Laws and Fosters. But mark you their conversation took place only a few days previous to your father's death. What that private teaching might have been, that those persons whom your mother named, were circulating in a clandestine manner, (since there has been so much said about a doctrine called the plural wife doctrine on this subject), I leave the reader to judge.

One other point I wish to notice in the conversation that took place while I was eating at your father's table, and that was, as the conversation turned upon Brigham Young, your father remarked that with regard to the charge brought against these brethren, that he expected that he would have trouble with Brigham Young, especially, and added that "should the time ever come that this man B. Young should lead the Church that he would lead it to hell." And these words I remember as plainly as though they were spoken but yesterday; as at this time I had not known that there could have been a charge of fault brought against the man. My association with this man Brigham Young for near three years previous, had been very limited, in consequence of our different localities and fields of labor.

These matters that I have thus named do not comprise the whole ground of the causes that led to your father's death; although in part it did, as this secret evil that had crept into the Church, by means of this private teaching, gave food and material for the Expositor press to pour out its vials of wrath upon the head of the prophet, making him responsible for the conduct and teachings of these secret and clandestine teachers. What fixes the stain of guilt upon these parties named in this letter making them more criminally murderous, is the part that the City Council at Nauvoo took in getting up the ordinance which resulted in the destruction of the Expositor press. And I wish here to name the fact that the principal instigators in getting up that ordinance were men who feared the revelations that this organ (Expositor) was about to make of their secret and ungodly doings to the world. The persons who were most conspicuous in the work, and were the means of bringing on the scenes that finally resulted in the bloody tragedy which took place at Carthage Jail were no other than John Taylor and Willard Richards, who by constant importunities prevailed upon your father to sign his own death warrant by placing his name to that accursed ordinance which resulted in his death and the death of your Uncle Hyrum.

To these importunities of Richards and Taylor I was a witness, and was present when Richards brought in the book containing the ordinance and asked for your father's signature to make it a law in the City of Nauvoo. I remonstrated with Richards at the time, against my brother Joseph putting his name down in such a place, as it would most certainly result in his death. Richards, failing to secure your father's name at this time, both he and Taylor called on your father the next morning, with feigned tears of desperation, expatiating upon the great necessity of having that Expositor removed, as a means to the further growth and prosperity not only of the City of Nauvoo, but of the cause of the Church abroad. Thus these men, with the sophistry of their lying tongues, like wolves in sheep's clothing, ensnared the prophet from off his watch tower, and led him as a lamb to the slaughter, they promising, also, to be his assistants in case he should fall into trouble, as a result of his name being placed to that ordinance. This accounts for the whys and the wherefores, that Taylor and Richards were both in the jail at the time your father and your uncle Hyrum were murdered. The principal reasons why these conspirators against your father's life did not suffer the same fate that your father and your uncle Hyrum did, are because, like cowards they hid themselves away -- Taylor under a bed that was in the room where the prisoners were confined and Richards behind the door. Thus you see, by the secret workings and secret doings of these men for years gone by, the Church was robbed of her prophet and patriarch, by a most hellish plot that had been in vogue for not only months, but years previous to the time of their deaths. When I see men whose finger stains show positive signs of their guilt in the death of the martyrs, now reveling in the spoils of the Church robbed from the innocent and unsuspecting saints, I cannot restrain my pen from writing the facts and incidents that I do know before God and man were the means of your father and uncle Hyrum's death.

There is one more fact I will notice and that is, that however strange or great the testimony that might be brought against these men, John Taylor and others, in this murderous affair, the Utah Mormons would not credit it though one rose from the dead to bear witness of it, and as for the redemption of any from their blindness, who have willingly given their names in support of this great apostasy, I am in much doubt that there are many who will be saved or forsake the great error they have fallen into.

And especially do I believe this in regard to the remnants of the Smith family in Utah, whose chances for knowing the erroneous position they are in, and with ample proof from the Word of God that their whole system of church organization is founded in corruption and fraud; and still they persist in their unholy alliance with that apostate and God-forsaken people. "There are none so blind as those who will not see."

This then, is the end of this epistle, and I conclude with many good wishes to you and to all good saints.

Your brother in bonds of love.

>Wm. B. Smith.
>Kingston, Caldwell Co., Mo.,
>March 25th, 1879

Book of Mormon as a Covenant

Transcript of a Lecture delivered in Columbia, SC
January 13, 2019

I have this portable triple combination that I brought with me because the copy that I have of the new Scriptures is so cumbersome, and we have to pack everything to catch the plane flights. So, although I really prefer the new Scriptures, for portability sake, I brought these.

One of the things that I have—and I want to point out to you these features in the new Scriptures in hopes that you will take note of the same kinds of things—one of the things that I have found is that when you get a new set of Scriptures, everything is laid out differently than the way that it used to be laid out in the set that you're accustomed to reading and using. As a result, what used to be on the top left-hand side is now on the bottom right-hand side. Everything is reoriented. And the new Scriptures do not have versification. They're divided into paragraphs in order to have complete thoughts gathered together. Now, the paragraphs are numbered in order to cite them, but the purpose was to divide it into paragraphs so that you've got a complete thought. Therefore, when you're reading something that you're used to seeing out of context as a… Some verses in the Scriptures are a phrase. They're not even a sentence; they're just a phrase. But the phrase belongs inside a sentence, and the sentence belongs inside a paragraph, and when you pick up the new Scriptures and you read them in this current layout, everything changes. You begin to see things…

I have read, one way, a passage in a January 1841 revelation—the entire time, over 40 some years—I read it the same way. I got the new Scriptures with the new layout, and I read the same material, and all of a sudden, it has a different meaning. I'm not gonna take the time to read it, but I want you to find it. It's the January 1841 revelation. When you have time, read it. And read the words about "they shall not be moved out of their place," which I've always read to mean the people who are in Nauvoo—and if they're faithful, the people who are in Nauvoo shall not be moved out of their place. In the new Scriptures, I read that, and I believe it is referring to Joseph and Hyrum Smith— that they would be preserved and not moved out of their place if the people were faithful. And if they were not, they were gonna lose Joseph and Hyrum. Now, it doesn't matter whether the words are referring to the people living in Nauvoo or to Joseph and Hyrum. The sign was that they would be moved out of their place, and both were. We lost Joseph, we lost Hyrum, and we lost Nauvoo. So, things like that happen when you've got the new Scriptures.

Last night, as I was listening to Jeff and others who spoke, one of the things that struck me is that almost all revelation—going back to the days of Adam and coming right down to today—come as a consequence of understanding Scripture. That was true even of Enoch —because Enoch had a record that had been handed down from Adam. And in the case of Abraham, the records belonging to the Fathers fell into his hands, and he studied them to gain the understanding that he had. Micah quotes Isaiah. Isaiah quotes Zenos and Zenoch. Jacob quotes the allegory of Zenos. Nephi quotes Isaiah. All of them study Scripture in order to get an understanding, and revelation is largely based upon expanding your understanding of Scripture. The Book of Mormon is really the keystone of the religion but also the keystone to revelation itself. It was intended to open our eyes to things that we couldn't see before. The Book of Mormon is really a giant Urim and Thummim intended for our benefit.

I was also struck by something that I went and found this morning. This is a passage in which Nephi is describing the saints at the very end, at the end of time, just before the scene wraps up:

> And it came to pass that I beheld the church of the Lamb of God, and its numbers were few, because of the wickedness and abominations of the whore who sat upon many waters; nevertheless, I beheld that the church of the Lamb, who were the saints of God, were also upon all the face of the earth; and their dominions upon the face of the earth were small, because of the wickedness of the great whore whom I saw.

> And it came to pass that I beheld...the great mother of abominations did gather together multitudes upon the face of the earth, among all the nations of the Gentiles, to fight against the Lamb of God.

> And it came to pass that I, Nephi, beheld [that] the power of the

*Lamb of God, that it descended upon the saints of the church of the Lamb, and upon the **covenant** people of the Lord, who were scattered upon all the face of the earth; and they were armed with righteousness and with the power of God in great glory.*

And it came to pass that I beheld that the wrath of God was poured out upon that great and abominable church, insomuch that there were wars and rumors of wars among all the nations and kindreds of the earth.

And as there began to be wars and rumors of wars among all the nations which belonged to the mother of abominations, the angel spake unto me, saying: Behold, the wrath of God is upon the mother of harlots; and behold, thou seest all these things. (1 Nephi 14:12-16 LE; see also 1 Nephi 3:28-29 RE, emphasis added)

These words don't say that the coming conflict is against the covenant people of God or the church of the Lamb. Nor does it say that the wrath of God consists of God picking a fight with the wicked. In the case of the wrath of God, people are stirred to anger against each other. They decide. The wicked destroy the wicked because the wicked decide that they cannot put up with peaceful co-existence anymore. Their hearts are so angry with one another that they manage to inflict violence and death and destruction upon one another.

Like the judgment that Mormon describes in Mormon chapter 9 (of the old set [LDS Edition]), God is a bystander. The wrath of God is manifest by the rejection of God and the violence that people turn upon one another. And the power of God and the glory of God— meaning the peace of God and the ability to live with one another in harmony without this raging conflict—that power is manifest among the people of God, the church of God, and the covenant people that belong to God. So, if you can maintain peaceful co-existence with one another as you worship God in the coming days, the power and glory of God will descend and be with you because you managed to extract yourself from the coming conflict, rage, hatred, polarization. And if you don't think those days are not commencing, then, well, you're not watching the news. It's just an ongoing political battle escalating continually.

Well, the Book of Mormon… This is the Book of Mormon Covenant Conference. The Book of Mormon tells you what it's for.

Oh, one last thought about the church of the Lamb of God. At the time that these words were being written by Nephi (and he had seen the vision, and he's talking about what he saw), at the time that he's writing that prophecy, the earliest stages of the Nephite civilization had just begun. Nephi's still living. He has a wife. He has some children. He has brothers. The total group that are involved is not much larger than the group that we have right here today [about 25 people]. He's looking down through history prophetically, and he's saying the saints —the covenant people of God, the people that the Lamb of God's church—that group is "few." Now, if it was 16 million people scattered globally, in the reality of Nephi's context, he would not describe them as few. He's not making a comparative analysis. He's simply describing what he saw. He said they're all around the world, but there's only very few of them, k? If you go to the Fellowship Locator and you look at what you see among those that have identified themselves with the last days' covenant, they're all over the world, but there's really very few of them.

We tend to think about numbers in the Book of Mormon as if their numbers were akin to what we're accustomed to seeing in our day. One of the distortions that comes in is the rank/the identification. If **we're** talking about someone who is a general, we would say he's a general, and we would expect a star to be on his shoulder. If **they're** talking about someone that is a general, they would call him a captain of 10,000. It does not mean that he has 10,000. A captain of a hundred does not mean that he has a hundred. It means a rank. A captain of 50 does not mean that he has 50. It means that he has a rank. When the pioneer companies were organized, and they divided into captains of 100's and captains of 50's and captains of 10's, those were simply identifying a role/a rank/a position. It didn't mean that you had a hundred people in your company. It didn't mean that you had 50 people that you were directing. It didn't mean that you had 10 people over whom you had charge. It was simply a way of dividing them. So, when we get to the end of the Nephite wars, with "this and his 10,000" and "that and his 10,000" and "someone else and their 10,000" and they're all slain, it doesn't mean that you're reading about hundreds of thousands or millions who are dying. It means that someone in a position of rank and authority and all of those under his command were slain. What those numbers amounted to, we don't know. But the designation that Nephi gives to what would be going on in the last days before the coming of Christ, when the wicked are destroyed by the wrath of God (meaning that the spirit withdraws, and as it withdraws, their level of cruelty and violence increases) is few, probably describing gatherings like we have here.

The Book of Mormon begins with a title page that was on the very last plate of the plates that Joseph Smith translated, and it appears as the first page of the Book of Mormon:

> AN ACCOUNT WRITTEN BY THE HAND OF MORMON UPON PLATES TAKEN FROM THE PLATES OF NEPHI. *Wherefore, it is an abridgment of the record[s] of the people of Nephi, and also of the Lamanite—Written to the Lamanites, who are a remnant of the house of Israel; and also to Jew and Gentile.* (Title Page of the Book of Mormon LE)

The Book of Mormon was written for three groups. Three targeted audiences are identified right at the outset: the Lamanites, the Jews, and the Gentiles. That's who the Book of Mormon was sent to. In the Teachings and Commandments section 158, there's a covenant offered to the Gentiles, to the remnant of the Lamanites, and to the remnant of the Jews. These are the words of that covenant:

> *Do you have faith in these things and receive the scriptures approved by the Lord as a standard to govern in your daily walk in life, to accept the obligations established by the Book of Mormon as a covenant, and to use the scriptures to correct yourselves and to guide your words, thoughts and deeds?* (T&C 158:3)

It also goes on to say:

> *But if you do not honor me, nor seek to recover my people Israel...then you have no promise.* (Ibid., vs. 19)

The people that the Book of Mormon established as the target audience are the Lamanites, the Jews, and the Gentiles. We have an obligation to try and reach out to the Lamanites, the Jews, and the

Gentiles.

The Title Page goes on to say:

> ...*Written by way of commandment, and also by the spirit of prophecy and of revelation—Written and sealed up, and hid up unto the Lord, that they might not be destroyed—To come forth by the gift and power of God unto the interpretation thereof—Sealed by the hand of Moroni, ...hid up unto the Lord, to come forth in due time by way of the Gentile—The interpretation thereof by the gift [and power] of God.* (Title Page of the Book of Mormon LE)

Did you get that? Almost in rapid succession—twice—we're told "to come forth by the gift and power of God unto the interpretation thereof" and "the interpretation thereof by the gift [and power] of God." Joseph Smith did not translate the Book of Mormon. **God** translated the Book of Mormon and told Joseph Smith what He wanted that interpretation to say.

I've read as many source documents as are currently available to review in print. There are some source materials I haven't looked at because they are in private collections, and you have to travel to see those. But we have this fanciful narrative about how the Book of Mormon was translated.

One of the things that went on in Kirtland was a "shouting Methodist" tradition. People would go into the woods, and they would shout praises to God in hopes that they obtained some kind of spiritual manifestation. The typical manifestation that they were able to create in this tradition was to be seized upon, bound up, and unable to move, which was considered a sign of God's grace and redemption because they were seized upon by some unseen power that had such marvelous power as to bind them up so they could not move. One of the other things that the "shouting Methodists" tradition in Kirtland, Ohio encountered was the idea that as you're out and shouting praises (oftentimes standing on the stump of a tree that's been cut down), there would be a scroll or parchment that would flutter down from heaven, and when it arrived, on the parchment, there would be words written, and you would read the words, and after you had read the words, the parchment would disappear; it would disintegrate. These were the kinds of manifestations that were the "shouting Methodist" tradition which, when Mormonism came to Kirtland, some of the Kirtland Mormon converts had similar experiences.

Well, one of the stories that gets told about the translation of the Book of Mormon is that Joseph Smith would look in a hat, a parchment would appear, he would read the words off the parchment, and then the parchment would disintegrate as soon as the translation was written down, and then a new parchment would appear. K?

At a conference in Kirtland, Hyrum Smith introduced his brother, Joseph. And as Joseph was coming up to talk, Hyrum said, "And Joseph is going to tell us about how the translation of the Book of Mormon took place." Joseph got up in front of the people, and he said, "It's not appropriate; it was translated by the gift and power of God," and then he went on. He refused to describe the process. If you want to know how the Book of Mormon was translated, the Book of Mormon tells you how: by the gift and power of God.

When pressed (after Joseph is dead and gone), and you want to sound like you know something, and you think back about the experiences of the "shouting Methodist" tradition in the early days in Kirtland, well, why not say, "Scrolls would appear, and then when he read them, they'd disintegrate"? There is so much that has crept into the reconstruction of events that are accepted by the LDS Church/that are accepted by historians/that are accepted by the scholars. There's only two people... I was gonna say "one person" that knows how it was done, and that was Joseph. But there are two; the second one is God. How did God interpret the Book of Mormon? And, by the way, would... If you took only the etchings that are on the plates of the Book of Mormon and you rendered a word for word translation of that set of inscriptions, would it read exactly like the Book of Mormon that we have? Or did God—in His mercy, understanding the weaknesses of our day—give us an interpretation that helps us to understand things in our language, maybe a little more clearly than if we had simply a word for word translation from the plates? These are things that Joseph may know, or he may not. But certainly God would know.

When people pretend to know everything there is to know about the translation of the Book of Mormon and then to mock the process, they're really inviting… They're putting their own foolishness on display, and they're inviting the ire of God. The fact is that **the** witness to how that process unfolded confined what he had to say to, "It was translated by the gift and power of God." And the source of these other fanciful tales (Oliver Cowdery, Martin Harris—two of the three witnesses to the Book of Mormon), they were commanded to bear testimony, and their testimony was to consist of "the interpretation thereof was by the gift and power of God." So, when they go beyond that to give details that they probably have no way of knowing a thing about, they're actually violating the restriction that God put upon it: "for a wise purpose."

Well, Joseph Smith was not the translator. It plainly states that God was the translator. It does not mean that what was composed by Nephi, Jacob, Enos, Omni, and others on the Small Plates—and by Mormon and Moroni on the rest (and their abridgment)—is necessarily exactly what was composed by them, because God used the interpretation of the text that He provided to state what **He** intended by His gift and power to be the message that we receive today. It is literally God's statement to us about the content He wants us to understand, adapted to our needs.

It goes on to say, in this Title Page,

> *An abridgment taken from the Book of Ether also, which is a record of the people of Jared, who were scattered at the time the Lord confounded the language…Which is to shew unto the remnant of the house of Israel what great things the Lord hath done for their fathers; …that they may know the covenants of the Lord, that they are not cast [out] forever—And also to the convincing of the Jew and Gentile that JESUS is the CHRIST, the ETERNAL GOD, manifesting himself unto all nations…now if there are faults they are the mistakes of men; wherefore, condemn not the things of God, that ye may be found spotless at the judgment-seat of Christ.* (Ibid.)

What are the covenants of the Lord that are supposed to be made known unto the remnant of the house of Israel that comes through the Book of Mormon? Well, the Book of Mormon tells you what they are:

It shall also be of worth unto the Gentiles, …not only unto the Gentiles but [also] unto all the house of Israel, unto the making known of the covenants of the Father of heaven unto Abraham, saying: In thy seed shall all the kindreds of the earth be blessed (1 Nephi 22:9 LE; see also 1 Nephi 7:3 RE). So, the purpose of the Book of Mormon is to alert the Gentiles and the Jews of the covenants that were made, specifically the covenants that were made with Abraham. OK?

One of the great things about the new set of Scriptures is that the Teachings and Commandments are laid out chronologically. There's this tradition that the last great revelation that Joseph Smith received was in January of 1841, in which the Lord outlined the commandment to build the temple and the signs that would be given if the temple were completed in sufficient time and how the Church would be accepted with their kindred dead (or rejected with their kindred dead, depending upon how they pursued this). That's supposedly his last great revelation. In the Teachings and Commandments, however, what you see in the layout of Joseph's revelations chronologically is that in 1842, the first installment of the Book of Abraham was published (and it appears in the Teachings and Commandments in its chronological layout), and then a few months later, the next installment of the Book of Abraham appears. And so, the last largest revelation given to Joseph, although there were others that are included in this same timeframe, is the text of the Book of Abraham.

The Book of Mormon points to a recovery of knowledge and understanding about the covenants God made with Abraham. The Book of Abraham **had** to be revealed. It **had** to come forward. In order for us to understand the covenants that God made with Abraham, we had to get the Book of Abraham, which did not roll out until the 1842-and-beyond time period. Joseph's work culminated in attempting to get on the ground ordinances that would have reflected more fully the covenants made with Abraham, but the Book of Abraham is part of vindicating the promises that were made in the Book of Mormon.

So, as you read the Teachings and Commandments and you see it unfolding chronologically, you see where the Lectures on Faith fit in. You see where the Book of Abraham fit in. You see how Joseph's ministry was taking on a trajectory that literally fits the pattern of what the Book of Mormon was promising would come forth and be vindicated.

In the Book of Abraham:

> *I have purposed to take thee away out of Haran, …to make of thee a minister to bear my name* [this is God's great gift to Abraham; He's going to make of him a minister to bear His name] *in a strange land which I will give unto thy seed after thee for an everlasting possession…* (Abraham 2:6 LE; see also Abraham 3:1 RE)

Ok. This is cumbersome language, but I want you to ask yourself: If the great gift that God gives to Abraham is to make of him a minister to bear His name, and then He mentions he's gonna bear His name in a strange land, followed with "…which I will give unto thy seed after thee for an everlasting possession," is the gift that He's giving to his descendants "the land" or "the ministry"?

> *…I will give unto thy seed after thee for an everlasting possession, when they hearken to my voice.*

Does that sound like land, or does that sound like the ministry relating to hearkening to God's voice? As He goes on to explain what his descendants are going to inherit:

> *…thou shalt be a blessing unto thy seed after thee, that in their hands they shall bear this ministry and Priesthood unto all nations; And I will bless them through thy name; for as many as receive this Gospel shall be called after thy name, and shall be accounted thy seed, and shall rise up and bless thee, as [unto] their father; And I will bless them that bless thee, and curse them that curse thee; and in thee (that is, in thy Priesthood) and in thy seed, (that is, thy Priesthood), for I give unto thee a promise that this right shall continue in thee, and in thy seed after thee…* (Ibid., vs. 10-11 LE)

The seed of Abraham are the people that hearken to the same God that Abraham hearkened to. If you hearken to that same God, you're the seed of Abraham. And the ministry that you're supposed to bear is the testimony that **THAT God lives**! And that **that God** is **THE God** over the whole Earth, that His work began with Adam and won't wrap up until the Second Coming of Christ in judgment on the world, to save and redeem those that look for Him.

We have to have the record of Abraham in order to understand the covenant that God made with Abraham in order to vindicate the promise that's made in the Book of Mormon. One of the sharp edges of criticism of Mormonism is directed specifically at the Book of Abraham. There are a lot of intellectual arguments that are being made out there, a lot of challenges for why the Book of Abraham ought to be thrown out, and how the Joseph Smith papyrus that got recovered is really, simply Egyptian *Book of Breathings* material that has very little to do with a record written by the hand of Abraham on papyrus, and so on. Well, if the Book of Mormon was translated by the gift and power of God, the Book of Abraham was translated no differently, except by the gift and power of God. And it includes information that's vital for us to understand in order for us to know what the covenants were that were made with Abraham—in order for us to inherit the same gospel that was given to Abraham, so that we can lay hold upon the same blessings that were given to Abraham, so that the covenants that were made with the Fathers can be understood/activated/realized, and we can obtain the blessings of those here in the last days.

All this stuff fits together, and Joseph's work had to necessarily include recovery of the covenants made with Abraham. Now, you may regard yourself as a Gentile, but the covenant that was made with Abraham makes **you** a descendant of Abraham **if** you hearken to that same God and receive that same gospel. And Nephi explains who the Gentiles are in relation to the family of Father Abraham, also. This is Nephi:

> *And it shall come to pass, that if the Gentiles shall hearken unto the Lamb of God in that day that he shall manifest himself unto them in word, and also in power, in very deed, unto the taking away of their stumbling blocks—*
>
> *And harden not their hearts against the Lamb...they shall be numbered among the seed of thy father; yea, they shall be numbered among the house of Israel; and they shall be a blessed people upon the promised land forever; they shall be no more brought down into captivity...* (1 Nephi 14:1-2 LE; see also 1

Nephi 3:25 RE)

Nephi's telling you, "If you are willing to receive what God has offered, then you're numbered among the house of Israel."

Jacob, the brother of Nephi, wrote about the Gentiles. He said:

> *He that fighteth against Zion shall perish, saith God. For he that raiseth up a king against me shall perish, for I, the Lord [God], the king of heaven, will be their king, ...I will be a light unto them forever.... Wherefore, for this cause, that my covenants may be fulfilled which I have made unto the children of men, that I will do unto them while they are in the flesh, I must needs destroy the secret works of darkness, and of murders, and of abominations. Wherefore, he that fighteth against Zion, both Jew and Gentile, both bond and free, both male and female, shall perish....*
>
> *...the Gentiles shall be blessed and numbered among the house of Israel. Wherefore, I will consecrate this land unto [them and] thy seed.* (2 Nephi 10:13-16,19 LE; see also 2 Nephi 7:2-4 RE)

So, Jacob, likewise, says Gentiles who are willing to receive this as their covenant: numbered among the house of Israel; no longer numbered among Gentiles. They change identities, just like the promise that was made to Abraham. You receive it, you're his seed.

Christ picked up the same thing in 3rd Nephi: *...that the Gentiles, if they will not harden their hearts, that they may repent and come unto me and be baptized in my name and know of the true points of my doctrine, that they may be numbered among my people, O house of Israel...* (3 Nephi 21:6 LE; see also 3 Nephi 9:11 RE).

The purpose of the Book of Mormon is to reveal that:

- God made a covenant with Abraham in the beginning, and
- At the end, God intends to vindicate the covenant that God made with Abraham by changing Gentiles into the house of Israel—by covenant.

When the Restoration began, the people... From the first publication in 1830 until September of 2015 [2017] in Boise, no one accepted the

Book of Mormon as a covenant. It had not been done. The Lectures on Faith got accepted. The Doctrine & Covenants got accepted. The church leaders got accepted. A First Presidency, a high council—all kinds of things got accepted—but **not** the Book of Mormon **as a covenant** until September... Was it...? What year was that? 2017. It was. (It was an odd year, but not '15.) September of 2017—it was the very first time in history that the Book of Mormon was received as a covenant. And in the words that I read you just a moment ago, Nephi mentions covenant people. You **have** to receive it as a covenant. God only works to bring people into His good graces by covenants. They have to be made. Without covenants, you **cannot** participate in what the Lord sets out.

Well, the Book of Mormon was intended as a record for our day to restore our knowledge to make it possible for us to enter back into a covenant relationship with God in order for the promises that were made to the Fathers to be vindicated. Abraham looked forward to having seed that would be countless. He had one son. But God told him, "Don't worry about that." The time will come when everyone who receives this gospel—that is, the gospel that Abraham had in his possession; the gospel that is unfolding in front of your eyes today— **that** will continue to unfold until all of its covenants, rites, obligations, privileges, understandings will all roll out. The Restoration will be completed. But the promise was made to Abraham that whenever that is on the Earth, those who receive it will acknowledge him (Abraham) as their covenant father—the father of the righteous.

Well, I want to comment about an issue that came up last night, both in remarks that got made by Jeff and comments that others made in the audience. During the early Kirtland era (when there were a lot of false spirits that wound up creating a lot of mischief), the people were really wanting to have these miraculous signs to be given. Faith does not come from signs. It's actually impossible for that—to have a sign, and that as a consequence of the sign, you now have faith—it doesn't work that way. That's one of the reasons why Christ—when He did something miraculous (like healing someone who was a leper or healing someone who was lame)—He would admonish them, "Don't tell anyone about this." Because if the person who underwent this miraculous event went out and talked it up, then the people who heard that would be damaged in their ability to have faith—because they now had a sign. And if what you do is run after signs, then you go from sign to sign, and you never develop the required faith.

By studying the Scriptures and plumbing the depths of the message that we have in the Scripture record that's in front of us, you can arrive at a point in your understanding in which it really doesn't matter if an angel appears to you or not. The angel's purpose is never going to be to produce faith in you. If the angel is going to produce faith in you because of their appearance, then the angel ought not appear, because they'll turn you into a sign seeker. On the other hand, if you have developed faith by the careful study of what we've been given in the Scriptures and the presence or absence of an angel will have no effect on your faith—you will believe; you will have confidence; your understanding reaches the same depth with or without the angel's presence—then there's no reason for the angel to withhold. There's no reason for him not to appear.

When the brother of Jared went to the Lord with an interior lighting problem and the Lord said, "What do you want as a solution?"—the brother of Jared did not need to see the finger of the Lord in order for him to have faith that the Lord was going to solve the problem. He went out, he molten the stones, he took them back, he presented them to the Lord. He asked the Lord to take care of it. Is there any greater faith in saying, "Oh, as the Lord touched the stones I saw His finger," or "Here are the stones that will light in the dark that the Lord has now taken care of." *Because of the knowledge of this man he could not be kept from beholding within the veil* (Ether 3:19 LE; see also Ether 1:14 RE). Well, what was the knowledge that he had? It was the fact that his faith had grown to the point where he was taking what is behind the veil and unseen, and he's pulling it into this world—a physical manifestation of God in **this** world—by the stones that he had molten and by the request that he had put to the Lord. And so, the Lord makes that manifestation here. He… His knowledge parted the veil because he had done the labor to make something in this world that connected God to it in order to bless the people. All of this was an act of service and sacrifice and faith for the blessing and the benefit of others. It was selfless. But it was selflessness in a way that drew into the physical world what lies beyond the veil.

And so, he sees God's finger, and it startles him. It startles him, and the Lord puts a question to him. It's a question that is reflected earlier in Nephi's writing. Nephi says, "God loveth all who will have him to be their God."

And the brother of Jared is asked, "Did you see more than this."

"No."

"Will you believe me if I show myself to you?"

"Yea, I know you're a God of truth, and you cannot lie; I'll believe all your words."

Why do you think the Lord posed the question, "If I show myself to you, will you believe in me?" Why do you think that Mormon writes about how He's spoken face-to-face in plain humility, as one man speaks to another? We want the thundering and the lightning and the ground-shaking on Sinai, and when the Lord appeared to the brother of Jared, before appearing, He asked him, "Now, when you see me, are you gonna believe me?" He loveth all who will have Him to be their God. "Well, I knew not that God was a man. You seem so much bigger and better when you were the burly thunderer from behind the curtain announcing that you are the great and powerful Oz. But now that the curtain's drawn aside and you're like... Man was created in your image," and it literally means that. It takes some of the varnish off it all.

God's greatness does not consist in striking awe in the eye of the beholder because of glory. It consists in the humility, the virtue, the goodness, the purity of the being. We worship God, not because He's powerful. We worship God because He represents everything that is pure and holy and good—everything that is desirable above all else. The purity of that fruit that was delicious (that father Lehi talked about and Nephi wrote about), it is so because of its goodness. Because it is exactly what the highest and the best and the most noble should be. That's who God is.

People that are brought into God's presence are convicted of their own inadequacies because you see here—at last, now—is a complete being, is a pure, just, and holy being. And in comparison, we all lack. We **all** lack. When Isaiah was caught up to the presence of the Lord, he's shouting, "Woe is me; I'm undone; I am a man of unclean lips; I dwell among people of unclean lips." He recognizes the enormity of the gulf, the gap between him and God. And so, God purges it. It's because of the faith and the confidence that he has in God that Isaiah afterwards says, "Here am I, Lord. Send me" It's not because Isaiah is suddenly a greater being than he was before. It's because Isaiah had faith that this Being can indeed make one as flawed as we are cleansed, holy, pure, confidence in him.

If I were to make one recommendation about "the process," I would say forget about asking for signs; study the depths of the Scriptures, and you'll find yourself in company with angels who will come help you to understand what is in these Scriptures—and in particular, above all, the Book of Mormon. The Book of Mormon is a giant Urim and Thummim; used in the correct way, you'll find yourself in company of angels who are helping to tutor you—in a conversation—as you look into an understanding of what's written in the Scriptures. And then there's no reason for them to withhold their presence from you. "Adam, having conversed with the Lord through the veil, desires now to enter into His presence." There's no reason—after you have conversed through the veil—for that presence to be denied you. But it follows an order. It follows a pattern.

We have now arrived at that moment when there are going to be competing meetings going on. I did say that we'd do questions if people had any. So, is there something someone wanted to have me talk about?

Yeah?

Question 1: I wondered if you would expound upon studying the Scriptures? One of the things I've found is [indecipherable] he's a Christian that's… From a young man, he started studying the New Testament and became a professor of theology, and in the process of studying, he ended up losing his faith instead of developing faith. And there seems to be that risk, also like Jeremy Reynolds and the CES letter. People that really look deeply into stuff sometimes lose their faith instead of developing it. I wondered what the… What's the difference? How do you develop faith instead of running into issues and contradictions that [indecipherable]?

Denver: The question is, Do you run any risks by studying? That you can just as easily study your way out of belief as you can study your way into belief.

The way that I think that works is: Everyone wants to understand, because of how proximate (how close) Joseph Smith is, everyone wants to understand how Joseph Smith did it. So, if we think we can figure out how Joseph Smith did it, then presumably, that will equip us to understand or put it into context. But most people who are studying to figure out how Joseph Smith did it are only interested in debunking it. "I want to know how he pulled this off because I'm a little skeptical that what he pulled off is actually genuine. And maybe if I can understand how Joseph Smith pulled that off, then I can understand how Jesus pulled it off. Then I can understand how Moses pulled it off. Then I can put it all to rest because I needn't worry about it." Or, "I want to understand how Joseph Smith pulled it off so **I** can pull it off. And when I **get** that and I figure it out and I try it and it doesn't work for me, **then** I can say Joseph made it up because it didn't work for **me**." I mean, there are a lot of pitfalls along the course of study.

The first and primary question you have to ask is: Take a look around this world and ask yourself if—in this world—it makes sense to you that there is no Creator. Does it make sense to you that everything that's going on here simply is a haphazard accident? That there is no creation? There's no Creator; there's no divine plan; there's nothing here that operates on any other basis than random chance? If you reach the conclusion that everything that's going on here **could** possibly be by random chance, then read *Darwin's Black Box*. There's a little over 200 different things that have to line up perfectly in order for your blood to clot. If any one of those 200 things don't happen simultaneously—it's a little over 200—if any one of those don't happen simultaneously, you will die. For some of those, if you get a cut and they're not present, you'll bleed out. You'll simply die because you will exsanguinate. For others of those, if you get a cut, your entire blood system will turn solid, and you will die (because clotting knows no end). *Darwin's Black Box* makes the argument that it is evolutionarily impossible for trial and error to solve the problem of blood-clotting because every one of the steps that are required, if nature simply experiments with it, kills the organism. And that ends that. You don't know that you're going to succeed until you've lined them all up, and you've made them all work. It's an interesting book: *Darwin's Black Box*. In essence, it's saying that the evolutionists require more faith, really, than do people that believe in God because the theory upon which they base their notion requires **far** too many things to occur by trial and error than is conceivably possible.

Well, **if** there is a creation, then there is a Creator. If there is a Creator, then the question is... I assume all of you have had a father or a grandfather—someone that you respected—a mother or a grandmother, an aunt or an uncle that, over the course of a lifetime, developed skills and talents and humor and character—someone that you admire. And then they pass on. How profligate a venture is it to create someone that you...a creation that you view as noble, as worthy, as admirable, as interesting, as fascinating; some person that you love... Take that, and just obliterate it. God, who can make such a creation, **surely** doesn't waste a creation. He's not burning the library at Alexandria every day by those who pass on. God had to have a purpose behind it all.

I don't know how many of you have had a friend or a loved one or a family member who passed on who, subsequent to their death, appeared to you, had a conversation with you, in a dream, in a thought. I can recall going to my father's funeral, and his casket with his body was in the front of the little chapel we were in, but his presence was not there; he... That may have been the hull he occupied while he was living and breathing, but I had no sense at all that my father was there. I **did** have a sense that he was present, but he wasn't in the coffin; he was elsewhere in the room. I couldn't see him, but I could have pointed to him and said, "He's here." I fact, I made a few remarks at my father's funeral, and I largely directed them at him.

Nature testifies over and over again:

- It doesn't matter when the sun goes down, there's going to be another dawn.
- It doesn't matter when all the leaves fall off the deciduous trees in the fall, there's going to come a spring. There's going to be a renewal of life.
- There are all kinds of animals in nature that go through this

really loathsome, disgusting, wretched existence, and then they transform. And where they were a pest before, now they're bright, and they're colorful, and they fly, and they pollinate. Butterflies help produce the very kinds of things that their larvae stage destroyed.

These are signs. These are testimonies. Just like the transformation of the caterpillar into the butterfly—the pest into the thing of beauty; the thing that ate the vegetables that you were trying to grow into the thing that helps pollinate the things that you want to grow—that's the plan for all of us.

So, when you study the Scriptures, the objective should not be, "Can I trust the text? Can I evaluate the text? Can I use a form of criticism against the text in order to weigh, dismiss, belittle, judge?" Take all that you know about nature, take all that you know about this world and the majesty of it all, take all that you know that informs you that there is **hope**, there is **joy**, there is **love**…

Why do you love your children? Why do your children love you? These kinds of things exist. They're real, they're tangible, and they're important. And they're part of what God did when He created this world. Keep **that** in mind when you're studying, and search the Scriptures to try and help inform you how you can better appreciate, how you can better enjoy, how you can better love, how you can better have hope. What do **they** have to say that can bring you **closer** to God?—not "Can I find a way to dismiss something that Joseph said or did?" As soon as Joseph was gone off the scene, people that envied the position that he occupied took over custody of everything (including the documents), and what we got—as a consequence of that—is a legacy that allowed a trillion dollar empire to be constructed.

Religion should require our sacrifice. It should not be here to benefit us. We should have to give—not get. And in the giving of ourselves, what we get is in the interior; it's in the heart—it's the things of enduring beauty and value. If your study takes you away from an appreciation of the love/the charity/the things that matter most, reorient your study.

Yeah?

Question 2: Can you talk to the phrase, "the pavilion of thy hiding place"?

Denver: Yeah. Yeah, see at that time, Joseph was in Liberty Jail, and he was longing for that earlier companionship that he had been involved with. Joseph made a remark one time about how the apostle Paul had seen the third heaven and that he (Joseph) had seen the seven heavens. There's a construct to the order of everything. And there are veils within veils within veils. I once analogized priesthood to fellowship— and there's more than one kind of fellowship beyond the veil, and there are councils, and there are places in the heavens where some are invited (and others will get there eventually). The "pavilion of God" is another way of saying you have moved/you have located yourself in a place— "high and lifted up" is one way that it gets described—in which God appears to be inaccessible at that moment; God appears to be outside of the range. Joseph was writing that in Liberty Jail because he felt like God had abandoned him.

In fact, the… One of the problems with the LDS version of the Doctrine and Covenants is that the language that appears right before God's answer to Joseph is gone. It's not in your D&C (but it's in the Teachings and Commandments). Joseph got a letter from friends. It was very consoling. He was complaining to God—because now he'd heard from his loved ones, but it made him reflect upon all the misery that had gone on in their being driven out of the state of Missouri while he's locked up in a dungeon and unable to do or say anything to help them. And his mind… He describes how his mind is aflame with anxiety; his mind is jumping from point to point with—the *Teachings of the Prophet Joseph Smith* says—"with the avidity of lightning." The real word that he used was "with the **vivacity** of lightning," but his mind is simply jumping from place to place to place because of the circumstances. And then just before the answer comes… See…

> *O God, where art thou? And where is the pavilion that covereth thy hiding place? How long shall thy hand be stayed…?* (D&C 121:1)

That is part of the letter. Between verse 6 and verse 7 (as it appears in the Doctrine and Covenants), there's this long explanation that Joseph gives about how his mind is stirred up. He's jumping from subject to subject. His anxiety… He's worked up into a frenzy. And then he says, "At last everything, all the anxieties lie slain," and he reaches a state of peace and reconciliation. And when he is finally calm and his mind has settled down, the voice of inspiration comes along and whispers,

> *My son, peace be unto thy soul; thine adversity and thine afflictions shall be but a small moment.* (Ibid., vs. 7)

The voice of God came to Joseph in Liberty Jail when his mind came to peace. Have you got that? The… Read just before the answer that God gives.

> *[He] grasps after the future with the fierceness of a tiger… retrogrades from one thing to another, until finally all enmity, malice, and hatred, and past differences, misunderstandings, and mismanagements lie slain victims at the feet of hope. And when the heart is sufficiently contrite, then the voice of inspiration steals along and whispers, My son, peace be unto your soul.* (T&C 138:11)

Finally, hope and peace. And then comes the answer. We have a lot of reasons to be anxious in every one of our lives. There is so much that troubles us. But the voice of inspiration steals along and whispers (when we finally are calm enough): "Be still, and know that I am God" gets read as, "Be Still!! And know that I am God!!" when what it's really saying is, "If you would like to know that I am God, quiet it all down. Because whatever pavilion I may occupy, I also occupy part of you." You live and breathe and move because God is sustaining you from moment to moment by lending you breath. He's in you, and He's with every one of us.

We've got about—probably—four more minutes before we need to start doing sacrament and some other things. Anyone else?

Yeah?

Question 3: So, you spoke of the need to plumb the depths of the Scriptures—particularly the Book of Mormon—and how it becomes a Urim and Thummim to us. And the Book of Mormon itself informs us that this is the "lesser things"; it's intentionally withholding much.

Denver: Yeah.

Question 3 (continued): And it specifically states the purpose is to try our faith.

Denver: Right.

Question 3 (continued): The faith having been "so tried," those who plumb the depths can expect more to come forth at some point—in terms of Scripture; in terms of record. I guess the question there is—and not to minimize what we've already been given, because it's clearly enough for our present state and more—but does that sort of thing/those sorts of records that are promised, is that a millennial sort of thing (after the Lord returns)? Is that the sort of thing that, if we finally take seriously enough what's been given now, can we expect more to come forth **before** the Lord comes?

Denver: I believe that how we respond to what we are given will drive that entirely. And whether we get it before the Millenium or after is dependent upon us. But I also think that... Look, the people who prepared the summaries on the plates—the abridgment—and the Lord (who provided the translation of that) **both** know what's being withheld. They abridged what they abridged with what was being withheld in front of their eyes. So, they can't tell you the abridged story without the content of what's being withheld present in their mind. If you go through the text carefully, you'll begin to see that there are patterns that start fitting together. I don't think that when the rest of what has been withheld is suddenly brought out into the light, if you've carefully looked at what's in the Scriptures already, you're not going to say, "Wow! That is shockingly different!" You're gonna say, "I always suspected that. And that fits in with this, and this fits in with that," and the picture begins to emerge a bit more clearly, and yeah, that just... "I've always sort of suspected that to be the case."

Well, when we read the Scriptures, keep in mind that the people writing them have in their mind the rest of the picture, and it leaks through. It... A great deal leaks through because you can't... If you know the rest of the story and you're telling the tale (but you're leaving out some of the big punch lines—but they're present in **your** mind), punch lines are gonna leak through. There's a lot that comes through in the Book of Mormon.

The character and the nature of God is probably better understood by what we have in the Book of Mormon—and it is **perfectly consistent** with the testimony of the gospel writers who knew Christ in mortality. And if you take what we've got in a fairly-battered New Testament record and the Book of Mormon (together) and what happened in the life of Joseph Smith and you weave them all together, you begin to understand that God is a very patient, loving, kindly being. And that the mysteries of God largely consist in developing the attributes of godliness in us. The things that matter the most are the things that make us more like Him: better people, more kindly. You want to know more of the mysteries of God? Serve your fellow man, and be of more value to them. In the process of blessing the lives of others, you find out that you know more of the character of God as a consequence of that.

Let me end by bearing testimony that God really **is** up to a work right now. And the work that is underway **can** culminate in Zion. Covenants were made. Promises were given. God has an obligation to the covenant Fathers that He **will** vindicate. God's words **will** be fulfilled— all of them; none of them are gonna fall to the ground unfulfilled. The question is not, "Will God bring about the culmination of all His purposes?" The question is, "Are we willing to cooperate with Him to bring those purposes to pass in our day?" It could…

The offer that God makes—this appears in Scripture nearly as often as the promise in Malachi—God says, "How oft would I have gathered you as a hen gathers her chicks under her wings, and ye would not." Could God have brought about His purposes and vindicated His promises in the days of Moses? Could He have done what He had promised to do when Christ was here on the Earth? Could He have done it in the days of Peter? Could He have done it in the days of Joseph Smith? The question is never whether God **will** vindicate His promises. The question is, "Will there ever come a people who will **respond** to the Lord's willingness to gather them as a hen gathers her chicks under her wings and **be gathered**, and **be content** with being gathered and being at peace with one another?"

We **have** that opportunity, but so many generations before us have had the same opportunity, and "they would not." The question isn't whether God **is** going to do it or whether God is **willing** to do it **now**. The question is, "Are **we** willing to cooperate with Him in that process to do **our** part?" We get really petty with one another, and we shouldn't be. We ought to value one another so highly that we'll do anything we can to support one another and to assist in bringing about the purposes of God. At the end of the day, "obedience to God" is simply "blessing one another by the way we conduct ourselves."

I like the Lamanite king's prayer, "I will give away all my sins to know you." We tend not to be willing to give away our sins. We want to harbor them and cultivate them and celebrate them. We ought to be more… We ought to love God more and our sins less. God **can** fulfill His promises in our day—before we leave this stage of the action. It can happen. Whether it happens or not is up to us and how interested we are in doing as He bids us.

Of that, I bear testimony, in the name of Jesus Christ, Amen.

Signs Follow Faith

Transcript of a Lecture delivered in Centerville, UT
March 3, 2019

The oldest Old Testament Scripture is the Book of Job. It's older than even the Pentateuch. There are three Old Testament texts in the King James Version of the Bible that are universally regarded as Wisdom texts: Job and Proverbs and Ecclesiastes. A total of seven Old Testament texts have been regarded as Wisdom literature (some of which are not in the King James Version).

Wisdom literature is about mature faith—where disappointments and difficulties are accepted and anger against God for life's setbacks is exposed as foolishness. Wisdom literature teaches about enduring, patient, determined, and resilient faith. Job's friends mistook his suffering with divine disfavor. One of the major themes is faithfulness through adversity and trials.

The first verse of the Book of Mormon echoes with Wisdom. It contains a profound lesson learned over a lifetime. Nephi explained: *Having seen many afflictions in the course of my days, nevertheless having been highly favored of the Lord in all my days* (1 Nephi 1:1 RE). He saw many afflictions. He was highly favored of the Lord in **all** his days, including those in which the affliction was visited on him.

How can one suffer "many afflictions" and be "highly favored of the Lord"? Wisdom literature would suggest that perhaps they are related to one another. Do those who are highly favored need to encounter afflictions to understand God's grace and favor toward them? **That** is a Wisdom theme.

When we say life should be easier, we are foolish. We're not wise.

In his final blessing to his son Helaman, Alma says something similar: *I...know that whosoever shall put their trust in God shall be supported in their trials, and their troubles, and their afflictions* (Alma 17:1 RE). Trusting God does not remove life's trials. Trusting God will not keep afflictions from you. Trusting God will not prevent troubles in your life.

The Book of Mormon explains a mature form of faith in God: resilient in the face of difficulty, enduring in the day of trouble, comforting in the moment of affliction. The faith of the Book of Mormon writers is not superficial, conditional, and weak. It bears up under trial; it is proven in troubles; it accompanies during afflictions.

The Book of Mormon is, among other things, a Wisdom text. What if trials, afflictions, and troubles are not negative? What if they are gifts provided as an opportunity to prove us therewith so that we and God may show what is in our heart?

Job asks: *Shall we receive good at the hand of God, and shall we not receive evil?* (Job 2:3 RE). Christ taught: *In this world there are difficult trials to be faced by my followers, but those who remain devoted will, like me, finish the path and experience the fullness of joy* (Testimony of St. John 10:29 RE).

Each person experiences religion uniquely. No two persons have read exactly the same library of materials, which is why study of Scriptures become a valuable common basis for understanding one another.

Reading Scripture calls forth from each person all their background, education, and experience as they study and learn from the text. If a Christian reaches deeply into the New Testament canon, they'll eventually be lead to study New Testament Greek. Then they will discover New Testament Greek is commonly believed to have been Koine, a dead form of language about which today we must make assumptions. There's also a theory that the New Testament was translated into Koine from Aramaic, and that theory is called the Peshitta Primacy (also known as the Aramaic Primacy). If the original was in Aramaic and the Koine version a translation, then there will be unresolved questions about the quality of that translation that we can no longer answer.

Assumptions make hardline Christians insecure, and therefore, they insist nothing (or very little) has been lost in understanding Koine Greek. We do not know for certain the correct pronunciations for some Koine words. We also do not know the full definitions or meanings for many of the words.

If we're humble about the challenges, we would admit we cannot fully know what the writers intended by what they wrote in the New Testament texts. We think we can get close, but we should be humble enough to acknowledge the imperfection we confront.

Scholars who delve deeply into the Old Testament find another challenge. The Old Testament was written in a form of ancient Hebrew that is a dead language. Although Hebrew has been revived, the Old Testament is written in a dead form. We do not know how many Old Testament words would be correctly pronounced. We do not know all the definitions for Old Testament language. If we're humble about the challenges, we would admit we can never fully know what the writers intended by what they wrote in the Old Testament texts. We think we can get close, but we should be humble enough to acknowledge the imperfection we confront.

The majority of Christians feel no need to read their Scriptures in the original Koine Greek or ancient Hebrew. Whether they are right about that or not, the more deeply you venture into textual scholarship, the more humble you should become about what you actually are able to understand.

In contrast, if you accept the Book of Mormon as Scripture, it presents **none** of these challenges. It was translated by the gift and power of God into English. The English spoken in 1830 is fully known and understood today, and dictionaries published in 1830 are still available today. Any slight shift in meaning between 1830 and 2019 can be fully determined.

In addition to varying forms of ignorance and study, diligence and sloth, interest and indifference that separates each of us in our religious beliefs, there are also false spirits that mislead and confuse.

The term "false spirit" is not limited to the idea of a devil, imp, or mischievous personage but includes the much broader attitude, outlook, or cultural assumptions that people superimpose atop religion. False spirits in the form of ignorant, incomplete, or incorrect ideas are easily conveyed from one person to another. People convey false spirits every time they teach a false idea and the student accepts the idea.

False spirits infect every religious tradition on Earth. This is not limited to Eastern religions that deny Christ but also include Christianity **and Mormonism**. So long as there is anything false or any error, a false spirit prevails. Different religious structures lend themselves to be overtaken by false spirits through different means.

If you have a hierarchy, only the top needs to be taken captive by a false spirit. If it is a diffused religion, then all you have to do is take captive the theological seminaries in order to spread the false spirit. But if the religion is individual and each person is standing on their own—accountable for their relation to God, accountable to learn, to pray, to reach upward, and to have God connect with them individually—then the only way to corrupt a ~~diffused~~ [individual] religion is to corrupt every single believer, every single practitioner.

In the new Scriptures, there is a section in which Joseph Smith discusses **at length** the topic of false spirits. It's an editorial he published in the *Times and Seasons* on April the 1st of 1842. This new section 147 in the Teachings and Commandments is worth careful study (the Teachings and Commandments being the new volume of Scripture recovering and restoring the text as it was originally; available, if you're interested, either for free online to read at www.scriptures.info, or if you want to purchase a copy, it's available through Amazon).

This new section of the Teachings and Commandments is worth careful study. Keep in mind the meaning of several words. Priesthood means "a fellowship." You can have a priesthood that is a fellowship of men. You can have a priesthood that is a fellowship between men and angels. You can have a priesthood that is a fellowship between man and Christ. And you can have a priesthood that is a fellowship between man and God the Father.

In section 147, Joseph Smith ties discerning of false spirits to priesthood, and therefore, when a person has an association with heavenly angels, they are not apt to be misled by fallen false spirits.

Joseph Smith also uses the term "keys" in section 147. Joseph used the term to mean "understanding"—the greatest "key" being the ability to ask God and receive an answer.

- In the Teachings and Commandments section 10, verse 1: *I have given him* [referring to Joseph] *the keys of the mysteries of the revelations which are sealed.*
- In section 141, Joseph (speaking about his ordination of Hyrum and endowing and in blessing him): *Joseph, who shall show unto him the keys whereby he may ask and receive...* (vs. 32).
- And then a reference again in that same section to another servant: *Let my servant William...also receive the keys by which he may ask and receive blessings* (vs. 33).

Joseph used the term "keys of the kingdom" to mean: When a person can ask and receive an answer each time he asks, they hold the keys of the kingdom—because the kingdom belongs to God, and God must direct its affairs for it to be His.

Here are some excerpts from Joseph's editorial (section 147):

> *One great evil is that men are ignorant of the nature of spirits: their power[s], laws, government, intelligence, [and so on], and imagine that when there is anything like power, revelation, or vision manifested, that **it must be of God.*** (vs. 4, emphasis added)

That is a great evil. After criticizing the experiences of Methodists, Presbyterians, and others, Joseph inquired about manifestations of false spirits:

> *They consider it to be the power of God and a glorious manifestation from God — a manifestation of what?* (Ibid.)

He's just described what these people take as glorious manifestations, and he says, despite their supernatural appearance, it's a manifestation of what?

> ***Is there any intelligence communicated?*** *Are the curtains of Heaven withdrawn or the **purposes of God developed?** Have they seen and conversed with an angel — [and] **have the glories of futurity burst upon their view?** No!* (Ibid., emphasis added)

In other words, nothing has advanced that is of God—edifying, instructing, and providing greater intelligence. It's simply spiritual voyeurism, and it's evil.

> *Nothing is a greater injury to the children of men than to be under the influence of a false spirit when they think they have the spirit of God.* (Ibid., vs. 5)

Then he extends this outward as he continued:

> *The Turks, the Hindus, the Jews, the Christians, the [Indian] — in fact all nations have been deceived, imposed upon, and injured through the mischievous effects of false spirits.* (Ibid.)

Then he (close to the end) says,

> *And we shall at last have to come to this conclusion, whatever we may think of revelation, that without it we can neither know nor understand anything of God, or the Devil; …it is equally as plain that **without a divine communication** they must remain in ignorance… The world always mistook false prophets for true ones, and those that were sent of God they considered to be [the] false prophets, and hence they killed, stoned, punished, and imprisoned the true prophets, and [these] had to hide themselves "in deserts, and dens, and caves of the earth," and though the most honorable men of the earth, they banished them from their society as vagabonds, whil[st] they cherished, honored, and supported knaves, vagabonds, hypocrites, impostors, and the basest of men.* (Ibid., vs. 6)

Read that section. False spirits are actively involved whenever God begins a work. And there are **many** false spirits—vying for your acceptance—now at work **among us**.

That having been said, it's time to stop dividing and begin uniting. There are enough divisions in Christianity and in Mormonism. This does not need to continue. The Restoration is intended to bring unity not division. Division needs to end.

In one of the accounts that Joseph Smith wrote about what precipitated his calling by God (that appears in the new Teachings and

Commandments as T&C 146), Joseph wrote this about what provoked him to go out and to pray to get an answer from God about which church to join:

> *I found that there was a great clash in religious sentiment: if I went to one society they referred me to one plan, and another to another, each one pointing to his own particular creed as the summum-bonum of perfection. Considering that **all could not be right and that God could not be the author of so much confusion**, I determined to investigate the subject more fully, believing that **if God had a church it would not be split up into factions**, and that if he taught one society to worship one way and administer in one set of ordinances, he would not teach [other] principles which were diametrically opposed.* (T&C 146:4, emphasis added)

That's what precipitated the Restoration. And there are those who say we have reached a point of stagnation, we have reached a point of corruption, or we have reached a point of apostasy in the various factions of the Mormon world. And people can agree something must be done; something needs to be done.

But people are crying as much *lo here, and…lo there* (Joseph Smith History 1:11 RE) in their current search to try and reconnect through the Restoration as were the Presbyterians and the Methodists and the Baptists at the time that Joseph went into the woods to pray.

What has come of the Restoration? It's reached exactly the point now that was a dead-end at the beginning. What is wrong with us that we can't overlook—based upon the individual experiences, the individual's study, the individual's comprehension, even the individual's prayerful reflection and guidance through that—and accept one another when, in sincerity, all of us are trying to follow God?

Why have we now managed to produce (among ourselves) contention, division, disruption? What is wrong with us? Better yet, what's wrong with me? Because whatever it is, it's wrong with every one of us. It's no different than the mess that Joseph Smith saw in the landscape of Christianity in 1820 when he went to the woods to pray.

We should be ashamed of ourselves. We should be **ashamed** of our division. It should repulse us so much, that I should be readily willing to embrace you even if you have some idea with which I disagree. I don't have your background. I don't have your experience. I haven't lived your life. I have to assume that you've reached the conclusion that you have reached because of the life you've lived.

And perhaps if you and I were to take a long enough walk with one another, we could reach an agreement. But **we** don't do that—just like the Christian's didn't do that—because we're unwilling to suffer the slightest variation to pass by without commenting on it, criticizing it, and rejecting it without ever considering that there may be a wealth of information that underlies that proposition. And if we understood that well enough, we might say, "Now that I understand, I see where your point fits into a larger gospel context, and I need to embrace it. I would like to embrace it but to do so in this fashion, because let me give you what underlies my experience, my background, and my education."

Why do we do this?

The vineyard that the Lord began the Restoration in was cumbered with all sorts of strange fruit. (I mean, I've spent a lifetime referring to it as the Jacob chapter 5. In the new T&C Book of Mormon layouts, it's one of the very few chapters that I can actually point you to from memory. It's Jacob chapter 3 in the new layout. So, I'm becoming familiar with it.)

Talking about the condition of this vineyard (and its cumbered with all sorts of strange fruit—none of it worth harvesting; none of it work keeping; none of it worth laying up and preserving against the harvest), the allegory says:

> *This is the last time that I shall nourish my vineyard, for the end is nigh at hand and the season speedily cometh. And if ye labor with your mights with me, ye shall have joy in the fruit with which I shall lay up unto myself against the time, which will soon come.*
>
> *And it came to pass that the servants did go and labor with their mights, and the Lord of the vineyard labored also with them. And*

they did obey the commandments of the Lord of the vineyard in all things. (Jacob 3:26-27 RE)

Well, that's fairly critical. The Lord's gonna labor with you, but He's gonna expect you to obey His commandments in all things. Have you recently read the Answer to the Prayer for Covenant? Are you determined to obey the Master of the vineyard and His commandments in all things? Maybe we ought to read that twice before we berate one another, belittle one another, argue with one another, dismiss one another. Otherwise, we're really not laboring with the Lord of the vineyard to help for the coming harvest. Instead, we're embracing a false spirit, and we're dividing one another, and we're trying...

Our ambition, whether we're willing to acknowledge it or not, our ambition is to set this into the same sort of divisive factions as the Lord condemned to Joseph in 1820. They have a *form of godliness but they deny the power thereof* (Joseph Smith History 2:5 RE). *They teach for commandments [doctrines] the doctrines [commandments] of men* (Ibid.). They're all corrupt.

> *And there began to be the natural fruit again in the vineyard. And the natural branches began to grow and thrive exceedingly, and the* **wild branches began to be plucked off and to be cast away**. (Jacob 3:27 RE, emphasis added)

Some of the plucking and some of the casting away is voluntarily done by those who submit to false spirits that stir them up to anger against one another, and they depart from fellowship thinking themselves justified before God when, in fact, all they're doing is being plucked and cast away.

> *And they did keep the root and the top thereof equal, according to the strength thereof.* (Ibid.)

We are seeking to keep it equal. Every one of us is on the same plane. No one's getting supported by tithing money. If they are, that's done by a local fellowship that has voluntarily determined that they have one among them in need. Because the tithes are gathered and used to help the poor. There's no general fund being accumulated, and there's no one who does anything that they get compensated for.

This is the only group of people whose religion requires—**incessantly**—sacrifice. No one gets paid. No one gets remunerated. Everything that is done is done at a price of sacrifice. If you're a person in need among a fellowship, the tithes are appropriately used because that's what they're for. They're for the poor. They're not for the leader.

You have to keep the root and you have to keep the top equal. If you allow inequality to creep in at the beginning, the end result is lavish palaces in which some fare sumptuously and others ask to eat the crumbs that fall from the table because they're treated so unequally, and their despair and their poverty and their need goes ignored.

Among us, it can't go ignored, because the money is gathered at a fellowship level, and if there is someone in need among you and you don't minister to their needs, you're cruel. You're…

> *And thus **they** labored with all diligence, according to the commandments of the Lord of the vineyard, even until the bad had been cast away.* (Ibid.)

If you can't tolerate equality, if you can't tolerate the top and the root being equal, if you can't tolerate peace among brethren, then go ahead and be bad and cast yourself away. If you feel moved upon to do that, well, that's the Lord of the vineyard getting rid of you.

> *Even until the bad had been cast away out of the vineyard and the Lord had preserved unto himself, that the trees had become again the natural fruit. And they became like unto one body, and **the fruit were equal**.* (Ibid., emphasis added)

That word "equal" shows up so often in the labor that the Lord of the vineyard is trying to accomplish with the people that you ought to take note. We ought to probably typeset it:

EQUAL

in double-sized font. We're not gonna do that, so **you** have to underline the word, or circle the word, or pay attention to it. The purpose is to go and become equal with one another. As soon as you set out to create rank and position and hierarchy—

Admittedly, within the parable, there is a top, and there is a root—admittedly; but the objective is to achieve equality. If you start out saying the one is greater or better than the other, you're never gonna arrive at the point that is the purpose of the parable, the purpose of the labor of the Lord of the vineyard: "…and the fruit were equal."

The Book of Mormon has had libraries of material written. And almost every single volume in the libraries of Book of Mormon material are filled with debates between polemics and apologists. All the literature basically debates the pro and the con. I spent decades studying the back and forth of polemicists and apologists. One of the fellows that I admire greatly is Hugh Nibley, and Hugh Nibley was one of the very first serious-minded Mormons to take the Book of Mormon seriously. If you read what I wrote about the Book of Mormon history of scholarship in *Eighteen Verses*, you find that, literally, it was Hugh Nibley that ultimately persuaded the First Presidency that the Book of Mormon should be studied and taken seriously.

There were stake presidents and bishops in the LDS tradition who never read the book at the time, and when Hugh Nibley mounted a defense of the Book of Mormon, then-President David O. McKay essentially said, "You talk about it like you think it's true," and Hugh Nibley defended it. At the end of the day, however, Hugh Nibley is an apologist. He's defending the faith. The Book of Mormon itself, on the other hand, has this passage from Alma where he invites you to experiment upon the word. He says, "You ought to plant it." Now, think for a moment what it means to plant something. Alma says:

> But behold, if ye will awake and arouse your faculties, even to an **experiment** upon my words, and exercise a particle of faith, yea, even if ye can no more than **desire to believe**, let this desire work in you, even until ye believe in a manner that ye can **give place for a portion of my words**…

Just think for yourself, for a moment, how you would do that?

*Now we will compare the word unto a seed. Now, if ye give place [unto that seed] that a seed may be planted in your heart, behold, if it be a true seed, or a good seed — if ye do **not cast it out by your unbelief**, that ye will resist the spirit of the Lord — behold, it will begin to swell within your breasts. And when you feel these swelling motions, ye will begin to say within [yourself], It must needs be that this is a good seed, or that the word is good, **for it beginneth to enlarge my soul**; yea, it beginneth to **enlighten my understanding**; yea, ...it beginneth to be **delicious [un]to me**. Now behold, would not this increase your faith? I say unto you, yea.* (Alma 16:27-28 RE, emphasis added)

And he goes on to describe what happens after that and how it converts into knowledge once you've gained experience with the process.

*For ye know that the word hath swelled your souls, and ye also know that it hath sprouted up, that your **understanding doth begin to be enlightened** and your **mind...begin to expand**. O then, is [this not] real? I say unto you, yea, because **it is light**; and whatsoever is **light is good**, because it is discernible; therefore, ye must know that it is good.*

*And now behold, after ye have tasted this light, is your knowledge perfect? Behold, I say unto you, nay; neither must ye lay aside your faith, for ye have only exercised your faith to **plant** the seed, that ye might try the experiment to know if the seed was good. And behold, as the tree beginneth to grow, ye will say, Let us nourish it with great care, that it may get root, that it may grow up and bring forth fruit unto us. And now behold, **if ye nourish it with [great] care**, it will get root, and grow up, and bring forth fruit. But if ye neglect the tree and take no thought for its nourishment, behold, it will not get any root; and when the heat of the sun cometh and scorcheth it, because it hath no root, it withers away, and ye pluck it up and cast it out. Now this is not because the seed was not good, neither is it because the fruit thereof would not be desirable, but it is because **your ground** is barren and ye will not nourish the tree; therefore, **ye cannot have the fruit thereof**. And thus it is: [and] if ye will not nourish the word, looking forward with an eye of faith to the fruit thereof, ye can never pluck of the fruit of the tree* *of life. But if ye will **nourish** the word, yea, **nourish** the tree as it beginneth to grow, by your faith, with great **diligence**, and with **patience**, looking forward to the fruit thereof, it shall take root; and behold, it shall be a tree springing up unto everlasting life. And because of your **diligence,** and your **faith**, and your **patience** with the word, in nourishing it that it may take root [ye shall] by and by…pluck the fruit thereof, which is most precious, which is sweet above all that is sweet, …which is white above all that is white, yea, …pure above all that is pure…And then you thirst not and you hunger not.* (Ibid., vs. 29-30, emphasis added)

Diligence, patience. Diligence, faith, patience.

We want a faith that will respond like Google. We don't want God to prepare a banquet; we want fast-food and a short-order cook and someone that will slap something on our plate fast, fast, fast! And the Book of Mormon is saying, "Slow down. Diligence isn't quick. Patience isn't fast." Planting the seed—

It's like the kids in elementary school that plant the pumpkin seed in the styrofoam cup. And every day they go over and look at the styrofoam cup, and nothing seems to be happening. And before long, a third of the class has killed the seed 'cuz they've dug it up to see what's going on.

Patience. Patience and diligence. Three times: diligence and patience. Diligence and patience.

I have had spiritual breakthroughs that are so profound and so sacred that when I've described them (one time), I did so with only nine words. But I can tell you why it happened:

I taught the Book of Mormon in a Gospel Doctrine class for four different years on cycles while I was a Gospel Doctrine teacher, each time pushing the Book of Mormon deeper and deeper, always (for the first couple of decades) being a little reticent, being a little skeptical. I mean, I accepted the arguments of the apologist. I knew, I understood, and I had studied the arguments of the polemicists.

But Alma was asking that I do something different. Alma was saying, "Hey, why don't you just experiment with this thing, and plant it **as if** you believed it. Plant it **as if** you had faith in it. So, forget about the pros and cons, accept the Book of Mormon at face value, and let the Book of Mormon define itself; let the Book of Mormon be the source from which you evaluate whether or not it enlightens you, whether or not it appeals to your heart, to your soul, and to your mind."

And so, I experimented on the word, and I took the Book of Mormon **as if** it were actually a revelation from God, translated by the gift and power of God, and delivered to me through no human instrumentality. Joseph Smith may have dictated it, and Oliver Cowdery may have penned most of it, but it was translated by the gift and power of God. Therefore, the book was translated into English by the Lord.

And so, I took the Book of Mormon seriously. I entertained no doubts. I employed no apologetics. I just accepted the book and tried to understand it. As I did so, going through the text of the Book of Mormon, there were moments when there were glints where something leapt off the page to me, as if someone had flashed the reflection of the sun off a windshield passing down the street and it aligns with the right angle of the sun. The text itself seemed to spark to me.

As I took it seriously, I could breathe the spirit of the writers. I beheld more as I went through that text than the text will yield to the cautious and wary reader. The Book of Mormon—like the spirits I referred to earlier—the Book of Mormon also has a spirit, and **that spirit is Christ**. If you want to relate to the spirit of Christ and not a false spirit, drop all your apprehensions, lower your guard, and see if the Book of Mormon does not yield the spirit of Christ. It was a better text than any other I had encountered in conveying the spirit of Christ. It is, in fact, the most correct book, and a man can get closer to God by abiding its precepts than any other book.

It can be trusted as a source of direct information in our language. We don't have to encounter uncertainties and hurdles in trying to manage the language and understand the vocabulary (as is always the challenge when you're looking at a New Testament or an Old Testament text).

The New Testament text has a statement that was made by Christ:

> *Think not that I have come to destroy the law or the prophets. I am not come to destroy, but to **fulfill**; for truly I say unto you, heaven and earth must pass away, but one jot or one tittle shall by no means pass from the law **until** all shall be fulfilled. Whosoever therefore shall break one of the least of these commandments and... teach men so to do, he shall by no means be saved in the kingdom of Heaven. But whosoever shall do and teach these commandments of the law until it shall be fulfilled, the same shall be called great and shall be saved in the kingdom of Heaven. For I say unto you, except your righteousness shall exceed that of the scribes and Pharisees, you shall in no case enter into the kingdom of Heaven.* (Matthew 3:17 RE, emphasis added)

That's a text from Joseph Smith's translation or Joseph Smith's Inspired Version of the New Testament. And he's added a few words in there, including the world "until."

The English word that gets used in this text about "fulfilled" was translated from the Greek word *pleroo*. Pleroo can be interpreted "to make fully known, proclaim fully" instead of "to accomplish." In that sense, a scholar might conclude from the Greek that Christ's statement has nothing to do with ending or with completing the law of Moses. And there are scholars who have taught that—Christians.

So, there's an ambiguity about whether Christ intended for the law of Moses to come fully to an end or if he was simply establishing it firmly by fulfilling it or adhering to it. Any ambiguity about what Christ intended is removed when His declaration to the Nephites is added to your understanding:

> *And it came to pass that when Jesus had said these words, he perceived that there were some among them who marveled, and **wondered what he would concerning the law of Moses**, for **they understood not the saying that old things had passed away** and that all things had become new. And he said unto them, Marvel not that I said unto you that old things had passed away and that all things had become new. Behold, I say unto you that **the law is fulfilled that was given unto Moses. Behold, I am he that gave the law**, and I am he who covenanted with my people Israel. Therefore, **the law in me is fulfilled**, for I have come*

*to fulfill the law; **therefore, it hath an end**…the covenant which I have made with my people is not all fulfilled, **but the law which was given unto Moses hath an end in me**.* (3 Nephi 7:2 RE, emphasis added)

Those who teach the Law of Moses has not come to an end are led by a false spirit. That having been said, someone that has been misled by a false spirit does not necessarily mean that they are an evil person; it only means that they have been misled. Recall Christ rebuking Peter and calling Peter "Satan" because Peter was advising the Lord against the determined trip to Jerusalem where he would be crucified; and Peter told him, advised him, counseled him, and objected, "Far be it from you Lord. Don't do this thing" (see Matthew 9:2 RE). And the Lord, responding to Peter, called him "Satan."

There are many people who are only kept from the truth because they do not know where to find it. The obligation of those who can teach truth is to teach it. Overcoming most false spirits is to be done by gentleness, meekness, pure knowledge, and persuasion, not by rebuking, condemning, and dismissing the honest seeker for truth. At some point, every one of us has emerged from a cloud of falsehoods into acceptance of some truth. We're no better than others who remain under that cloud, but we have an obligation to invite them to join in receiving light and truth. Likewise, we have an obligation to continue to search for truth. Until you have an understanding of all things, you're still misled, at least in part.

The prophets are not all fulfilled and there will yet be many things returned and restored. This will include holy days—when we have a holy place to observe (in proper order) the things practiced between the time of Adam until the time of Abraham.

Now, I want to talk for a moment about signs that are in the New Testament canon involving Christ, in order to get to a principle that we need to understand. In Matthew:

And when Jesus departed from there, two blind men following him, crying and saying, Jesus, son of David, have mercy on us. And when he [was] come into the house, the blind men came to him, and Jesus said unto them, Do you believe that I am able to do this?

They said unto him, Yea, Lord. Then he touched their eyes, saying, according to your faith, be it unto you. And their eyes were opened. **And sternly he charged them, saying, Keep my commandments and see you tell no man in this place, that no man know it.** (Matthew 4:13 RE, emphasis added)

"You need to obey my commandments! You don't tell anyone! You don't tell anyone."

And again departing from the borders of Tyre and Sidon [this is from Mark], *he came unto the sea of Galilee, through the middle of the region of Decapolis. And they brought unto him one that was deaf, and had an impediment in his speech. And they petitioned him to put his hand upon him. And he took him aside from the multitude…put his finger into his ears, …spit and touched his tongue. And, [he] looked up to Heaven, he sighed and said unto him, …(that is, Be opened). And immediately his ears were opened, and the string of his tongue was untied [that] he spoke plain. And* **he charged them that they should tell no man.** *But the more he charged them, so much the more a great deal they published him, and were beyond measure astonished, saying, He has done all things well. He makes both the deaf to hear and the dumb to speak.* (Mark 4:14 RE, emphasis added)

This is from Mark, returning from the Mount of Transfiguration:

And as they came down from the mountain, **he charged them that they should tell no man what things they had seen** *until the Son of Man was risen from the dead.* (Mark 5:6 RE, emphasis added)

In Luke, after raising a dead man's daughter:

Her parents were astonished, but **he charged them they should tell no man what was done.** (Luke 6:12 RE)

In Luke, after healing a leper:

He charged him to tell no man. (Luke 4:10 RE)

Christ said to tell no one because it would attract the wrong kind of follower. It would attract the adulterers. It would attract the sign seekers. It would attract the wrong kind of people.

Satan tempted Christ, asking Him for signs that were self-serving: bread for the Lord to eat when the Lord was hungry; a show of angelic support when He would be cast off the Temple's pinnacle. At His death, the wicked demanded signs from Him. "Spare yourself from the crucifixion; heal yourself." Signs are (by their very nature) self-serving and attention-grabbing, and it is just inevitable. They attract followers, and the Jews knew this and feared Christ's miracles would result in Him becoming greatly popular.

> Then many of the Jews who came to Mary and had seen the things which Jesus did, believed on him. But some of them went their ways to the Pharisees and told them what things Jesus had done. Then gathered the chief priests and…Pharisees a council, and said, What shall we do? For this man does many miracles. If we let him alone, **all men will believe on him**, and the Romans shall come and take away both our place and nation. (John 7:7 RE, emphasis added)

But these would be the wrong kind of follower. The Gentiles **crave** that sort of thing. Gentiles who try to get a sign to follow do so because their hearts are wrong. **Signs follow faith**. Signs follow faith by the will of God, not of man. From the Teachings and Commandments: *And these signs **shall** follow them that believe: in my name they shall do many wonderful works* (T&C 82:22, emphasis added).

You want a sign that someone is a follower of Christ? Go ask the single mother with children who's being helped by the tithes of a fellowship that go directly to help her whether that is a wonderful work in her life and in her experience—and that's the **first** sign, perhaps the primary sign, perhaps the greatest sign—because it's relieving the need of someone that needs it.

> In my name they shall cast out devils, [and] in my name they shall heal the sick, [and] in my name they shall open the eyes of the blind and un-stop the ears of the deaf, and the tongue of the dumb shall speak, and if any man shall administer poison unto them, it

*shall not hurt them, and the poison of a serpent shall not have power to harm them. But **a commandment I give unto them that they shall not boast themselves of these things, neither speak them before the world,** for these things are given unto you for your profit and for [your] salvation.* (Ibid., emphasis added)

They are not given to you to boast about.

Melchizedek and the order of priesthood he obtained is described in the book of Genesis chapter 7 (in the current set of Scriptures, the Old Covenants):

> *For God…[swore] unto Enoch and unto his seed, with an oath by Himself, that everyone being ordained **after this order and calling,** should have **power, by faith,** to **break mountains*** (Genesis 7:19 RE, emphasis added).

We have no direct account of when the mountains have been broken by those after that order. We have one indirect reference in the book of Genesis, referring to Enoch:

> *And he spoke the word of the Lord, and the earth trembled, and the mountains fled even according to his command, and the rivers of water turned out of their course* (Genesis 4:13 RE).

You need to be careful how you parse that Scripture. Enoch spoke the word of the Lord. The word of the Lord is spoken. And in response to the word of the Lord having been spoken, the Earth trembled, and the mountains fled even according to His—the Lord—His command. And the rivers of water turned out of their course. Enoch preached, earthquakes followed, mountains moved. In Jacob 3:2 RE, there is another reference:

> *We obtain a hope and our faith becometh unshaken, insomuch that we truly can command in the name of Jesus and the very trees obey us, or the mountains, or the waves of the sea.*

That's Jacob illustrating that the faith they have has this effect. He doesn't describe that effect having occurred, simply that it's there. Nephi explained this is the power that God entrusted him with in Helaman:

> *For behold, the dust of the earth moveth hither and thither, to the dividing asunder, at the command of our great and everlasting God. Yea, behold, at his voice doth the hills and the mountains tremble and quake, and by the power of his voice are broken up and become smooth, yea, even like unto a valley.* (Helaman 4:10 RE)

He was given the sealing power. He was told that the Earth will obey you—because He knew that he would not do anything with that power other than what God willed. And shortly after being entrusted by God to this, Nephi prays to God and asks God to send a famine to stop the people from killing one another. So, here's someone who can speak the word of God and the Earth itself will obey him, and he uses that to get on his knees and pray and ask God. He doesn't command anything.

That kind of endowment of priestly authority is done because God expressed His faith in the man. Can God have faith in you? Can God trust you?

So, the list goes on:

- The mountains is the first thing.
- *To divide the seas.* We have an example of that with Moses.
- *To dry up waters.* We have an example of that with Joshua when they reached the river Jordan.
- *To turn them out of their course*, which was done again at the time of Enoch.
- To put at *defiance the armies* of nations—Elijah.
- To *divide the earth*.
- To *break every band*.
- To *stand in the presence of God*.
- To do all things according to *His will, according to His command*…

When it comes to breaking every band, keep that in mind—because we're gonna return to that in a moment.

And then it says:

- to *subdue principalities and powers*—these are in the spiritual realm: commanding devils, subduing principalities and powers.

These are rebellious spirits cast down from Heaven. These are those that pretend to be and often are false ministering spirits or angels.

...And this by the will of the Son of God, who was from before the foundation of the world. And men having this faith, coming up unto this order of God, were translated and taken up into Heaven. (Genesis 7:19 RE, emphasis added)

Not always the case—the only reason translation occurred is because a mission was assigned to them (but that's outside of this).

Any one of the foregoing signs is a **confirming** sign. It's not required for **all** these signs to be given before **faith is confirmed**. And because these are gifts from God, it is God who decides when the sign will be given. God determines if, when, what, and how often a sign will be given—not the will of men.

Notice that the Brother of Jared's moving of the Mount Zerin is not recorded in his record or Moroni's abridgment of that record. It is only mentioned in passing as an illustration (see Ether 5:6 RE). Even if we have faith to participate, the signs are God's. We are only witnesses. God sent Moses to deliver signs to Egypt, but the signs were God's. There is only one way in which a mortal can have discretion to invoke God's power, which involves one of the three kinds of sealing power I've previously discussed. (That third kind is described in the book of Helaman and involves Nephi, and I've previously talked about that.)

The reason Nephi was granted this authority was explained by God when he said, *Thou shalt not ask that which is contrary to my will* (Helaman 3:19 RE). When Nephi used that authority shortly afterward, he deferred to God, prayed, and asked God if **He** would cause a famine to stop the violence of the degenerate people of his generation.

One of the signs that someone has this authority is that they can break every band. An illustration of this is in Nephi. In the First Book of Nephi, when Nephi (in the wilderness) is bound by his brothers, left behind so that wild beasts would kill him:

*And it came to pass that they did lay their hands upon me, for
behold, they were exceeding[ly] wroth; and they did bind me with
cords, for they sought to take away my life, that they might leave
me in the wilderness to be devoured by wild beasts. But it came to
pass that I prayed unto the Lord, saying, O Lord, according to my
faith which is in thee, wilt thou deliver me from the hands of my
brethren? Yea, even give me strength that I may burst these bands
with which I am bound? And it came to pass that when I had said
these words, behold, the bands were loosed from off my hands and
feet, and I stood before my brethren and I spake unto them again.*
(1 Nephi 2:4 RE)

Nephi is evidencing one of the signs of a person who is entrusted with
that ordination of priesthood or that order of priesthood to which
Melchizedek had been previously ordained. So, we have a sign, and we
have a testimony, and he's broken the band, and it confirms who he is.

But later, on the boat, Nephi was bound again, and a tempest came up:

*Nevertheless, they did not loose me. And on the fourth day which
we had been driven back, the tempest began to be exceedingly sore.
And it came to pass that we were about to be swallowed up in the
depths of the sea. And after we had been driven back upon the
waters for the space of four days, my brethren began to see that the
judgments of God were upon them, and that they must perish save
they should repent of their iniquities. Wherefore, they came unto
me and [loosened] the bands which were upon my wrists, and
behold, they had swollen exceedingly; and also mine ankles [which]
were much swollen, and great was the soreness thereof.* (1 Nephi
5:30 RE)

Nephi could not break the bands, and he suffered because of it. Why
would that same God (who entrusted to Nephi the power and the
authority to demonstrate one of the signs that he was beloved and
trusted of God, ordained to the order of Melchizedek, and could break
the bands) leave him in a bound condition for days while his hands
and his feet are swelling? Why would He do that? Why is God not
Google? Why is God not fast-food? Why is God not a short-order cook
that can be bossed around by those to whom He has entrusted this
authority? Why does God leave them always subordinate to the will of

God? Why does the conferral of the sealing power upon Nephi and Helaman state that it is only because he will obey God? Why must all men always remain subordinate to God?

Moroni explained this principle:

> *Wherefore, dispute not because ye see not, for ye receive no witness — not until after the trial of your faith. For it was by faith that Christ shewed himself unto our fathers and after he had risen from the dead, and he shewed not himself unto them until after they had faith in him; wherefore, it must needs be that some had faith in him, for he shewed himself not unto the world but because of the faith of men...Behold, it was by faith that they of old were called after the Holy Order of God. Wherefore, by faith was the Law of Moses given. But in the gift of the Son hath God prepared a more excellent way, and it is by faith that it hath been fulfilled. For [there is] no faith among the children of men, God can do no miracle among them; wherefore, he [showeth] not himself until after their faith.* (Ether 5:2 RE)

I have witnessed many miracles. I have been ministered to by angels and have been both in the presence of and received instruction from Jesus Christ. I've been shown unspeakable things, but I **know** that **I am nothing**. I fear God, and I pray continually and submit to His commandments even when it's difficult. I disagree with, I argue with, and I provide my best advice and counsel when I honestly believe something asked of me is unwise or when I believe I'm not the right person to be doing an assignment.

God is willing to speak plainly as one man speaks to another. God has been patient, faithful, and willing to reason with me as one man reasons with another. I can't tell you how often God's words to Isaiah have been vindicated: *For my thoughts are not your thoughts, neither are your ways my ways, says the Lord. For as the heavens are higher than the earth, so are my ways higher than your ways, and my thoughts than your thoughts* (Isaiah 20:2 RE).

God knows and understands every one of us. God knows and understands when healing would prove to be a curse and not a blessing. God knows and understands when some person of faith, like Job, is called upon to endure something. Christ in the garden **begged** that the cup be taken from Him, and **the Father refused that request**.

Have any of you ever witnessed the miracle of healing? Because I have. I've participated in some of those. But there are people I know who I would love to have healed, who I begged God for the blessing that they be healed. I've gotten answers. I've been told why they will not be healed. But I don't have the ability to require God to heal at my insistence—nor do any of you; nor has any man ever, in all the account of Scripture. Christ could not heal some people in some instances, and He was the Son of God. In all of Scripture, there is only one moment when it appears that anyone could be healed no matter what their condition was—only one time. And at that moment, Christ was resurrected, and He was appearing as a resurrected being, not still as a mortal. As a mortal, Christ could not heal some. As a mortal, Christ could not persuade the Father to change the Father's will.

Some of you, like the antagonists of Job, have said to others of you that you don't have enough faith to be healed. You're worm-tongue. You're a false spirit. You're an accuser of the brethren. You have absolutely no right to make that assertion. Would you tell Christ (when He could not perform a healing), "Jesus, your problem is you don't have enough faith." Because that's essentially what you're saying. You're saying, "Men ought to be sovereign; not God." You're saying, "Signs, which surely are given, signs follow people of faith incessantly."

I don't know how many times… (I'm looking at Rob over there taking notes. Hey, Rob, do you know I'm here? He hasn't looked up.) I don't know how many times you and I, in company with one another, have witnessed signs. Signs are given. Signs exist. You know what? I've told a few family members; I assume Rob's told a few family members. It's never been on the Internet; it's never been advertised, never found its way into one of my talks. And you know why? Because people that are only interested in signs are corrupt, and if someone will go perform some great sign and boast about it and that's of interest to you, then take your gentile, adulterous predisposition, and go follow them. But you will not witness the miracles of God unless you submit to the commandments of God, and if you do that, signs will follow.

Don't judge another because you think God can be turned into an obedient servant that must heal if you have faith. It doesn't work that way. It didn't work that way for Christ. It won't work that way for us. Go humbly to the throne of God, and petition Him for intercession. If you have faith, He will either heal or (if you have faith) He will explain to you in an answer why it's denied. You will know. You will come away with intelligence. What you cannot do is ignore Heaven and demand that you have your way. God has been patient, faithful, and willing to reason with me. And God will be patient, faithful, and willing to reason with you.

There's no institution for us, and none is planned. We are all on our own, accountable to individually accept the responsibilities of discipleship. We should help one another in that effort. But we are not powerless when strange fruit comes and cumbers our fellowships. If a teaching does not conform to the Book of Mormon, you are entitled to reject it, to correct it, to be done with it. The Book of Mormon is the standard for our faith, for our day. It is the rule for our beliefs and practices. It is a covenant for our day.

One of the greatest events that has occurred in history is that in our day—in your lifetime—new Scriptures have become available. The extent to which that is a good work can hardly be put into words. Moses recovered Scripture that had been lost. The Old Testament record originates beginning with Moses. Prior to Moses' day, the only volume of Scripture that we can definitively say is preceding Moses' five books is the Book of Job.

In the Book of Mormon, there is another prophet who may also have preceded Moses, and that's Zenos. The Book of Mormon quotes— directly—writings of Zenos. Somewhere over three thousand words of Zenos are quoted directly in the Book of Mormon. He may also be older than the five books of Moses.

All of the Scripture that was recovered through Moses was recovered again, a second time, through Ezra. There had been a great deal lost as a consequence of the Babylonian captivity, and when a remnant returned, one of the things that a leader in that remnant did was to recover Scripture. So, the Old Testament canon that we're familiar with is really a recovery by Ezra of what had been originally produced in part at the time of Moses. All these texts get corrupted over time.

We have a third attempt to recover the Scripture that occurred through the Prophet Joseph Smith. The Prophet Joseph Smith was commanded to go through the Old and the New Testament and to make inspired corrections to it, and we have that. But the saints were condemned in ~~1831~~ [1832] because they did not respect the Book of Mormon and the former commandments, not only to say but to do, and that condemnation rested upon all.

One of the things that has been discovered in the effort to recover the Scriptures and to get them in a form that closely… (At this point, it's hopeless to make it "exactly," but it is "extremely close" to what was here originally.) One of the things we've learned is that the condemnation was for two things: failure to say and the failure to do. Most people think that the problem was the failure to do (like, "You're condemned because you say it, but you don't do it"). That's not what it meant. God condemned them because they weren't **saying** it, **and** they weren't **doing** it. In other words, the Book of Mormon and the former commandments that had been entrusted to the saints: they failed to say it, and they failed to do it, because the text of the Book of Mormon had become "roughed up" in the process.

An extraordinary effort was required in order to try and get it back to the beginning. We **know** that we did not (because you cannot, at this point) fully recover the original—can't be done. We got as close as we could, and in the process of that recovery effort and praying about it (as a sign to us of divine approval), God made edit corrections to the text of the Book of Mormon, and those have been put into… Divinely, recently obtained corrections to the text have been put into the Book of Mormon, almost every one of which are quotes of Christ. He fixed what He said into a correct set of instructions for us.

The original revelations of Joseph Smith were mishandled, mistreated. They were interlineated by people that probably shouldn't have done that. A great deal of conscientious effort went into trying to get that recovered. We now have, for the first time—it didn't happen while Joseph Smith was alive—we now have as close and as accurate a set of Scriptures as can be recovered at this late date that are remarkably faithful to the Restoration that the Lord intended through Joseph Smith.

The Joseph Smith Translation of the Bible (the Old and the New Testament), when the Latter-day Saints left and came out West, that manuscript remained in the possession of Emma Smith. Emma Smith handed it down to her son, Joseph Smith III, and ultimately, the church that he led (the Reorganized Church) published the Joseph Smith Translation or the Inspired Version of the Bible. But when they published it, the committee that did the publication left out a number of the changes and corrections that Joseph Smith had made. Likewise, they felt it their prerogative to insert some editorial changes of their own. And so, the Inspired Version of the Bible that people purchase and look at today is actually not what Joseph Smith did. The new Scriptures **have** what Joseph Smith **did**—all of his punctuation changes; all of his alterations—and Joseph never published it during his lifetime and continued to make changes to the text right through the sermons that he delivered in Nauvoo.

Several times in his sermons he would say/read a verse from the Bible or the New Testament, and he would say, "I could give a plainer translation," and then he says something about the verse that is plainer or more correct. For the first time, **all** of those Nauvoo-era alterations that he said is "plainer or more correct" or "it should read…" all of those have been gathered and put into the New Testament and Old Testament of the New Covenants and Old Covenants text that are published. This is a great work. This is a sign. Whether you respect the effort that it took or the fact that it has finally rolled out or not, it is a remarkable, historical occurrence in your lifetime.

Now, I wrote a book… I wrote a book that got me into a lot of trouble. It was an intellectual exercise; it was a historical exercise. I was attempting to start from the theoretical standpoint that the Book of Mormon text and the prophecies of Joseph Smith foretell events that will occur when the Gentiles obtain the Restoration of the gospel. And so, as a matter of curiosity, investigation, study, and effort, I posed the question, "What would it look like if the things that are prophesied **have** occurred?"

Passing The Heavenly Gift is a text attempting to answer the question, "What if it's already happened? How would you tell the story of the Restoration?" It is not put out as a dogmatic claim that [in Cronkite's voice], "This is our history, and you better look at it as though it's the truth." (That's my best Walter Cronkite. He was the guy that everyone trusted, at one point.)

[In McConkie's voice] "I did not regard it as my responsibility to declare the history and your responsibility to accept what I declared," —as if I were some, you know, McConkie figure.

I did it as conjecture, to see: Does it fit? Would it work? Can the story be told that way? And I never reach a conclusion in that book. I simply say, "Look at what might have happened." The fact that it fits hand-in-glove may be incredibly persuasive (alarming, distressing…), but it doesn't assert that it's true, and that book took like 200,000 words to tell the story of the Restoration.

Well, when the ~~Nauvoo~~ Kirtland Temple was dedicated (Joseph didn't live long enough for the Nauvoo Temple to be completed, much less dedicated), but when the Kirtland Temple was dedicated, Joseph Smith thought that that occasion required a formal prayer to be given. And so, Joseph prepared a formal prayer for the dedication of the Nauvoo Temple, and he said that that prayer—that dedicatory prayer—was actually a revelation, that the content (it's in the D&C; it's section 109 of the Doctrine and Covenants), it was an inspired prayer.

I wrote a book that was 200,000 words. I thought that petitioning God for His approval of the new Scriptures required a formality akin to the formality of the dedication of the Kirtland Temple. And so, I knew that there needed to be a prayer presented.

I was prayerful about considering the content of the prayer, and one evening I sat down to compose a prayer for presenting the Scriptures (which I intended to present to the Scripture Committee for their approval before presenting it to the Lord—and to get their input on the prayer). When I sat down, the prayer was revelation. It was what God wanted us to ask. Well, that left me no choice to go to the committee and say, "Hey, give me your input." Because I don't have the right to change what God wants the prayer to include. It's part of the new Scriptures.

That prayer tells the same story, in an inspired way—with far fewer than 200,000 words with footnotes and chapter divisions. It is God's view of what we have done with the Restoration.

I do not assert that *Passing The Heavenly Gift* is good, true, and faithful history. But I testify to you that the Prayer for Covenant is, in fact, a revelation from God that tells you what the history of the Restoration has consisted of. And if you want to know what has happened, read the Prayer for the Covenant that describes the project, and you'll know what God thinks we have done and what we have not done.

The new Scriptures is a historical event that—throughout the entirety of history, going back to the time of Moses—has only happened three times:

- It happened with Moses.
- It happened with Ezra.
- It happened through the prophet Joseph Smith and
- Through the faithful diligence of a remnant of the people who sought to reconnect, in our day (and to honor that third restoration through Joseph Smith).

It is beyond historic. It is something designed to alter the course of history. But some people look upon signs like that as inconsequential and easy to dismiss.

I can testify to you that the heavens themselves rejoice at what happened there—even if you're dismissive; even if you're nonchalant about it. It is, nevertheless, one of the greatest developments to occur in history, and it happened in your lifetime. The saints were rejected in 1844. Nothing has been done to repair the condemnation in ~~1831~~ [1832] or to reclaim people since the rejection in 1844. No one has attempted to repent and remember the former commandments—not only to say but to do—until today.

Stop your damn squabbling! Don't go back and revert to pre-1820 Christian conduct that aroused God's ire! (I use the word "damned" in the scriptural sense because that's exactly what it is.) Stop squabbling!

Stop disagreeing! Surrender your pride! If you think you're right/if you think someone needs to be corrected/if you think you have a higher, holier, better way—stay and persuade. Be meek. Be humble. Solicit other people, and appeal to their heart.

We should welcome everyone. We should welcome Latter-day Saints. We should welcome Community of Christ. We should welcome Catholics. We should welcome Presbyterians. We should welcome every kind of person and then treat them with respect and kindness and understanding. Let them bring their ideas, and let you teach them those truths that you presently understand. The religion of Joseph Smith which—it's in that video that was shown just before the opening prayer—the religion of Joseph Smith is to accept all truth. Just because it hasn't entered into your hard heart and your closed mind yet doesn't make it untrue.

There are truths in rich abundance that hail from all quarters of the Earth. As religions have discarded truths, many of them have sought and fought to retain the most important core. And the most important core of many faiths and the highest aspiration and the highest ideal—

It doesn't matter if you're talking the Cherokee tradition, the Hindu tradition, the Islamic tradition, the Polynesian/the Hawaiian tradition. It doesn't matter. The highest aspiration remains for the individual to connect to God and for God to recognize and connect with the individual. There's really no difference. If we welcome one another, and we treat each other kindly—

Someone that may have a religion that is very strange to us, if they bring with them the aspiration to know God and we can persuade them that God has done a work among us through Joseph Smith—through the labor that has been done to recover that Restoration—maybe they'll labor alongside us as the Restoration wraps up.

There is a great deal left to be done. And there is no one seriously entertaining the possibility of constructing a city of holiness, a city of peace, a people that are fruit "worthy to be laid up against the harvest." No one has made the effort until now. And while you may look at us and say, "You've done a crude job; you've done a rudimentary job; it needs improvement..." then help us improve it! Stop sitting back and throwing rocks! This is a time to gather, not to disperse. The same garbage that existed at the beginning (when Joseph looked around and saw confusion and disharmony) wants to creep in among us. Recognize that's a false spirit.

If you'll cast it out of yourself and if you'll look at the words of the covenant that was offered in September of 2017, what you'll find is that Christ wants us—like the Book of Mormon explains—to be meek, to be humble, and to be easily entreated.   And therefore, entreat one another to honor God, and recognize that all of us aspire to be equal, whether you're at the top or at the root. The aspiration is the same: to be equal.

Well, the time's far spent, and we need to be out of here in less than an hour, and there's some work that has gone on behind the scenes that needs to continue. So, I'm gonna wrap this up.

Let me end by bearing testimony to you that what I've said has not been just me up here giving a talk. Guidance has been given and content has been provided from a higher source than myself, and I hope you take seriously the things that have been said today.

Because this is a Sunday, as an act of rebellion, I wore a tie; and because it was a Sunday, I had someone give an opening prayer, and we're going to have someone give a closing prayer.

But if you want to know the history of the Restoration from God's perspective, read the Prayer for the Covenant that's in the Teachings and Commandments, and you'll see what God thinks the history is. If you want to know my research project and how I parsed it together in a lot more words than that, you can read *Passing the Heavenly Gift*. I don't know how many footnotes are in there, but it's a research project.

Thank you.

Response from the Lord on Acceptance of Scriptures

Revelation received through Denver Snuffer, Jr., recorded on the morning of 6 April 2019 in response to his supplication on behalf of the Scriptures Project completion.

You have asked to know if the Scriptures are acceptable and approved or if there is more to be done:

The work that has been done is acceptable and sufficient for the labor now underway. You were permitted to update language, select a current vocabulary, and you were warned not to change any meaning. I reminded you that you do not understand the glory to be revealed unto my covenant people. You were instructed to complete the agreed-upon labors, and you have done as was required.

These Scriptures are sent forth to be my warning to the world, my comfort to the faithful, my counsel to the meek, my reproof to the proud, my rebuke to the contentious, and my condemnation of the wicked. They are my invitation to all mankind to flee from corruption, repent and be baptized in my name, and prepare for the coming judgment.

False witnesses will be exposed, and the imaginings of the wicked heart will prove a curse unto them. A corrupt and foolish world will be brought to harvest, while the faithful who receive my words, obey my voice, covenant with me, and abide my law shall be preserved. I come as a thief in the night, and none can stay my coming.

I ordained this work and labored beside you. No man should condemn these words or see the weakness of my laborers when I judge their hearts. All their weakness, foolishness, and vanity are before me, and none of it is hidden to me. To vindicate the promises I made to the fathers, I will bear patiently with all of you for my name's sake. If I accept their work, despite their weaknesses, that I may fulfill my promises to gather my people under my wings, then stop murmuring and complaining against those who labor. If you expect mercy, then show mercy to others. I, your Lord, am pleased with all those who are grateful and merciful and who will have me be their God. I am meek and lowly of heart.

Celebrating the Family of Joseph and Emma Smith

Transcript of a Lecture delivered in Independence, MO
April 10, 2019

My name is Denver Snuffer. I'm an attorney from Sandy (in Salt Lake; it's a suburb of Salt Lake). I graduated from Brigham Young University's law school. And I'm an excommunicated Mormon— because one of the things they taught me to do in law school was to critically-think. And as a result of critically-thinking, I followed a number of historical issues through to their logical conclusion. I wrote an alternative history of the Restoration (explaining how I think it might better fit within the scriptural model that says the Gentiles were going to behave in a certain way), and I was told, "Either withdraw that book from publication or we're going to excommunicate you from the Church." And I had contracts in place that obligated me to leave it in publication, so I got the boot.

Now, I didn't come to Mormonism from birth. I was born to a Baptist mother. And I **learned** that Joseph Smith was a ne'er-do-well founder of a cult and someone to be feared, not admired. I grew up in Idaho. I was in the military during the Vietnam conflict, but I was stationed stateside. I was in New Hampshire and ran into a Mormon fellow who sicced Mormon missionaries on me12 who proceeded to pamphleteer and filmstrip me. And over the course of a number of months, they finally persuaded me to actually take Joseph Smith seriously.

I was at the birthplace of Joseph Smith in Sharon, Vermont; spent a weekend there. It was a Aaronic Priesthood Commemoration, and this was, more or less, a campout. While I was there, I went to a visitor's center, took a copy that they gave me (for free) of a triple combination, in which the fellow that was befriending me suggested I read section 76: the Vision of the Three Degrees of Glory. I read the Vision of the Three Degrees of Glory, and it struck me that a **scoundrel** could not write this. A **fraud** could not write this—the loftiness of the content, the beauty, the symmetry, the light that came through. This shook me up because I'd been very dismissive of the whole Joseph Smith thing, and now here I have something (from the very scoundrel) that read like a transcript from heaven. It was disturbing. But I finally resolved to seriously investigate whether or not Joseph Smith amounted to much.

I was baptized into the LDS version of Mormonism when I was 19-years-old. I was baptized on September the 10th of 1973. I was excommunicated from the LDS Church on September the 10th of 2013—40 years, to the day, from the time I came into the LDS Church to the time that I went out. But where I "came in" reluctantly accepting Joseph Smith to be an actual messenger from God, I "went out" firm in the conviction that Joseph Smith was everything he purported to be and probably more. He probably understated it.

If you read the words of Joseph Smith—

One of the best places to get your hands around Joseph is to get one of the Joseph Smith history versions (that you find in the LDS publication of the Joseph Smith-History) and just read the account of the visit of John the Baptist when Aaronic priesthood is bestowed. Then (in the LDS version) they give you a footnote, and the footnote is Oliver Cowdery's account of the very same thing. Joseph Smith's version is **remarkably understated**—simple words, small vocabulary, homespun, plain. It reeks of honesty and simplicity. And then you read Oliver's account of the very same thing—it's ornate, it's flowery, it's overstated, it's lawyered. (I mean, to his discredit, after he left the Church, Oliver Cowdery wound up practicing law. And we all know what the Scriptures have to say about lawyers. So, Oliver certainly fell from grace.)

Joseph Smith is an enigma. He is a blank screen onto which you project who **you** are, literally. I have read probably every document that Joseph Smith ever authored. I have studied every journal that was written for him. I've read all of what the critics and the anti-Mormons had to say about Joseph Smith. Anytime a new Joseph Smith biography rolls out, I'll get it, and I'll read it.

If you take the moment that Joseph Smith died (June the 27th of 1844), if you take that moment and you go backward in time and you say, "How do I construct the history of Joseph Smith from the beginning of his birth in 1805 until June the 27th of 1844, using only materials that existed at or before the moment of his death?" you come away from that endeavor saying, "Joseph **could not possibly** be a polygamist."

You heard him say a moment ago that Joseph Smith III and David and Alexander—they came out to Utah. You know that when they came out to Utah, it so upset the apple cart that their first cousin (Joseph F. Smith—who would subsequently become president of the LDS Church) began—in the same 1860s when they came out—to go around to get affidavits (in an affidavit book) of women who would swear an oath that Joseph Smith practiced polygamy and/or was their plural husband and/or taught them about polygamy. All of these affidavits were created in the 1860s. Brigham Young had the notion of polygamy taught publicly for the first time in 1853. Joseph Smith had been dead for nine years by the time it became public news. Well, the best way to get people who are loyal to Joseph Smith to accept a principle that you want to advance is to pin it on Joseph Smith, whether it belongs there or not. But the people who knew Joseph best had a very different view of where that originated.

On that evening when the angel visited him in his home, Joseph Smith recorded (and this was in 1838), he recorded: *He called me by name...* This is the angel Nephi—turned into Moroni, subsequently—but the angel Nephi:

> *He called me by name, and said unto me that he was a messenger sent from the presence of God to me, and that his name was* [in the original, it said "Nephi"; in this version it now says] *Moroni; that God had a work for me to do; and that my name should be had for good and evil among all nations, kindreds, and tongues, or that it should be both good and evil spoken of among all people.* (JS-H 1:33 LE; see also Joseph Smith History 3:3 RE)

First words out of his mouth. First words out of the angel's mouth: "Get used to it, Joseph. People are gonna say things. They're gonna say things that are good about you, and they are going to speak evil about you." And the angel goes on to describe a few other things.

The light gathers around him; he departs. And then the light starts up again, and the angel shows up again. And when he shows up again,

> *He commenced, and again related the very same things which he had done at [the] first visit, without the least variation[s]...* (Ibid. vs. 45; see also 3:7 RE)

...which means that the **second** visit that occurs that night, the angel tells him the **same thing** about how people are going to talk about him, both good and evil.

Then he ascends, and he returns a third time. And the third time:

> But what was my surprise when again I beheld the same messenger at my bedside, and heard him rehearse or repeat over again to me the same things as before; and added a caution... (Ibid. vs. 46; see also 3:8 RE)

...not to try and get the plates to get wealthy. Three times that night, and it starts out the very same way all three times, "Joseph, your name is gonna be had for both good and evil"—on the same night.

Then Joseph, the next morning—he's tired; he goes out to work. When he goes out to work, his father says, "You're unable." And he sends him home. On his way back home, he collapsed from exhaustion. When he wakes up from that collapse:

> First thing...I can recollect was a voice speaking unto me, calling me by name. I looked up, and beheld the same messenger standing over my head, surrounded by light as before. He then again related unto me all that he had related to me the previous night... (Ibid. vs. 49; see also 3:10 RE)

So for the fourth time, he gets told the very same thing.

Yeah, yeah?? [responding to a raised hand in the audience]

Audience Member: So, why was it Nephi, when we've always thought it was Moroni, then?

Denver: The name got changed to Moroni **later**. In all of the early accounts, the name of the angel is Nephi. Joseph Smith wrote that the name of the angel was Nephi; he wrote that.

Audience Member (continued): In his history?

Denver: Repeatedly. In multiple accounts of his history, the name was Nephi. One of the little known facts about the visit of the angel is that before the Three Witnesses got their vision of the plates, the angel that would show those plates to the Three Witnesses appeared to the Whitmers' mother. Mother Whitmer saw the angel, and he identified himself to her also, and he identified himself by the same name—as Nephi.

Well, I have a supposition, and I'll give you my supposition, okay? Moroni was the last one to write in the book. He was the one to finish the record, and he was the one to bury it. And therefore, someone got to thinking: if he was the one that buried it and if Nephi had lived long ago and wasn't around when the book got finished—wasn't around when Mormon condensed it, wasn't dealing with the text at the end—and Moroni buried it up, maybe we should say it was Moroni, 'cause he was the one that put it in the ground. Makes more sense; he'd know where it was.

But there's a **problem** with that. Joseph Smith was very clear about the intangibility of a spirit. A spirit is not composed of the same stuff as are resurrected beings (who are composed of physical matter after the resurrection). Moroni lived 400 years **after** Christ's resurrection. There is only going to be a general resurrection (that will include him [Moroni]) at the Second Coming. Nephi, on the other hand, lived 600 years **before** Christ. And at the resurrection of Christ… It's recorded in Matthew that many of the saints that slept arose and went into the city and were seen by people. So, people in Jerusalem saw that there were resurrected beings.

And then, in His discussion with the Nephites, Christ said, "Hey, Samuel prophesied that when I arose from the dead that there would be others who were resurrected. He prophesied of that, and it happened! And that's not in your record." And so, the Book of Mormon has that commentary by Christ. As He looks at the records, He says, "You have omitted the fact that there were those who would be resurrected." Well, Nephi would have died at a point that he would be one of the candidates for resurrection, which means that he could **easily** handle the plates.

The Three Witnesses saw the plates and were shown them by an angel who took the plates and opened and turned the pages to show them each one of the pages that had been translated. And so, it makes sense that the name of the angel would have been Nephi. If you think that

Nephi couldn't be told where to go and find the plates, I mean, that's just plain silly. You do not need the **last** guy who handled them and put them under the stone in the box to be the only guy who... "Shhhh, keep it a secret. I buried the plates there. No one knows." And so, I think the reason the name got changed was someone thought it through and concluded it makes more sense to have the fellow who buried the plates be the one who restores the plates, instead of thinking it through the rest of the way and saying, "Wait a minute; he would be a spirit being in spirit prison and incapable of physicality."

Audience Member (continued): So, the Mormons have—don't they have Moroni at the top of the temple?

Denver: Yes, they do. It's silly. Yeah.

Audience Member (continued): So, well, that should've been Nephi, then?

Denver: It should've been, yeah. It should've been.

Audience Member: I guess they could always say it's Nephi?

Denver: No, no, they are very clear: It's Moroni. Yeah, think he's got a name tag on, representative of... I shouldn't be irreverent like that, actually.

Okay, so, four times he appears to him.

By the way, John Whitmer was called to be the historian for the Church. John Whitmer had all of the records that existed in the LDS Church (the Church of Jesus Christ of Latter Day Saints—no hyphen, small 't'—unlike what the LDS claim today). And he was excommunicated, disaffected, in the 1838 timeframe. So, the history of Joseph Smith that you read in the LDS version was Joseph Smith sitting down to re-write the missing history that they couldn't get back from John Whitmer, and it's a replacement history. It was written in 1838. And in 1838, he said it was Nephi. It was copied; he proofread the copy in 1839—it was again Nephi. He published his history in the *Times and Seasons*—it was Nephi. The first time that it shows up with the name Moroni, I believe, was in the *Messenger and Advocate*. I think that's where it first shows up, and that paper was edited by someone other than Joseph. So, it crept in there.

So, Joseph composes a replacement history in 1838. The Missouri conflict breaks out later in 1838. And Joseph winds up arrested and confined—ultimately confined in the Liberty Jail. While he's in the Liberty Jail, he writes a very lengthy letter—it's written in two parts, but it's a single letter, portions of which have been added to the LDS version of the Scriptures. And in one portion—after Joseph has been pouring his heart out about the circumstances and asking God why he's being put through this gosh-awful mess and why his people have been put through what the people have been put through and why isn't God answering him and doing something and pouring out His anger on the people—Joseph gets a letter from home. It excites his mind. The letter is brilliantly written about how his mind... It's going from one offense to the next to the next like lightning; he just... He cannot keep his mind composed until finally, he says, he sits down (exhausted from the mental anguish of it all) and then—**then**—the still small voice creeps in, and he hears God in it, and God says:

> *The ends of the earth shall inquire after thy name, and fools shall have thee in derision, and hell shall rage against thee; While the pure in heart, and the wise, and the noble, and the virtuous, shall seek counsel, and authority, and blessings constantly from under thy hand. And thy people shall never be turned against thee by the testimony of traitors.* (D&C 122:1-3; see also T&C 139:7)

Why would the wise, the noble, the virtuous—why would they want blessings from under the hand of Joseph Smith if Joseph Smith is not himself a wise and noble and virtuous man? It makes no sense.

Well, I have read histories that have attacked Joseph Smith as one of the vilest characters that has ever lived, and they make a plausible case for that. And I have read histories that make Joseph out to be noble and virtuous (although in my estimation none of those **adequately** capture who he really was), and they make a plausible case. The problem is not that there isn't source material from which to write a positive or a negative history of Joseph Smith. The problem is that you can't reconcile them; they can't be the same man. You literally are forced to choose. When it comes to Joseph Smith, the blank canvas that Joseph Smith is that's standing in front of you, you have to pick up and color it. And whatever you color it with is more a reflection of **you** than it is of him.

I've reached the conclusion to color in Joseph Smith using the most wise, the most noble, and the most virtuous version that I can construct of the man—the man who helped write the denunciations of John C. Bennett, the man who removed the authority of Sampson Avard in order to prevent Sampson Avard from going out and extracting vengeance that led to the Missouri conflict. I choose to view Joseph as someone who **was** noble, who **was** a peacemaker, who—when the Missouri militia showed up—chose to have his people surrender their arms rather than to have open conflict. I choose to view Joseph as the one who surrendered the muskets and surrendered the cannons of the Nauvoo Legion (even though they outnumbered the United States Army at the time) rather than to have armed conflict. I choose to view Joseph as the one who said, "I go as a lamb to the slaughter with a conscience void of any offense against my fellow man or of God" (see D&C 135:4). I don't think an adulterer and a liar and a thief could have made such a statement. I choose to color the picture in of Joseph as what I believe him honestly to be: a man of extraordinary virtue.

Well, in that Joseph Smith-History, he begins his account by talking about the religious conflict that existed at the time that provoked him to go out and pray and try to get an answer about which church to join. And he makes this point after talking about the *Lo, here!…Lo, there! Some [going to] the Methodist[s], some [going to] Presbyterian* (JS-H 1:5 LE; see also Joseph Smith History 1:11 RE), and he says:

> *It was seen that the seemingly good feelings of both the priests and the converts were more pretended than real; for a scene of great confusion and bad feeling ensued; priest contending against priest, and convert against convert; so that all their good feelings one for another, if they ever had any, were entirely lost in a strife of words and a contest about opinions.* (JS-H 1:6 LE; see also Joseph Smith History 1:11 RE)

Look, the legacy of Joseph Smith has been turned into over 80 different denominations that claim Joseph Smith as their founder. And if you don't think that Mormonism today—in the landscape, taking them all into account—aren't engaged in a strife of opinions with all of the seeming-good feelings one towards another entirely gone, then you aren't paying any attention to what these various sects are saying, claiming, and doing. The headquarters in Salt Lake City is a multi, multi-billion dollar organization. They have enough resources that they're about to develop a community in Florida that will have everything necessary for a half-a-million people to live in the community. It's a commercial development. They're not building it for members; they're building it as a real estate developer to sell to the public—a half-a-million-population community that will include streets and water tanks and utilities and schools, that will include business districts, that will include gas stations, that will include everything you need in order to have a community of half-a-million people living.

Audience Member: Where is that in Florida?

Denver: It's just outside Orlando. It's on a former cattle farm that they're now converting over to commercial development. It will pencil in, over the course of the development, in excess of a trillion dollar investment. A **trillion** dollar investment, 'k?

Mormonism—The Church of Jesus Christ of Latter-day Saints—is a small subsidiary (admittedly, it's a tax-free subsidiary, but it's a small subsidiary) venture of the Corporation of the President of The Church of Jesus Christ of Latter-day Saints. They own Bonneville Communications. They own universities. They own banking interests. They own a **lot** of real estate interests. And they have this tax-free subsidiary called the "Church"—and the only thing that's required for them to do to maintain that is every six months provide some meaningful, uplifting talks in their general conferences and get the sustaining vote. And they get it automatically. But they're becoming increasingly more vacuous.

Yeah?

Audience Member: Sorry.

Denver: No, it's fine.

Audience Member: OK, a couple things: first, with Joseph Smith, you know, at Liberty Jail he says, I, Joseph Smith, Jr., you know—young Joseph, you'll be the next prophet. Okay, so when you see that and know that he is a member, you know, of the Reorganized Church of Jesus Christ of Latter-day Saints, wouldn't you say that if you resolved already about Joseph Smith, wouldn't you say that this [Community of Christ] is the true church then, because Joseph Smith, Jr., you know, brought it up?

Denver: I think all of us fall into the institutional trap. It's that old game: "Button, Button, Who's Got the Button?" Are you trying to determine who is it that has the prerogative? Who is it that has the right?

The Book of Mormon has a message about Christ. And the revelations through Joseph define the church not in a corporate sense but in a believing sense. All who will repent and come unto Him are His church. Does that church necessarily have to have a hierarchy? Does it have to have structure? Does it have to have offices? Well, each one of the denominations contend and say, "You **have** to have... And **we're it**." The Book of Mormon and the revelations through Joseph Smith dial that back to…

If you belong and support and fellowship in the Community of Christ (and I used to belong and can't fellowship within the LDS Church), but you and I can agree on the fundamentals of the religion and agree on who Christ is and that salvation is through Christ alone, there's no reason why you and I can't have fellowship with one another. There's no reason why we ought to be dividing ourselves.

Eighty different denominations. The most wealthy one has fairly little regard for the substance of the religion anymore. **All** of them have their pet causes, their hooks, what they claim: "This is why we are the **best** version of that." But what if the best version of that doesn't exist in an institutional way, with someone presiding over someone else? What if the best version of that consists of you and me viewing each other with equal dignity, equal care, equal concern, and that we can fellowship across any boundaries?

What if I can offer baptism that reflects **all** of the Restoration, but the person that comes to me is Catholic and their family's Catholic and their friends are Catholic; and they would like to continue to fellowship with the Catholics, but they believe in the Restoration, and they believe in Joseph Smith, and they accept the Book of Mormon? Why can't I baptize him or her and let them **fellowship** with who they want to fellowship with and rejoice that both of us have found in each other a brother or sister in which we accept Joseph, we accept the Restoration, we accept the work of God?

Why does denominational differences occupy the center (instead of just the outer) periphery? Why isn't denominational affiliation largely superfluous? And what matters is understanding that God did a work through Joseph Smith, and it didn't get completed? It **did not** get completed. Much of what we argue over are the beginning stages of something that's supposed to develop into—ultimately—one heart, one mind, no poor among us. What if our denominations don't want there to be no poor among us? What if our denominations are interfering with our ability to be of one heart?   What if they **purposefully** do not want us to be of one mind?

If you are the adversary, if you're the enemy, if what you fear above all else is the coming of Zion, what's the best way to hedge up the way and to prevent the coming of Zion? It's to make sure that all of the good feelings that people have towards one another are entirely lost in a contest of opinions and a strife of words, in which what separates us is far more important than accepting the things that matter, that are eternal, that are divine. How are we going to become of one heart and one mind if the only thing that's on our mind is our differences? How are we going to become of one heart if our hearts can never become united because, well…you accept that brand, and I don't, and there's something wrong with that brand!

Audience Member: So, what is the attraction of the Mormon Church that brings so many of them in?

Denver: They have some bundle of truth. All of these Restoration groups, even…

You can take the most odious version of Restoration Mormonism Sectarianism, take the worst of the group—that's probably that "Warren Jeffs thing" that went on in Colorado City with the giving and taking of child brides. It's odious; it's repulsive. And yet, the Book of Mormon is a better teaching document to understanding Christ and the universal nature of Christ and the fact that Christ (post-resurrection) ministered globally, than anything that we've got in the New Testament. The revelations through Joseph give us more information. I mentioned a while ago the Vision of the Three Degrees of Glory; it supplies greater answers. You take someone from out of that odious cult headed by Warren Jeffs and you let them sit through a Presbyterian meeting, and they're gonna say, "My religion holds more. It gives me more truth. There's more substance to it." Even though there's a darkness to that cult, it still appeals. **All** of the Restoration denominations offer something that has value, and it's value above what you get merely from a New Testament church.

But the plan of the adversary is to stop the culmination of what the Restoration's intended to accomplish: unity. The Community of Christ does a far better job of giving lip service to unity than do probably any other of the various sects. But it's still the same problem; it's still exactly the same thing. You put a brand on you, and that brand is "I belong to this denomination," and you instantly feel like you need to be competitive.

Right now, the only church that I ever joined, I got thrown out of. I was too candid, I was too honest, and they couldn't tolerate that. And the man who is the president of that organization, Russell Nelson, is the one that came to my stake with my membership records and gave them to a new stake president. He released my old one, and he called a new one. (My old stake president defended me and refused to kick me out.) He called a new one, handed him my membership records, and said, "The committee thinks this guy has to be disciplined."

And so, I'm "un-churched." I am as committed a believer in the **Restoration**. I think I know as much or more than many of the Mormon historians that are regarded as **authorities** on Mormonism. I read every volume of the *Joseph Smith Papers* as they come into publication, and I make notes all over the margins. They are inconsistent in their storytelling. I pick out the problems. My notes and my version of the *Joseph Smith [Papers]* volumes are flooded with notes that are correcting the problems that the Church Historian's Office makes as they put these things into print.

But, at the end of the day, what matters is not who can make the better argument. What matters isn't who can make the better historical claim. At the end of the day, what matters is **who** among **us** accepts the Restoration through Joseph Smith, accepts the Book of Mormon, accepts the teachings, and are willing to live them. And who among us is willing to fellowship with anyone else that they have a common belief in God's work currently underway. Because **that's** what matters.

I went to Lamoni and talked, and I was happy to do that. I've come here during the general conference of the Community of Christ, and I'm happy to do that. I've been to Dallas to talk to Baptists. I've been to Atlanta.

Audience Member: So, have you heard of the Baptist preacher that read the Book of Mormon, yes?

Denver: Yeah.

Audience Member (continued): I think he's started a movement of where it's every sect, you know, come together with the Book of Mormon.

Audience Member: You're talking about Lynn Ridenhour?

Denver: That's Lynn Ridenhour, yeah.

Audience Member: Sidney Rigdon did that type of conversion; brought his whole church on.

Denver: Yeah, he did.

Well, look, one of the problems with the history-writing of Joseph Smith that happened is that there are villains in the story of Joseph. There are a number of villains. Some of those villains figured out that they could take the villainy that they were accused of and they could ascribe it to Joseph and to make **him** the responsible party for what they were up to. When Joseph was confined in jail and they were going through the preliminary hearing…

The preliminary hearing's purpose is only to determine if there's a plausible case that can be made against him for treason. Witness after witness after witness failed to make out a plausible case, and Joseph Smith was likely to be released because there wasn't a good enough case to hold him on the charge of treason in Missouri—until one of the disaffected Mormons not only stepped forward, but came to the courthouse to testify. And it was because of the villainy that that man had been up to (that he said Joseph Smith was the author of) that Joseph was ultimately able to be held to stand trial on the charge of treason. Well, the state of Missouri lost their stomach for that, and they let Joseph escape, and he never was tried. But that allowed them later to make trumped up charges that said he evaded prosecution, and so they tried to get him back in Missouri in that 1842/3/4 time frame.

The same thing happened with John C. Bennett, the mayor of Nauvoo. When he got caught with his philandering, John Bennett did exactly the same thing. He attributed his villainy (his sexual improprieties) to Joseph Smith. He said, "Joseph was… I learned this from Joseph." And so, you get people who themselves are guilty of wrongdoing, improprieties, and villainy saying that it's not their sins; they learned this from Joseph—and Joseph is the sinner.

Again, it's the same thing—Joseph would be both good and evil spoken of. And you can find villains that say, "No, no, I'm not the real villain; he is. Blame him for what I've done." And you can…

Yeah?

Audience Member: The Laws and the Higbees did that when the *Expositor* was…

Denver: In fact, one of the reasons why Law was not sealed to his wife by Joseph was because he was an adulterer. And so, when Law got his ambition (to have the sealing) turned down, Law accused Joseph of what Law was up to. It's the same thing over and over again.

I was… I left my cell phone at home. I was planning to do and bring some things with me including…

I have written a book, and I was going to bring copies to hand out to anyone that said they'd read it. I've written a book about Joseph Smith called *A Man Without Doubt*. In *A Man Without Doubt*, I take three things—three of the longest things that Joseph Smith ever wrote—and I lay out a background/a history/a context for why the document got written and then simply give you Joseph's document to read: the Joseph Smith history, the Lectures on Faith, and the letter from Liberty Jail. But I give you a context beforehand so that you can see the history. What were all the circumstances that were going on? What was happening at the moment that led to Joseph writing the document? And then I get out of the way, and I let Joseph speak. Joseph writes things of surpassing, heavenly value. You can't take a corrupt heart and produce the beauty and the light that Joseph Smith produced, that he called down from heaven. Can't be done.

Audience Member: Promise, last question. So then, what is your purpose in having these meetings—like you've been to Lamoni, you're here, so what...?

Denver: Well, one of the observations that... I've been kicked out, and I'm un-churched. The couple who have spoken before me, the Bartels, are actually now affiliated with the Community of Christ. One of the things that I have seen and learned from them and from others (I have seen it in the LDS Church; I've heard about it in the Community of Christ) is that Joseph Smith is occupying an increasingly lower estimation in the eyes of **all** the Restoration people.

Audience Member (continued): So, that's what you share, your belief of Joseph Smith and that he was the man that…

Denver: Joseph Smith was everything that he said he was, and he was probably much more. His tendency to understate when he described things, his tendency to be hesitant to step out of that role of the meek teacher, his hesitancy to call down glory on himself…

One of the things that has become apparent to me is that Emma Smith was a stronger personality than Joseph Smith, and Joseph deferred to her. Joseph viewed her advice and counsel with extraordinary respect and seriousness. The caricature that some people turn Joseph Smith into is mirrored by the caricature that they turn Emma Smith into. Emma's not even recognizable in the stories that you get from the Utah community; it's a distortion.

I would like to see everyone who believes in the Restoration say, "Let's stop picking fights. Let's try to get down to the highest, the most noble, the most virtuous, the most wise view of what the Restoration was and where it was headed so that we, perhaps, stand a chance of, at some point, having one heart, one mind, and coming together in a way that would allow us to have no poor among us." Because if we're waiting on the denominations to do that, it will never happen. It will **never** happen. The institutional self-interests will not permit it.

I see within the Community of Christ a drift that is trying to accommodate and obtain popularity from the world. They want to fit in within the current cultural and political climate. That same thing is taking place in the Salt Lake church. The ones that are trying hardest to hold the line against accommodating the world are the most virulent forms of Mormonism—they're militant; they're isolated; they're polygamist. They're an aberrant form of the Restoration, and they're ugly. The ones that are **succeeding** are **destroying the Restoration** because they want to hold on and to grab more success.

If you and I don't rise up above this clamor, if you and I don't find common fellowship and value in the words of the Book of Mormon, in the revelations through Joseph, in the things that we were bequeathed as our common inheritance and forget about what separates us and try to find unity, if we don't do that, it's not going to happen. **Won't**.

Yeah?

Audience Member: The Community of Christ sponsors the John Whitmer Historical Association. And a few decades back there was the Community of Christ or the RLDS version of it, and then there was the LDS version of it—and different groups have their version of history. But over the last few decades, I guess, there has been an intentional effort to…

Denver: Bridge the gap.

Audience Member (continued): …say we accept everyone, from wherever you are coming from—whether you came from here and moved over there, or came from there and moved over here. We accept all who want to study this history together, and let's find out what we can, warts and all.

Denver: That's true, but the needle…

Audience Member (continued): There has been an effort to…

Denver: The needle on polygamy has moved to the version Brigham Young and his affiants gave. And the Community of Christ is now more or less **conceding** that Joseph Smith was the author of some things that, **I still believe**, there's not an adequate historical record to pin upon Joseph.

Audience Member (continued): We need to get involved in that…

Audience Member: Not everybody is following this.

Audience Member (continued): Well, I felt like Joseph Smith was a true, divine prophet. He came along… But with the rise of power and prestige… I mean, Nauvoo was bigger than Chicago in its day.

Denver: Yeah, it was.

Audience Member (continued): And so, all of these people that were clamoring to make a fortune and that type of thing and had their own villainy—as you put it—kind of led us a little bit off the track in that really short, whatever, fourteen years of time.

Denver: Yeah, it was. Yeah.

Audience Member (continued): And so, when Brigham Young, who actually, when they had trouble in Missouri, he organized all of the people to move over to Nauvoo. So, he was already seen as an apostle that was an organizer/leader and took them over there. So, when Joseph was killed, he took the role again of taking us out of danger and moving everybody out to Utah. So, that's why he had the rise in popularity when Joseph was in jail and other places.

Denver: But he also didn't… He didn't claim that he was going to run the show. He was saying that he would be a caretaker and that Joseph Smith III would ultimately (or sons of Joseph would ultimately) come and assume their position. He was an incremental grabber of power. He was not an abrupt one.

Audience Member (continued): Why did Brigham Young or one of his top people… I think one of them gave Joseph Smith III a knife that missed, like a switchblade that didn't work right. Another one gave him a gun that didn't fire right—I hope there's no bad things that happened to the young boy. But when he went out to Utah, there may have been that intention, that he was a caretaker, but it translated into them just taking over. Whereas the majority of the Church, I heard 115 splinters, you know, people claiming leadership when Joseph died…

Denver: There were…

Audience Member: Wasn't Brigham Young the president of the Twelve, council…?

Audience Member: He was at the time, and that's why he had his club.

Audience Member: He wasn't such a peacemaker out there in Utah, either…

Denver: Oh, no, no, no. He wasn't.

[Crosstalk]

Audience Member (continued): …because there was people that went out there thinking that they would find the true church—whatever you want to determine that to be—the true church and had to leave during the night on their own, however you want to say it because it was dangerous.

Denver: Just one point that I want to clarify. At the time that Joseph Smith died, you had Sidney Rigdon (who was back in Philadelphia) who was one claimant. You had James Strang (who was up in the timber mission in Wisconsin) who was one claimant. You had William McClellan (who was down in Texas—Joseph had sent him down to Texas, presumably, to find a place to go to, and he just never left; and he was a member of the Twelve, and he stayed a member of the Twelve for quite some time until they finally got around to throwing him out). And there was Brigham Young. And Emma Smith was solicited by all of the various claimants to come. But those were the five main at the time; and Emma stayed behind, refusing to fall in line with any of them.

Audience Member: And maybe they moved away to be a little bit safe for a little while, because her husband was killed. But they all wanted, ultimately, the seed of Joseph to lead them forward. That was the thing. And they all came back when young Joseph was a little older and solicited for him to be **their** leader because that would give them the ultimate…

Denver: During the (what was called) the Mormon Reformation at the —

Brigham Young and the leadership of the Church were running out of time. Brigham Young and the leadership of the Church took the position that the reason they were having droughts, the reason why all the cattle got killed in the hard winter and they were starving, the reason why the elements were treating them so poorly was because God was mad. And God was mad because the members weren't faithful. And so, he began a program called the Home Missionary Program, in which there was a list of questions that home missionaries were supposed to go around and interview people. The purpose of that list of questions was to find out if you were doing something that was unforgivable that required your blood to be spilled on the ground through blood atonement—because Brigham Young instituted, literally, a reign of terror.

When Johnston's Army came out to Utah, the people who were resident in Utah viewed that, among some quarters, as liberation. The spring following Johnston's Army's arrival in Utah, there were over 3,400 people that left to go back east. They have records of that because the…or they know the numbers on that because the migration to the east occurred in wagon trains and other supervised exits that they kept numbers on. But there was likely an even larger number than that, that evacuated out to California, going west to escape the kingdom of Brigham Young.

I wrote a paper called "Brigham Young's Telestial Kingdom" that I presented at the Sunstone Symposium. I've got a website. You can... It's on a page called "Downloads"—there's a bunch of papers I've written. One of them is "Brigham Young's Telestial Kingdom": denversnuffer.com.

Audience Member: Do you have a business card?

Denver: I don't have it.

Audience Member: Well, isn't it on the bottom of your flier?

Denver: Is it?

[crosstalk about the information]

Denver: Yeah, denversnuffer.com. Just all one word.

Audience Member: Well, Brigham Young was not so very nice to Emma either.

Denver: Oh, no, no, no! He called her a wicked, wicked, wicked woman! He said that "Joseph once said he'd go to hell to be with Emma, and if he wants to be with Emma, that's exactly where he's gonna have to go." Brigham Young and Emma Smith...

Audience Member: He was not nice to her.

Audience Member: They didn't get along.

Denver: They did not get along. If Brigham had persuaded her to go west, he would've required her to marry him.

Audience Member: Well, anything that had Joseph Smith's name on it, Brigham tried to take from the, you know, he tried to take back. There was some things that I think Emma got out of all of that because she had kids to support.

Denver: Yes, she was able to get **some** property transfers. Joseph Smith had a pending petition for bankruptcy when he died because of all of the losses that they'd suffered in Missouri. Emma Smith got a number of assets transferred to her before Joseph filed for bankruptcy (to engage in some asset protection before that). And Emma was able, because of the transfers to her, to hold onto some of the property, which is why she was able to relocate back to Nauvoo. She owned a lot of property in Nauvoo.

Audience Member (continued): She didn't give up the Mansion House.

Denver: She did not. Listen, thank you for coming out. It was wonderful to spend some time with ya, and I hope it was useful.

Thank you.

Civilization

Paper presented at "A Hope in Christ: The Temple"
General Conference[1], Grand Junction, CO
April 21, 2019

[Because everything we do is voluntary and because no one gets paid to do any of the things that are done as part of the endeavor that we share together, in order to host a conference like this, those that choose to do so, do so at their own expense with volunteers doing everything that gets accomplished—arranging for the use of all the facilities that get used (including this one today)—and sacrifice in order to be able to host an event like this. This was a remarkable conference for the last three days now. And everything that has been done and everything that got organized and all of the facilities that were made available were done by the local group here that chose to sacrifice in order to make it possible. I wanted to start out by expressing my appreciation for all those who have worked to make this possible and all of the events and participants. I think it's been a marvelous conference, and I appreciate the opportunity to be invited.]

We study the Old Testament to learn about individual salvation from God. We study the New Testament to learn about individual salvation through Christ. We read the Book of Mormon to reassure ourselves that, like those who lived before us, we can be individually saved in our day. We study the revelations of Joseph Smith to learn about individual salvation.

Historic Christianity and the various Mormon traditions have all focused on individual salvation. Christians have been "born again" and found salvation through God.[2] Mormons have had their "calling and election made sure" and claim God has saved them.[3] Throughout the Judeo-Christian landscape, individual salvation is the great quest, the overarching yearning, and the religious end to be obtained.

Salvation **is** individual. There is only individual salvation and no such thing as collective salvation.[4] While I accept this as true, there is something else that is equally true: God wants "people" to collectively be His.

In the revelations of July 14, 2017 (T&C 157) and October 4, 2018 (T&C 176) received from God, the emphasis has been on "people." Both responses by the Lord have gone beyond individual salvation to focus on people, Zion, and the New Jerusalem. Consider these words from the Answer to the Prayer for Covenant addressing the importance of God's people:

> I, the Lord, say to you: You have asked of me concerning the scriptures prepared on behalf of all those who seek to become **my covenant people**, and therefore I answer you **on behalf of all the people**, and not as to any individual. For there are those who are humble, patient, and easily persuaded. Nevertheless, people who are quarrelsome and proud are also among you, and since you seek to **unite to become one people, I answer you as one**.

> I covenanted with Adam at the beginning, which covenant was broken by mankind. Since the days of Adam **I have always sought to reestablish people of covenant among the living**, and therefore have desired that man should love one another, not begrudgingly, but as brothers and sisters indeed, that I may establish my covenant and provide **them** with light and truth.

> …For the sake of the promises to the fathers will **I labor with you as a people**, and not because of you, for you have not yet become what you must be to live together in peace. If you will hearken to my words, **I will make you my people** and my words will give you peace. Even a single soul who stirs up the hearts of others to anger **can destroy the peace of all my people**. Each of you must equally walk truly in my path, not only to profess, but to do as you profess.

> …there are many things yet to be restored **unto my people**. It is ordained that some things are **only to be given to people who are mine** and cannot otherwise be given to mankind on earth. You do not yet understand **the glory to be revealed unto my covenant people**.

> …It is not enough to receive my covenant, but you must also abide it. And all who abide it, whether on this land or any other land, will be mine, and I will watch over **them** and protect **them** in the

*day of harvest, and gather **them** in as a hen gathers her **chicks** under her wings. I will number you among the remnant of Jacob, no longer outcasts, and you will inherit the promises of Israel. You shall be **my people** and I will be your God, and the sword will not devour you. And unto **those** who will receive will more be given, until **they** know the mysteries of God in full.*

*…You pray each time you partake of the sacrament to always have my spirit to be with you. And what is my spirit? It is to love one another as I have loved you. Do my works and you will know my doctrine, for you will uncover hidden mysteries by obedience to these things that can be uncovered in no other way. This is the way **I will restore knowledge to my people**. If you return good for evil, you will cleanse yourself and know the joy of your Master. You call me Lord, and do well to regard me so, but to know your Lord is to love one another. Flee from the cares and longings that belong to Babylon, obtain a new heart, for you have all been wounded. In me you will find peace, and through me will come Zion, a place of peace and safety.*

…Be of one heart, and regard one another with charity. Measure your words before giving voice to them, and consider the hearts of others. Although a man may err in understanding concerning many things, yet he can view his brother with charity and come unto me, and through me he can with patience overcome the world. I can bring him to understanding and knowledge. Therefore, if you regard one another with charity, then your brother's error in understanding will not divide you. I lead to all truth. I will lead all who come to me to the truth of all things. The fullness is to receive the truth of all things, and this too from me, in power, by my word, and in very deed. For I will come unto you if you will come unto me.

*Study to learn how to **respect your brothers and sisters and to come together** by precept, reason, and persuasion, rather than sharply disputing and wrongly condemning each other, causing anger. Take care how you invoke my name. Mankind has been controlled by the adversary through anger and jealousy, which has led to bloodshed and the misery of many souls. Even strong* *disagreements should not provoke anger, nor to invoke my name in vain as if I had part in your every dispute. Pray together in humility and together meekly present your dispute to me, and if you are contrite before me, I will tell you my part.* ((T&C 157:1-2,19,44,48,51,53-54, emphasis added)

These are God's words in the Answer to the Prayer for Covenant. The focus is on the community and not on the individual. It has taken me years to notice that. This focus is different for a reason. Our traditions have not and cannot bring Zion. That will require viewing God's work in a new way. Individuals may be saved individually—and have been throughout history. But Zion is not about individual salvation. Zion is about covenant people of God: individually saved, as a prerequisite, then gathered together to live in peace.

As part of the same revelation, there is the covenant language. It also moves the focus to community instead of individual:

Do you covenant with [the Lord] to cease to do evil and to seek to continually do good?

Second: Do you have faith in these things and receive the scriptures approved by the Lord as a standard to govern you in your daily walk in life, to accept the obligations established by the Book of Mormon as a covenant, and to use the scriptures to correct yourselves and to guide your words, thoughts, and deeds?

*Third: Do you agree to assist **all others** — **who covenant to likewise accept this standard to govern their lives** — to keep the Lord's will, to **succor those** who stand in need, to **lighten the burdens of your brothers and sisters** whenever you are able, and to help **care for the poor among you**?*

*Fourth: And do you covenant to **seek to become of one heart with those who seek the Lord to establish His righteousness**?*

If you agree, please stand wherever you are located, either here or in a remote location, to be recognized and numbered by God and His angels.

All those standing please confirm you are willing to accept this covenant by saying, Yes.

Please be seated.

Now, hear the words of the Lord to those who receive this covenant this day:

All you *who have turned from your wicked ways and repented of your evil doings, of lying and deceiving, and of all whoredoms, and of secret abominations, idolatries, murders, priestcrafts, envying, and strife, and from all wickedness and abominations, and have come unto me, and been baptized in my name, and have received a remission of your sins, and received the holy ghost, are* ***now numbered with my people*** *who are of the house of Israel. I say to you:*

Teach your children to honor me. Seek to recover the lost sheep remnant of this land and of Israel and no longer forsake them. Bring them unto me and teach them of my ways, to walk in them.

And I, the Lord your God, will be ***with you*** *and will* ***never forsake you****, and I* ***will lead you*** *in the path which will bring peace to you in the troubling season now fast approaching.*

I will ***raise you up*** *and* ***protect you****,* ***abide with you****, and* ***gather you*** *in due time, and this shall be* ***a land of promise to you as your inheritance*** *from me.*

The earth will yield its increase, and ***you will flourish*** *upon the mountains and upon the hills, and* ***the wicked will not come against you*** *because the* ***fear of the Lord will be with you****.*

I will visit my house, which ***the remnant of my people shall build****, and I will dwell therein, to be* ***among you****, and no one will need to say, Know ye the Lord, for* ***you all shall know me****, from the least to the greatest.*

I will ***teach you*** *things that have been hidden from the foundation of the world and* ***your understanding*** *will reach unto Heaven.*

*And you shall be called **the children of the Most High God**, and I will **preserve you** against the harvest.*

*And the angels sent to harvest the world will gather the wicked into bundles to be burned, but will **pass over you** as my peculiar treasure.*

*But if **you do not honor me**, nor seek to recover my people Israel, nor teach your children to honor me, **nor care for the poor among you**, nor help **lighten one another's burdens**, then you have no promise from me and I will **raise up other people** who will honor and serve me, and give unto them this land, and if **they** repent, I will abide with **them**.* (T&C 158:2-19, emphasis added)

People claim they have kept the covenant, but such claims cannot possibly be true. God's covenant is for and about people: His people. It is not possible for **an individual** to keep the covenant. Everybody rises together, or everybody fails together. The covenant can only be kept as a community. Individuals acting alone can never accomplish what is required of the group.

The October 4, 2018 revelation (T&C 176) also focuses on community. It begins by addressing "people" and not the individual. The Lord's voice to the people begins and ends with two questions. After asking the questions a second time, He gives an answer to what ought to have been learned. Here are the Lord's words to the people:

*You ask on behalf of **my people**, and therefore I answer **my people**. Hear, therefore, my words: What have you learned? What ought you to have learned?*

*…I ask again, What have you learned? What ought you to have learned? I say to you that there is need for but one house, and I accept the statement you have adopted, and approve it as your statement to be added. But I say again, there was honor in the labor of others. Whereas I look upon the heart and see faithful service, **many among you** do not look at, nor see, nor value what I, the Lord, love in **the hearts of my people**. As I have said before, I say again: **Love one another**, labor willingly **alongside each***

other. *Learn what you ought, and when I ask you to labor, do so wisely, even if you know not beforehand what you will find. I do not ask what you cannot do. Trust my words and proceed always in faith, believing that with me all things are possible. **All who have been faithful are mine**.* (T&C 176:1-2,12-13, emphasis added)

[Just as an aside, when the sacrament was passed and the group of brethren who came up here to perform that came up on stage in flannel and shorts and motley-colored shirts—to look upon that, to me, was a delight. It was a statement of the fact that righteousness holds no costume up to pretend to be something it isn't. Righteousness comes in divergent forms and manifests itself in unexpected ways. Had any one of those individuals come up to pass the sacrament (among some congregations) dressed as they were today, they would have excited the judgment, the censure, the horror of someone observing them in that garb. But to us, it's accepted, and it's acceptable. I would hope that if one among us chose to wear a white shirt and a tie to come up to pass the sacrament while standing among them, that none of us would look upon that judgmentally and with disfavor, but that everyone would be welcomed, everyone would be accepted, and that we would be just as tolerant of others and their idiosyncrasies as we are of what we expect to be among us.]

God mentions His "people" in order to get our attention. The prophecies of God's last-days' work and the fulfillment of God's covenants with the Fathers are not merely for individual salvation. The covenants are about "people" or a divinely organized community. Righteous individuals (isolated and scattered throughout the world) are incapable of vindicating the promises God made to the Fathers. There must be people gathered together and living the correct pattern before the Lord returns.

Enoch saw the crucifixion, resurrection, and ascension of Christ into heaven. He wanted to know if Christ would return again from heaven to save the Earth. In response to Enoch's inquiry, the Lord gave a promise and covenant that is still unfulfilled. Here is the account; Enoch asks:

*Wherefore, I ask you if you will not come again on the earth? And the Lord said unto Enoch, As I live, even so will I come in the last days, in the days of wickedness and vengeance, to fulfill the oath which I have made unto you concerning the children of Noah. And the day shall come that the earth shall rest. But before that day, the heavens shall be darkened, and a veil of darkness shall cover the earth; and the heavens shall shake, and also the earth. And great tribulations shall be among the children of men, but **my people will I preserve**. And righteousness will I send down out of Heaven. Truth will I send forth out of the earth to bear testimony of my Only Begotten, his resurrection from the dead, yea, and also the resurrection of all men. And righteousness and truth will I cause to sweep the earth as with a flood, **to gather out my own elect** from the four quarters of the earth **unto a place which I shall prepare, a holy city, that my people** may gird up their loins and be looking forth for the time of my coming. For there shall be my tabernacle, and it shall be called Zion, a New Jerusalem. And the Lord said unto Enoch, Then shall you and all your city **meet them** there, and we will **receive them** into our bosom. And **they shall see us**, and we will fall upon **their necks**, and **they** shall fall upon our necks, and we will kiss each other; and there shall be my abode. And it shall be Zion which shall come forth out of all the creations which I have made, and for the space of a thousand years shall the earth rest.* (Genesis 4:22, emphasis added)

The Lord has every intention of keeping His promise to Enoch. There will be those who are gathered. There must be people gathered to a place, a holy city that meets the description and fulfills the promises God made. The people must gird up their loins or, in other words, must be living the godly religion that declares things as they really are —a religion founded on truth. Truth requires us to know things as they were, as they are, and as they are to come.[5] Many past things that are hidden from the world must be revealed. God's people must know ancient truths so their hearts can turn to the Fathers. But it will be to covenant people, not individuals, to whom this outpouring will be given. A covenant body will belong in a New Jerusalem. The City of Enoch will "meet **them** there," and then they and the Lord "will receive **them** into our bosom." This is something more than individual salvation. Those involved will be individually saved, but the community itself must exist as something greater than individuals. There must be a "body" or "bride" for the Bridegroom to embrace.[6]

The focus on community or people in these two latest revelations is similar to that throughout the Old and New Testaments. It is everywhere. It is particularly clear that the prophecies about the last days' Zion require a people to belong to God and be regarded by Him as His.

In Isaiah, foretelling the future Zion:

> *And then shall they say, How beautiful upon the mountains are the feet of him that brings good tidings unto them, that publishes peace, that brings good tidings unto them of good, that publishes salvation, that says unto Zion, Your God reigns! Your watchmen shall lift up the voice; with the voice together shall they sing, for* **they shall see eye to eye** *when the Lord shall bring again Zion. Break forth into joy, sing together, you waste places of Jerusalem, for the Lord has comforted* **his people**, *he has redeemed Jerusalem. The Lord has made bare his holy arm in the eyes of all the nations, and all the ends of the earth shall see the salvation of our God. Depart, depart, go out from there, touch no unclean thing; go out of her midst; be clean, you that bear the vessels of the Lord. For you shall not go out with haste, nor go by flight; for the Lord will go before you, and the God of Israel will be your rear guard.* (Isaiah 18:8, emphasis added)

John also revealed how a group must depart from Babylon to be saved:

> *And I heard another voice from Heaven, saying, Come out of her,* **my people**, *that you be not partakers of her sins, and that you receive not of her plagues, for her sins have reached unto Heaven and God has remembered her iniquities.* (Revelation 7:2, emphasis added)

This theme is also throughout the Book of Mormon and revelations through Joseph Smith. Christ describes the end-times Zion and its accompanying sign in 3 Nephi:

> *And verily I say unto you, I give unto you a sign, that ye may know the time when these things shall be about to take place, that I shall gather in from their long dispersion **my people**, O house of Israel, and shall establish again among **them** my Zion. And behold, this is the thing which I will give unto you for a sign: for verily I say unto you that when these things which I declare unto you...shall be made known unto the gentiles, that they may know concerning this **people** who are a remnant of the house of Jacob, and concerning this **my people** who shall be scattered by them...that the gentiles, if they will not harden their hearts, that they may repent, and come unto me, and be baptized in my name, and know of the true points of my doctrine, that **they** [gentiles] **may be numbered among my people**, O house of Israel — and when these things come to pass, that thy seed shall begin to know these things, it shall be a sign unto **them** that they may know that the work of the Father hath already commenced unto the fulfilling of the covenant which he hath made unto [all] **the people** who are of the house of Israel. (3 Nephi 9:11, emphasis added)*

["All" of them of the house of Israel (in Christ's prophecy) includes the Gentiles who have accepted a covenant with Him.]

In a prophecy from Joseph about those who will be in Zion:

> *The Lord hath brought again Zion. The Lord has redeemed **his people** Israel according to the election of grace, which was brought to pass by the faith and covenant of their Fathers. The Lord hath redeemed **his people**, and Satan is bound, and time is no longer. The Lord has gathered all things in one. The Lord has brought down Zion from above, the Lord has brought up Zion from beneath. The earth has travailed and brought forth her strength, and truth is established in her bowels, and the Heavens have smiled upon her, and she is clothed with the glory of her God, for he stands in the midst of **his people**. Glory, and honor, and power, and might be ascribed to our God, for he is full of mercy, justice, grace, and truth, and peace, for ever and ever. Amen. (T&C 82:28, emphasis added)*

These are just examples. The Scriptures foretelling a return of God's "people" are in all passages of prophecy describing the latter-day Zion.

You cannot keep the covenant. **I** cannot keep the covenant. Only **we** can keep the covenant. The covenant was apparently designed by God to require **all** to labor together. This is a long way off, but God is working to bring His people along so that they may be able to keep the covenant together.

Creating unified people who qualify to worship God in truth (that is, knowing accurately the past, present, and future) is an extraordinary challenge. Only God can do it, and He must have willing people. It will require a new civilization. Prophecy likens that civilization to a stone carved out of a mountain that will roll out to destroy all the corruptions of Babylon, Medes and Persians, Greeks, Romans, and modern societies.

Anciently, civilizations were founded around the temple. Hugh Nibley studied ancient temples because of the LDS temples. He saw the effect temples had in the ancient world. In *Temple & Cosmos*, he explained their role:

> It is the hierocentric point around which all things are organized. It is the *omphalos* ("navel") around which the earth was organized. The temple is a scale model of the universe, boxed to the compass, a very important feature of every town in our contemporary civilization, as in the ancient world. (Years ago, Sir James George Frazer noticed a definite pattern among ancient religious cult practices: they all followed the same patterns throughout the whole world. He explained that as representing certain stages of evolution in which the mind naturally expressed itself in those forms. But since then the gaps between these various cultures have been filled in, to show that civilization was far more connected.) Civilization is hierocentric, centered around the holy point of the temple. The temple was certainly the center of things in Babylonia, in Egypt, in Greece—wherever you go.
>
> ...It is the scale model of the universe, for teaching purposes and for the purpose of taking our bearings on the universe and in the eternities, both in time and in space.

...The temple is the great teaching institution of the human race; universities are much older than we might ever expect. A university began as a Greek *Mouseion*, a temple of the Muses, who represented all departments of knowledge. The Egyptians called it the "house of Life." It was an observatory, a great megalithic complex of standing stones (later columns and pylons), with amazingly sophisticated devices for observing and recording the motions of the heavens.

...The creation hymn was part of the great dramatic presentation that took place yearly at the temple; it dealt with the fall and redemption of man...

...In short, there is no part of our civilization which doesn't have its rise in the temple. Thanks to the power of the written word, records were kept. And in the all-embracing relationship to the divine book, everything is relevant; nothing is really dead or forgotten. In the time of gathering of all things together, we gather everything good that ever was—not just people—that nothing be lost but everything be restored in this last dispensation. In an all-embracing relationship nothing is ever really dead or forgotten. Every detail belongs in the picture. ... Where the temple that gave us birth is missing, civilization itself becomes a hollow shell.

The temple must be there. It is not just a myth, it is the core of all of our civilization.[7]

[I read that—from *Temple and Cosmos*—because I agree with those words.]

The Lord is equal to the challenge. He will establish a new civilization. It will be founded on the fullness of His gospel. Lost truths will be restored. The path of righteousness will be returned.

Society is broken. Everywhere we see corrupt cultures based on corrupt laws, corrupt religions, corrupt values, and ultimately, corrupt thought. Beginning again requires re-civilizing people. To be free from corruption requires a change in thinking. If the Lord is to accomplish this, there will need to be a new temple at the center of that new civilization.

The Lord talked with Enoch regarding His return and started with a description of His temple: *For there shall be **my tabernacle**, and it shall be called Zion, a New Jerusalem* (Genesis 4:22). It can only become Zion and a New Jerusalem if the Lord's tabernacle is there. His temple will be where He teaches all that must be understood to please God. Then, when people rise up to become what the Lord expects, His risen Tabernacle of glory—the Lord Himself—will come to dwell there.

There is a great deal of work to be done to establish a foundation. And an even greater work thereafter. When God has His people, they are always commanded to build a temple. Joseph Smith explained:

> What was the object of gathering the...people of God in any age of the world? ...The main object was to build unto the Lord a house whereby He could reveal unto His people the ordinances of His house and the glories of His kingdom, and teach the people the way of salvation; for there are certain ordinances and principles that, when they are taught and practiced, must be done in a place or house built for that purpose.[8]

Joseph Smith taught the Relief Society, "That the church is not now organized into its proper order, & cannot be until the temple is completed."[9] Some believe that meant temple rites would fit inside the existing church organization. However, it is possible (if the temple had been completed) the people might have been organized in a new and different order, resembling the order in the age of the patriarchs. Joseph never had the opportunity to participate in that advancement. Before the temple was finished, Joseph was dead, and those who were leading had no intention or ability to reorganize the church into the "proper order."

The need for covenant people to cooperate in building a temple has been the same in any age. Temple builders founded the earliest civilizations. They did this to imitate the antediluvians. The Book of Abraham account suggests there was something in Egypt below the floodwaters worth waiting for the water to recede.[10] Some observers claim there is physical evidence that the earliest temple-complex structures in Egypt were built prior to the flood. They use archeological evidence at the Giza site to conclude the place was once under water, consistent with the description in the Book of Abraham.[11]

Whether the first temples were built or inherited by ancient civilizations, the center of life, government, education, culture, and art was the temple. This was handed down from the first generations. The temple was the foundation before and will need to be the foundation again. When there has been an apostasy, temple-building has been part of restoring. A new civilization will only become possible through teachings learned in the future House of God. The necessary ordinances can only be restored in that setting. There you will receive an uncorrupted restoration of the original faith taught to Adam and the patriarchs.[12]

Joseph Smith was told that God intended to restore what was lost (meaning the fullness of the priesthood), but it was only to be accomplished through a temple. These were the Lord's words to Joseph:

> For, for this cause I commanded Moses that he should build a tabernacle, that they should bear it with them in the wilderness, and to build a house in the land of promise that those ordinances might be revealed which had been hid from before the world was. Therefore, verily I say unto you that your anointings, and your washings, and your baptisms for the dead, and your solemn assemblies, and your memorials for your sacrifices by the sons of Levi, and for your oracles in your most holy places wherein you receive conversations, and your statutes and judgments for the beginning of the revelations and foundation of Zion, and for the glory, and honor, and endowment of all her municipals, are ordained by the ordinance of my holy house, which my people are always commanded to build unto my holy name. (T&C 141:12)[13]

Joseph was martyred before there was a place where God could come to restore what had been lost. Joseph began to roll out a portion of temple ceremonial worship, but it was never completed. Uninspired men who have changed, deleted, and added to what remained from Joseph have corrupted those incomplete ceremonies.

The gospel is for redemption. Redemption from the fall returns man to God's presence.[14] Ascending the heavenly mount is always taught in a properly-organized-temple's ceremonies. Ascending to heaven, redemption, and becoming part of the Family of God are all part of the ancient temple rites and must also be part of future temple rites.

The concept of "adoption" is widely recognized as part of Christianity. The term is employed loosely to mean a person believes in Christ and recognizes Him as their Savior. The language of Paul is often cited and understood to claim believers are adopted into God's family.

> *For you have not received the spirit of bondage again to fear, but you have received the spirit of adoption, whereby we cry, Abba, Father. The Spirit itself bears witness with our spirit that we are the children of God. And if children, then heirs — heirs of God and joint-heirs with Christ, if so be that we suffer with him, that we may be also glorified together.* (Romans 1:34)[15]

Language in the Book of Mormon has also been used to support a loose understanding of the term "adoption." *Marvel not that all mankind, yea, men and women — all nations, kindreds, tongues, and people — must be born again, yea, born of God, changed from their carnal and fallen state to a state of righteousness, being redeemed of God, becoming his sons and daughters* (Mosiah 11:28).[16]

The loose understanding of "adoption" was considerably tightened around October 1843 when Joseph Smith expanded his use of sealing authority. It grew from establishing marriages to include also man-to-man sealing through adoption.[17] The last eight months of his life, Joseph sealed or "adopted" other men to himself. There was no settled, formal ordinance that has been preserved, and the proof of Joseph's practice is mostly post-mortem, as those who were exposed to the practice only vaguely recalled what he had done.

Nearly a decade after Joseph died, when temple ceremonial work resumed in the Endowment House in Salt Lake, Brigham Young declared that adoption was the crowning ordinance. It was more important than the other temple rites, including washing, anointing, endowment, and marriage sealing:

This Chain must not [be] broken for mankind Cannot be saved any other way. This Priesthood must be linked together so that all the Children may be linked to Father Adam. …we will seal men to men by the keys of the Holy Priesthood. This is the highest ordinance. It is the last ordinance of the kingdom of God on the earth and above all the endowments that can be given you. It is a final sealing an Eternal Principle and when once made cannot be broken by the Devil.[18]

In that talk, Brigham Young taught that the "turning of hearts to the fathers" foretold by Malachi was only to be fulfilled through adoption. He also taught the fulfillment of God's promise to Abraham regarding "his seed"[19] would only be fulfilled through the temple ordinance of adoption. LDS Church leaders unsuccessfully tried to sort out how to practice adoption.[20]

In a meeting of the reorganized School of the Prophets in Salt Lake on January 20, 1868—attended by the Church Presidency (Brigham Young, Heber C. Kimball, and Daniel H. Wells), along with Elders John Taylor, Orson Hyde, George A. Smith, Erastus Snow, George Q. Cannon, Phineas Young, and Joseph Young—the topic of adoption was discussed. President Wells conjectured: "On Adoption he supposed it had reference to the linking together of the Priesthood now living that it might reach back to the link that had long since been broken, that it might present one unbroken chain."[21] In response, Orson Hyde said, "The Doctrine of Adoption he knew but little about and should decline touching it until the line is chalked out."[22]

Scholars struggle to make sense of what Joseph was doing, and the attempts to reconstruct Joseph's later adoption innovation are insufficient to give any firm understanding of what took place, how, or why.[23] Thirty years before he would become church president, Wilford Woodruff concluded that adoptions would be something a resurrected Joseph Smith would return to sort out during the millennium. "Man also will have to be sealed to man until the chain is united from Father Adam down to the last Saint. This will be the work of the Millenium and Joseph Smith will be the man to attend to it or dictate it."[24]

A half-century after Joseph's death, the apostles struggled to know how it ought to work, who should be sealed to whom, how and what effect it would have in the afterlife.[25] In a meeting on June 1, 1893 (attended by Lorenzo Snow, Franklin D. Richards, Francis M. Lyman, John W. Taylor, Marriner W. Merrill, Abraham Cannon, George F. Gibbs, John D. T. McAllister, Nephi W. Clayton, and James Jack), they "had some talk about the ordinance of adoption in the temple. Joseph F. Smith said Pres. [Brigham] Young had told him to follow in ordinance work for the dead the rules which will ordinarily govern similar work for the living."[26] The practice was to seal faithful children to their parents, and faithful parents to Joseph Smith.[27] Woodruff explained, "I was sealed to my father, and then had him sealed to the Prophet Joseph."[28]

The concept of adoption affected how people understood the afterlife. This led some people to view adoption as a chance to pursue their self-interests. People began to aspire to improve their post-mortality by recruiting and acquiring descendants using adoption. The Logan Temple President was told to end his practice of recruiting adoptees.[29] Eventually, President Wilford W. Woodruff announced a final adoption practice on April 8, 1894: "Pres. Woodruff announced the doctrine of the sealing of children to parents as far back as it is possible to trace the genealogy, and then seal the last member to the Prophet Joseph [Smith]."[30]

Family relationships were reckoned by sealing, not biology. For example, Heber J. Grant was the biological son of Jedediah Grant, but because his mother was sealed to Joseph Smith, he was regarded as Joseph Smith's son.[31]

What Joseph Smith understood about adoption did not get passed to subsequent church leaders clearly enough to preserve the practice intact. In September 1887, two months after John Taylor died, his son-in-law, John M. Whitaker, wrote in his diary:

> I went back to the office where I found [Apostle] Brother Lorenzo Snow and [First Council of the Seventy member] Jacob Gates. They conversed a long time. He finally entered into a deep subject on "The Law of Adoption." Brother Gates said he didn't believe in it as did also Brother Snow. He referenced back to the time that Brigham Young was in Kirtland...he had a person asked him about it and he said "I know nothing about it." President Taylor on one different

occasion had a letter written to him for the following reason: it was [two undecipherable words] of Prophet J Smith or rather Sister Eliza R. Snow Smith (Brother Gates didn't know which)…a about [sic] 70 persons were adopted into President J Smith's [family]…Sister Snow Smith said "she didn't understand the law" but had no objections to them being sealed to her husband. And this led Brother Gates to write to President Taylor asking him if he knew anything about it. He never answered the letter. But on another occasion Brother Gates saw him and asked him plainly. President Taylor said he knew nothing about it. And also just lately when asked by Brother Snow, President Wilford Woodruff knew nothing about it. ["]It hadn't been revealed to him." I know this at this time to say [or show] a prevailing feeling among the Twelve that they don't understand it. George [undecipherable] Cannon also said he didn't understand it.[32]

As John Taylor's health was declining in the last month of his life, Wilford Woodruff recorded in his journal on June 8, 1887: "I wrote 4 Letters to Jaques Emma Clara & Roskelly. I did not rest well. To much deep thinking to Sleep."[33] Roskelly was employed as the recorder in the Logan, Utah temple. That letter included the following mention of adoption:

> So in relation to Adoptions, most, if not all, of the Presidency and Twelve, have had men adopted to them, and all these Sealings and Adoptions are for the Salvation of the living and the dead. I have never asked any man to be adopted into my family that I can recollect of; but I have had a number of families of friends adopted into my family, as have other men, without any regard to whether it will, in the future, cost me one dollar or a million. What we have done in this matter has been for the salvation of man. It may possibly be a correct doctrine that a man's Kingdom will consist of only the fruit of his own loins. Yet Jesus Christ died to save the whole world, and if we, as Apostles and Elders, do nothing for the human family only for the fruit of our own loins, we shall not do much towards magnifying the Holy Priesthood God has given us for saving the souls of men—either the living or the dead. …I have

adopted this rule in Sealing and Adoptions: to take such as the Lord has given me, and leave the result in His hands. …Paul talked a good deal about Adoptions, but we did not understand much about it, until the Lord revealed it to Joseph Smith, and we may not, perhaps, understand it now as fully as we should. Still the Sealings and Adoptions are true principles, or our Prophets have been badly deceived.[34]

Adoption became progressively more controversial as time passed. Since the idea was not well understood by church leaders, they could provide no answers to questions on the subject. While bishop, Edward Bunker denounced the idea altogether, resulting in an 1892 church court that the Church President and one of his counselors attended. The former bishop was charged with teaching false doctrine and, in his defense, wrote a letter to the high council stating:

The adoption of one man to another out of the lineage, I do not understand and for that reason I would not enter into it. And adopting the dead to the living is as adopting the father to the son. I don't believe there is a man on earth that thoroughly understands the principle. If there is, I have never heard it taught as I could understand it. I believe it is permmited [sic] more to satisfy the minds of the people for the present until the Lord reveals more fully the principle.[35]

In his summary of the court [proceeding], Wilford Woodruff relegated the subject of adoption to one of the "mysteries" which church members ought to avoid discussing because they cause difficulties. He wrote: "June 11, 1892 We Met in the Tabernacle at 10 oclock on the trial of Bishop Bunker on Doctrin. We talked to them Plainly of the impropriety of indulging in Misteries to Create difficulties among the Saints. They professed to be Satisfied."[36]

Although John Taylor perpetuated the practice,[37] over time it diminished and then disappeared (beginning with Wilford Woodruff's presidency). Woodruff changed the policy in April 1894 to seal within biological families as far back as were known, then to seal/adopt the last parents to Joseph Smith. This made adoption less of an issue and the genealogical search for ancestors of greater concern. By 1922, the de-emphasis on adoption allowed it to be ignored altogether. The practice

Woodruff announced in 1894 was deleted from the account published by the Utah Genealogical Society[38] and from Clark's *Messages of The First Presidency*.[39] Today, adoption has vanished from the LDS Church and was never practiced by the RLDS or other branches of the Restoration.

Joseph Smith did not leave the Christian practice of "adoption" as a loose idea, with believers becoming sons of God by conversion, belief, or baptism. He tied it to both authority to seal and an authoritative ordinance. Both of those were lost when Joseph and Hyrum were killed.

If adoption is (as Brigham Young thought in 1856) the highest ordinance—above all the endowments that can be given—if it is needed for the gospel as taught to Abraham to be restored, then the loss of adoption rites is indeed a sign of apostasy. Brigham Young taught adoption would bind a person beyond the devil's power to break.[40] But adoption was abandoned before the end of the 1800s. Adoption will need to be restored as a rite with an accompanying authoritative ordinance and sealing in order for the things Joseph Smith alone understood and taught to be renewed.

The LDS Church has attempted to preserve other ordinances Joseph Smith began. Unfortunately, those ordinances have also been poorly preserved, changed, and compromised.[41]

Joseph did not live to [see the] complete Nauvoo temple, and he never finished the temple ceremonies.[42] Thirty-three years after Joseph died, Brigham Young explained that he was the one who finished the ceremony using what he could recall from Joseph's initiation:

> ...when we got our washings and anointings under the hands of the Prophet Joseph at Nauvoo, we had only one room to work in with the exception of a little side room, or office, where we were washed and anointed, had our garments placed upon us, and received our new name. And after he had performed these ceremonies, he gave the key words, signs, tokens and penalties. Then, after we went into the large room over the store in Nauvoo, Joseph divided up the room the best that he could, hung up the veil, marked it. Gave us our instructions as

we passed along from one department to another, giving us signs, tokens, penalties, with the key words pertaining to those signs.

After we had got through Bro. Joseph turned to me (Pres. Young) and said, "Bro. Brigham this is not arranged right but we have done the best we could under the circumstances in which we are placed, and I wish you to take this matter in hand and organize and systematize all these ceremonies with the signs, tokens, penalties and key words." I did so, and each time I got something more, so that when we went through the temple at Nauvoo I understood and knew how to place them there. We had our ceremonies pretty correct.[43]

["Pretty correct." "Approximately good."]

About a year and a half after the martyrdom of Joseph and Hyrum Smith, Brigham began to introduce the endowment to the general church membership. This was done in the attic of the unfinished Nauvoo Temple using canvas partitions. As these endowments proceeded, Brigham continued to make additions, changes, and alterations to the ceremony Joseph had introduced. By [the] time of the exodus from Nauvoo [in February of 1846], over 5,000 members had been endowed. Endowment ordinances resumed in 1852 in the Council House in Utah and then in the Endowment House, which was completed in 1855.

When there were a large number of ordinances being performed, Brigham Young admitted the ceremony was the best he could do but would be fixed when Christ returned and Joseph was resurrected. He explained,

> After Joseph comes to us in his resurrected body He will more fully instruct us concerning the Baptism for the dead and the sealing ordinances. He will say be baptized for this man and that man and that man be sealed to that man and such a man to such a man, and connect the Priesthood together. I tell you their will not be much of this done until Joseph comes. He is

our spiritual Father. Our hearts are already turned to him and his to us.[44]

From May 1842 until 1877, the temple rites were transmitted orally. Wilford Woodruff recorded on January 14, 1877, "Spent the Evening with Presidet Young. He requested Brigham jr & W Woodruff to write out the Ceremony of the Endowments from Beginning to End."[45] Putting the ceremony down in writing [in 1877] was necessary to standardize the variations between sessions. Those variations concerned Brigham Young. Once there was a manuscript, Brigham Young introduced a 30-minute lecture that was delivered before the veil as the endowment concluded. Because he added his Adam-God teaching as part of this lecture, it was subsequently removed. Also, because some who participated in killing Joseph and Hyrum Smith were still alive, he added an oath of vengeance.[46] This was also subsequently removed when it became public knowledge during the Reed Smoot Senate Confirmation Hearings before the U.S. Senate.

Because Brigham Young was only able to get "our ceremonies pretty correct" (as he described it), it is clear he did not preserve exactly what Joseph Smith introduced. He said that he expected the rites to be fixed by a resurrected Joseph Smith for the Millennium.

Brigham Young's successor, John Taylor, also saw the temple rites in a somewhat disorganized and incomplete state. Forty years after Joseph's death, he explained to the School of the Prophets,

> The reason why things are in the shape they are is because Joseph felt called upon to confer all ordinances connected with the Priesthood. He felt in a hurry on account of certain premonition that he had concerning his death, and was very desirous to empart the endowments and all the ordinances thereof to the Priesthood during his life time....[47]

His remarks concluded with, "Had Joseph Smith lived he would have had much more to say on many of those points which he was prevented from doing by his death."[48] Though survivors made a sincere effort to copy what Joseph had begun, they admitted it was not altogether correct and would need further help from a resurrected Joseph Smith before it could be recovered. Had Joseph survived, he may have been able to provide a ceremonial tour back through the seven heavens to the Throne of God.[49]

Succeeding generations of LDS leaders who were not taught by Joseph Smith have likewise taken advantage of the idea that the ceremonies were not perfectly preserved and could be "corrected" from time to time. The result has been numerous alterations of the temple endowment, washings, anointings, and sealings—the most recent of which were adopted four months ago.[50]

Although the ceremony was first put into writing in 1877, portions of it were not written down because it was initially considered taboo to include the descriptions of specific signs and penalties. These remained unwritten through at least 1923.[51] Changes in the written form of the ceremony began during the Reed Smoot Confirmation Hearings when the oath of vengeance was removed. Changes have continued to be made by the LDS Church,[52] the latest implemented in January 2019.[53]

Christ taught parables that include invited guests being barred from attending the wedding feast. In one, the guests are called "virgins" to suggest they possess moral purity and would be welcomed to the event. In another, there are strangers on the highway invited because others refused to come. Both parables, however, have some who are ultimately excluded from the "wedding" (a symbol of Christ's return). These parables raise an important issue about the Lord's return. There is a reason why five of the ten virgins could not enter into the wedding celebration.[54] Likewise, those invited to attend the wedding feast that arrive without a wedding garment will be excluded.[55] In both cases, those excluded were not welcome, as they were unprepared.

There have only been two societies in recorded history that became Zion. Because of the age of the world at the time, both were taken [up] into heaven. We have very little to help us understand why these two succeeded. Apart from describing them as of "one heart, one mind, and no poor among them," we know little else. But perhaps that is one of the most important things we can know about them. Maybe the point is that nothing and no one stood out as remarkable or different within the community. There were no heroes and no villains, no rich and poor, no Shakespearian plot lines of betrayal, intrigue, ambition, conflict, and envy. There was no adultery, theft, robbery, murder, immorality, and drunkenness—in other words, nothing to entertain us because all our stories, movies, music, novels, television plots, and social media are based upon and captivated by everything that is missing from these societies.

The centuries-long period of peace described in the Book of Mormon occupies only a few short pages in Fourth Nephi. Their society was marked by the presence of peace, the absence of conflict, and abiding stability. This is what they attained:

> There were no contentions and disputations among them, and every man did deal justly one with another. And they had all things common among them; therefore, there were not rich and poor, bond and free, but they were all made free and partakers of the Heavenly gift. (4 Nephi 1:1)

Because there was no future ministry for them to perform, their Zion society was not taken to heaven. Because the world was not yet ready for the Lord to return in judgment, neither Enoch nor Melchizedek returned with their people to fall on their necks and kiss them.[56]

These people were most remarkable for what they lacked. How they grew to lack these divisions, contentions, and disputes is described in a very few, simple words:

> They did walk after the commandments which they had received from their Lord and their God, continuing in fasting and prayer, and in meeting together oft, both to pray and to hear the word of the Lord. And it came to pass that there was no contention among all the people in all the land…. (Ibid. vs.2)

What were the names of the leaders? We don't know because, apparently, there were none. Who were their great teachers? Again, we don't know because they were not identified. Who governed? Apparently, no one. They had things in common, obeyed God's commandments, and spent time praying and hearing the word of the Lord. They were so very unlike us.

To make the point clear for us, the record of these people explains,

There was no contention in the land because of the love of God which did dwell in the hearts of the people; and there were no envyings, nor strifes, nor tumults, nor whoredoms, nor lyings, nor murders, nor any manner of lasciviousness. (Ibid. vs.3)

All the negatives were missing because the love of God dwelt in their hearts. Something else describes them,

And surely there could not be a happier people among all the people who had been created by the hand of God. (Ibid.)

Consider those words carefully. You cannot be happier than by allowing the love of God to dwell in you. The happiest people who have ever lived did so by the profound peace they displayed, equality they shared, fairness they showed one another, and love of God in their hearts.

This is a description of our social opposites. Reviewing the Answer to the Prayer for Covenant, the Covenant, and the recent Parable of the Master's House shows that the Lord is pleading for us to become this. It is not easy. It will require civilizing the uncivilized. However, it is necessary to become the wise virgins and the invited guests wearing the wedding garment.

Five of the virtuous virgins who were expecting the wedding party to arrive were nevertheless excluded. They were virgins like the others. But the others were allowed to enter, and they were not. They did not lack virginity. They did not lack notice. They were not surprised by an unexpected wedding party arriving. But they lacked "oil," which is a symbol of the Holy Ghost. They failed to acquire the necessary spirit with which to avoid conflict, envy, strife, tumult, and contention. To grow into the kind of people God will want to welcome into His dwelling requires practice, experience, and effort. People have not done it. Devout religious people are not prepared to live in peace with all things in common with no poor among them. God is trying to create a civilization that does not yet exist.

It is a privilege for God to give guidance to help prepare His people. There has always been a promise from the Lord that those who inherit Zion will be given commandments from Him to follow. He declared:

Yea, blessed are they whose feet stand upon the land of Zion, who have obeyed my gospel, for they shall receive for their reward the good things of the earth, and it shall bring forth in her strength. And they also shall be crowned with blessings from above, yea, and with commandments not a few, and with revelations in their time, they that are faithful and diligent before me. (T&C 46:1)[57]

Those who mock or criticize efforts to complete the Restoration are defining themselves as unworthy by their own words. No matter how good they may otherwise be, when they embrace conflict, envy, strife, tumult, and contention, they cannot be invited to the wedding of the Lamb.

We need more commandments from God to prepare for what is coming. The example in Fourth Nephi commends those people who walk after the commandments received from our Lord and God. There should be fasting and prayer. People should meet together, pray, and review the words of the Lord. Every step taken will make us more like those virgins who have oil in their lamps and less like the foolish virgins who took no effort to make the required preparation.

It is not enough to avoid outright evil. We have to be good. Being "good" means to be separate from the world, united in charity toward each other, and to have united hearts. If we are to be ready when the wedding party arrives, we must follow the Lord's commandments to us. They are for our good. He wants us to awaken and arise from an awful slumber.[58]

The third such society will not be taken into Heaven. Instead, it will welcome the return of the first two to the Earth. Why would ancient, righteous societies caught up to Heaven want to leave there to come and meet with a city of people on Earth? Why would they fall on their necks and kiss that gathered body of believers? And above all else, why would Christ want to occupy a tabernacle and dwell with such a community? Obviously: because there will be people living on Earth whose civilization is like the society in Heaven.

The Ten Commandments outline basic social norms needed for peace and stability. Christ's Sermon on the Mount was His exposition on the Ten Commandments. He expounded on the need to align the intent of the heart with God's standard to love your fellowman, do good to those who abuse you, and hold no anger. He took us deeper. Where the Ten Commandments allow reluctant, resentful, and hard-hearted conformity, the Sermon on the Mount requires a willing readiness to obey. Christ wants us to act with alacrity to follow Him. He taught us to treat others as you want to be treated.[59]

The answer to these questions is easy to conceptualize and easy to verbalize. But living the answer is beyond mankind's ability to grasp. We do not want to lay down our pride, ambition, jealousy, envy, strife, and lusts to become that community.

Enoch prophesied about the last-days' Zion. He saw the Earth was pained by the wickedness upon her. He wrote this account:

> *Enoch looked upon the earth and he heard a voice from the bowels thereof, saying, Woe, woe is me, the mother of men. I am pained; I am weary because of the wickedness of my children. When shall I rest and be cleansed from the filthiness which has gone forth out of me? When will my Creator sanctify me, that I may rest, and righteousness for a season abide upon my face? And when Enoch heard the earth mourn, he wept, and cried unto the Lord, saying, O Lord will you not have compassion upon the earth?* (Genesis 4:20)

The answer describes things that have not happened but may happen in our day if we choose to follow the Lord. The opportunity has been offered. The Lord's answer to Enoch was in the form of a covenant. That covenant will be vindicated but only by those who will rise up to obey Him. God's words will not fail, and this will happen:

> *And the Lord said unto Enoch, As I live, even so will I come in the last days, in the days of wickedness and vengeance, to fulfill the oath which I have made unto you concerning the children of Noah. And the day shall come that the earth shall rest. But before that day, the heavens shall be darkened, and a veil of darkness shall cover the earth; and the heavens shall shake, and also the earth. And great tribulations shall be among the children of men, but **my people** will I preserve. And righteousness will I send down out of Heaven. Truth will I send forth out of the earth to bear testimony*

*of my Only Begotten, his resurrection from the dead, yea, and also the resurrection of all men. And righteousness and truth will I cause to sweep the earth as with a flood, to gather out my own elect from the four quarters of the earth unto a place which I shall prepare, a holy city, that **my people** may gird up their loins and be looking forth for the time of my coming. For there shall be my tabernacle, and it shall be called Zion, a New Jerusalem. And the Lord said unto Enoch, Then shall you and all your city meet **them** there, and we will receive **them** into our bosom. And they shall see us, and we will fall upon **their** necks, and **they** shall fall upon our necks, and we will kiss each other; and there shall be my abode. And it shall be Zion which shall come forth out of all the creations which I have made, and for the space of a thousand years shall the earth rest.* (Ibid. vs.22, emphasis added)

The last-days' Zion and her people were planned, foretold, and chosen thousands of years ago to live on Earth when righteousness would come down out of Heaven. They will be here when truth is sent forth out of the Earth to bear testimony of Christ. And like a flood, righteousness and truth will sweep the Earth. Any who have witnessed a flood know that floodwaters carry a great deal of debris, dirt, and detritus. Today there is a flood of information, recordings, and teaching sweeping the Earth.[60] The Internet has made it possible for an individual sitting at a keyboard to speak to the entire world. Righteousness is sweeping the Earth while floodwaters are disturbing the whole world.

In Joseph Smith's day, it was required for an army of messengers to be sent. There was a practical limit on how many [people] Joseph could personally teach. Outside the direct sound of his voice, only printed words could carry the message. He and those who followed him invested in a press to publish newspapers and books to carry the truth. But that still was not enough; it required an organized body of missionaries to take the publications, repeat the message, and convey what new truths came through revelation to Joseph Smith. Even with the enormous investment of time and resources made while Joseph was alive, there were places and people who never heard a thing about the Restoration while Joseph lived.

Today we must still warn others. However, we have much greater means available to us. We can use a keyboard to reach the whole world. There are people in Africa, Asia, Europe, Australia, South America, and across North America who participate in our conferences. I send greetings to these brothers and sisters in Africa, Asia, Europe, South America, Australia, New Zealand, and elsewhere who cannot travel to be with us.[61] The flood overflowing the world today includes the promised righteousness and truth, but it requires the Lord's elect to distinguish between the filth, folly, and foolishness to find freedom from sin through Christ, who is the foundation of righteousness and truth.

Prophets have described how this will happen. Isaiah described a coming age of peace when righteousness and truth have had their opportunity to bear fruit. He spoke of Christ and of the power in Christ's teachings to transform the world itself. That same world that Enoch heard lamenting, pained by the violence on her face, will find rest. Isaiah foretells what will happen just prior to the Lord's return:

And there shall come forth a rod out of the stem of Jesse, and a branch shall grow out of his roots. And the spirit of the Lord shall rest upon him — the spirit of wisdom and understanding, the spirit of counsel and might, the spirit of knowledge and of the fear of the Lord — and shall make him of quick understanding in the fear of the Lord. And he shall not judge after the sight of his eyes, neither reprove after the hearing of his ears, but with righteousness shall he judge the poor, and reprove with equity for the meek of the earth. And he shall smite the earth with the rod of his mouth, and with the breath of his lips shall he slay the wicked. And righteousness shall be the girdle of his loins, and faithfulness the girdle of his reins. The wolf also shall dwell with the lamb, and the leopard shall lie down with the kid; and the calf, and the young lion, and the fatling together, and a little child shall lead them. And the cow and the bear shall feed, their young ones shall lie down together, and the lion shall eat straw like the ox. And the sucking child shall play on the hole of the asp, and the weaned child shall put his hand on the cockatrice's den. They shall not hurt nor destroy in all my holy mountain, for the earth shall be full of the knowledge of the Lord as the waters cover the sea. And in that day, there shall be a root of Jesse who shall stand for an ensign of the people; to it shall the gentiles seek, and his rest shall be glorious. (Isaiah 5:4; see also 2 Nephi 9:21)

How will Christ smite the Earth with the rod of His mouth? By teaching peace to people who are willing to obey and live at peace. What will it take to see the wolf dwell with the lamb? Why does the wolf kill the lamb today? The wolf kills because it is hungry. If the same shepherd who feeds the lamb also fed the wolf, then the wolf would not need to kill.

Wolves can be domesticated. I once owned a mixed wolf/Malamute we named Cicely (after the fictitious town in Alaska that was the setting for the TV show *Northern Exposure*). Cicely looked entirely like a wolf, and her behavior was lupine. She was very gentle with her clan: our immediate family and friends. My children were still young then, and our neighborhood had other young children who came over. Cicely recognized them and accepted them as belonging. However, an adult man trying to read an electrical meter once entered our backyard, and Cicely regarded this as a threat to her clan. The man scarcely escaped through the gate! Wolves are intelligent animals and, inside their clans, are capable of treating young children with gentle, protective care. They are also capable defenders against threats.

Under the peaceful guidance of a kindly shepherd, the wolf and the lamb could learn to lie down together. Lions have been domesticated, as have bears. When Adam was given dominion over the Earth, all the animals that came to him for naming dwelt together peacefully. Why do we assume nature is violent? Why regard it as "red of tooth and claw?"[62]

The Scriptures speak of an idyllic time in the beginning when man and nature were entirely at peace with one another. The Scriptures also foretell of a coming idyllic age when that peace is restored again. Why do we accept these bookends as true without ever considering the role of man in destroying the original peace? Why do we assume we have no obligation imposed on us to reform Creation back to the original? The prophecy of Isaiah is not magic imposed by God upon a reluctant Creation. It will require shepherds to care for the Creation.

Who are "they" in this passage: "They shall not hurt nor destroy in all my holy mountain"?

And why is the passage, "They shall not hurt nor destroy in all my holy mountain" followed by the statement, "for the earth shall be full of the knowledge of the Lord as the waters cover the sea"?

These are connected thoughts.

It should be obvious to you that this can only be fulfilled by a different civilization than the one in which we live. Ours can never produce such results.

Isaiah also describes what it will be like after the Lord's return. After He has come to dwell with those prepared to welcome His return, events will unfold in this way:

> *For behold, I create new heavens and a new earth, and the former shall not be remembered nor come into mind. But be glad and rejoice for ever in that which I create; for behold, I create Jerusalem a rejoicing and her people a joy. And I will rejoice in Jerusalem and joy in my people, and the voice of weeping shall be no more heard in her, nor the voice of crying. In those days, there shall be no more from there an infant of days, nor an old man that has not filled his day; for the child shall not die, but shall live to be a hundred years old. But the sinner living to be a hundred years old shall be accursed. And they shall build houses and inhabit them, and they shall plant vineyards and eat the fruit of them. They shall not build and another inhabit, they shall not plant and another eat; for as the days of a tree are the days of my people, and my elect shall long enjoy the work of their hands. They shall not labor in vain, nor bring forth for trouble; for they are the seed of the blessed of the Lord, and their offspring with them. And it shall come to pass that before they call, I will answer, and while they are yet speaking, I will hear. The wolf and the lamb shall feed together, and the lion shall eat straw like the bullock, and dust shall be the serpent's food. They shall not hurt nor destroy in all my holy mountain, says the Lord. (Isaiah 24:9)[63]*

The same words are used to describe the prepared people before the Lord's return and those with whom He will dwell after His return. Neither [of these] "shall not hurt nor destroy in all my holy mountain, says the Lord." What will they be like who do not hurt nor destroy? Can you imagine such a society? Isaiah's description reflects this incident involving Joseph Smith and Zion's Camp.

> In pitching my tent we found three massasaugas or prairie rattlesnakes, which the brethren were about to kill, but I said, "Let them alone—don't hurt them! How will the serpent ever lose his venom, while the servants of God possess the same disposition, and continue to make war upon it? Men must become harmless, before the brute creation; and when men lose their vicious dispositions and cease to destroy the animal race, the lion and the lamb can dwell together, and the sucking child can play with the serpent in safety." The brethren took the serpents carefully on sticks and carried them across the creek. I exhorted the brethren not to kill a serpent, bird, or an animal of any kind during our journey unless it became necessary in order to preserve ourselves from hunger.[64]

Last year while my wife and I were hiking the Bonneville Shoreline Trail in Draper, Utah, she was in the lead. We were going at a rapid pace. [(She always does that—that's why she's in the lead, because she wants to set the pace.) We were going at a rapid pace, and] she passed a rattlesnake so quickly that when it began to rattle its warning, she had already passed; but I heard it before I reached it, lying only inches off the trail, and I stopped to look. Growing up in Idaho, rattlesnakes were common. After watching it for a few moments, I started to talk to it in a calm voice and made no menacing movement toward it. As I took the time to talk calmly without advancing toward it, its nervous rattle began to slow and eventually stopped. Then it uncoiled, which only happens when the snake is not defensive. I suppose the calm of my voice and my non-threatening demeanor relieved the little animal's fear. It began to slowly move away, and I encouraged it to stay off the trail because another passing hiker or bicyclist would probably try to kill it.

I thought of Joseph Smith's words when I encountered that snake. How will the serpent ever lose his venom? Men must become harmless. Men must lose their vicious dispositions and cease to destroy.

I know however well I may treat an animal, another will soon come by and mistreat the same animal. Nature will refuse to be at peace with mankind while mankind continues to slay, abuse, and misuse the animal kingdom.

But the prophecy is about God's "holy mountain." It raises the question, if there were a place occupied by people who do not hurt or destroy in that holy mountain, could nature reach peace with the people in that place?

Cicely acted to protect the children in my yard from what she regarded as an intruding threat. It was her nature to do so. She wanted her clan to be safe. Toward her clan she showed affection, played, and gave us all companionship. But to the threat, she was menacing.

In the first Zion, the people were at peace with nature. But that place was apparently protected by nature. What Scripture describes is not magic or "fairy dust" but a perfectly natural process. This Creation has been ordained by God and framed with intelligence to follow certain principles established before the foundation of the world. Any people in any age who follow the same pattern will receive the same result. What is described in this passage about Enoch and his city?

> *And so great was the faith of Enoch that he led the people of God, and their enemies came to battle against them, and he spoke the word of the Lord, and the earth trembled, and the mountains fled — even according to his command — and the rivers of water were turned out of their course, and the roar of the lions were heard out of the wilderness. And all nations feared greatly, so powerful was the word of Enoch, and so great was the power of the language which God had given him.* (Genesis 4:13)

Would a lion that had been befriended by Enoch and his people be inclined by its nature to protect the people it viewed as part of its clan? Would a bear protect its shepherd and guardian? Would a wolf?

Is it possible for a civilization to exist that does not hurt nor destroy in all their land? If they would not hurt nor destroy in all their land, would it be a holy place?

We live in a very different civilization from the one described in prophecy. But the one described prophetically will not just one day appear. It will require effort, learning, obedience, and sacrifice to change.

The Earth rejoiced at Enoch's people. The Earth protected those people. Earthquakes, landslides, and floods stopped the wicked, and the animal kingdom—including predators like the lion—rose up to protect the City of Enoch.

For those who prepare to receive the people of Enoch and Melchizedek and those who will welcome the Lord to dwell among them, that can and will happen again.

Everybody will have to make changes. The most important changes have been provided in a blueprint revealed in the Answer to Prayer for Covenant, including the terms of the Covenant. Those changes are required before a temple can be built. We are expected to remember and obey these words:

> My will is to have you love one another. As people, you lack the ability to respectfully disagree among one another.
>
> …Wisdom counsels mankind to align their words with their hearts, but mankind refuses to take counsel from Wisdom.
>
> …there have been sharp disputes between you that should have been avoided. I speak these words to reprove you that you may learn, not to upbraid you so that you mourn. I want my people to have understanding.
>
> …There is little reason for any to be angry or to harshly criticize the labor to recover the scriptures, and so my answer to you concerning the scriptures is to guide you in other work to be done hereafter; for recovering the scriptures does not conclude the work to

be accomplished by those who will be my people: it is but a beginning.

...Satan is a title and means accuser, opponent, and adversary; hence, once he fell, Lucifer became, or in other words was called, Satan, because he accuses others and opposes the Father. I rebuked Peter and called him Satan because he was wrong in opposing the Father's will for me, and Peter understood and repented.

In the work you have performed there are those who have been Satan, accusing one another, wounding hearts, and causing jarring, contention, and strife by their accusations. Rather than loving one another, even among you who desire a good thing, some have dealt unkindly as if they were the opponents, accusers, and adversaries. In this they were wrong.

You have sought to recover the scriptures because you hope to obtain the covenant for my protective hand to be over you, but you cannot be Satan and be mine. If you take upon you my covenant, you must abide it as a people to gain what I promise. You think Satan will be bound a thousand years, and it will be so, but do not understand your own duty to bind that spirit within you so that you give no heed to accuse others. It is not enough to say you love God; you must also love your fellow man. Nor is it enough to say you love your fellow man while you, as Satan, divide, contend, and dispute against any person who labors on an errand seeking to do my will. How you proceed must be as noble as the cause you seek. You have become your own adversaries, and you cannot be Satan and also be mine. Repent, therefore, like Peter and end your unkind and untrue accusations against one another, and make peace. How shall there ever come a thousand years of peace if the people who are mine do not love one another? How shall Satan be bound if there are no people of one heart and one mind?

...For you are like a man who seeks for good fruit from a neglected vineyard — unwatered, undunged, unpruned, and unattended. How shall it produce good fruit if you fail to tend it? What reward does the unfaithful husbandman obtain from his neglected vineyard? How can saying you are a faithful husbandman ever produce good fruit in the vineyard without doing the work of the

husbandman? For you seek my words to recover them even as you forsake to do them. You have heretofore produced wild fruit, bitter and ill-formed, because you neglect to do my words.

I speak of you who have hindered my work, that claim to see plainly the beams in others' eyes. You have claimed to see plainly the error of those who abuse my words, and neglect the poor, and who have cast you out — to discern their errors, and you say you seek a better way. Yet among you are those who continue to scheme, backbite, contend, accuse, and forsake my words to do them, even while you seek to recover them. Can you not see that your works fall short of the beliefs you profess?

…you have not yet become what you must be to live together in peace. If you will hearken to my words, I will make you my people and my words will give you peace. Even a single soul who stirs up the hearts of others to anger can destroy the peace of all my people. Each of you must equally walk truly in my path, not only to profess, but to do as you profess.

The Book of Mormon was given as my covenant for this day and contains my gospel, which came forth to allow people to understand my work and then obtain my salvation. Yet many of you are like those who reject the Book of Mormon, because you say, but you do not do. As a people you honor with your lips, but your hearts are corrupt, filled with envy and malice, returning evil for good, sparing none — even those with pure hearts among you — from your unjustified accusations and unkind backbiting. You have not obtained the fullness of my salvation because you do not draw near to me.

The Book of Mormon is to convince the gentiles, and a remnant of Lehi, and the Jews, of the truth of the words of my ancient prophets and apostles, with all the records agreeing that I am the Lamb of God, the Son of the Father, and I was sent into the world to do the will of the Father, and I am the Savior of the world. All must come unto me or they cannot be saved. And how do men come unto me? It is by faith, repentance, and baptism, which bring the holy ghost, to then show you all things you must know.

...Hear therefore my words: Repent and bring forth fruit showing repentance, and I will establish my covenant with you and claim you as mine.

...It is not enough to receive my covenant, but you must also abide it. And all who abide it, whether on this land or any other land, will be mine, and I will watch over them and protect them in the day of harvest, and gather them in as a hen gathers her chicks under her wings. I will number you among the remnant of Jacob, no longer outcasts, and you will inherit the promises of Israel. You shall be my people and I will be your God, and the sword will not devour you. And unto those who will receive will more be given, until they know the mysteries of God in full.

But remember that without the fruit of repentance, and a broken heart and a contrite spirit, you cannot keep my covenant; for I, your Lord, am meek and lowly of heart. Be like me. You have all been wounded, your hearts pierced through with sorrows because of how the world has treated you. But you have also scarred one another by your unkind treatment of each other, and you do not notice your misconduct toward others because you think yourself justified in this. You bear the scars on your countenances, from the soles of your feet to the head, and every heart is faint. Your visages have been so marred that your hardness, mistrust, suspicions, resentments, fear, jealousies, and anger toward your fellow man bear outward witness of your inner self; you cannot hide it. When I appear to you, instead of confidence, you feel shame. You fear and withdraw from me because you bear the blood and sins of your treatment of brothers and sisters. Come to me and I will make sins as scarlet become white as snow, and I will make you stand boldly before me, confident of my love.

I descended below it all, and know the sorrows of you all, and have borne the grief of it all, and I say to you, Forgive one another. Be tender with one another, pursue judgment, bless the oppressed, care for the orphan, and uplift the widow in her need, for I have redeemed you from being orphaned and taken you that you are no longer a widowed people. Rejoice in me, and rejoice with your brethren and sisters who are mine also. Be one.

You pray each time you partake of the sacrament to always have my spirit to be with you. And what is my spirit? It is to love one another as I have loved you. Do my works and you will know my doctrine, for you will uncover hidden mysteries by obedience to these things that can be uncovered in no other way. This is the way I will restore knowledge to my people. If you return good for evil, you will cleanse yourself and know the joy of your Master. You call me Lord, and do well to regard me so, but to know your Lord is to love one another. Flee from the cares and longings that belong to Babylon, obtain a new heart, for you have all been wounded. In me you will find peace, and through me will come Zion, a place of peace and safety.

...I have given to you the means to understand the conditions you must abide. I came and lived in the world to be the light of the world. I have sent others who have testified of me and taught you. I have sent my light into the world. Let not your hearts remain divided from one another and divided from me.

Be of one heart, and regard one another with charity. Measure your words before giving voice to them, and consider the hearts of others. Although a man may err in understanding concerning many things, yet he can view his brother with charity and come unto me, and through me he can with patience overcome the world. I can bring him to understanding and knowledge. Therefore, if you regard one another with charity, then your brother's error in understanding will not divide you. I lead to all truth. I will lead all who come to me to the truth of all things. The fullness is to receive the truth of all things, and this too from me, in power, by my word, and in very deed. For I will come unto you if you will come unto me.

Study to learn how to respect your brothers and sisters and to come together by precept, reason, and persuasion, rather than sharply disputing and wrongly condemning each other, causing anger. Take care how you invoke my name. Mankind has been controlled by the adversary through anger and jealousy, which has led to bloodshed and the misery of many souls. Even strong disagreements should not provoke anger, nor to invoke my name in vain as if I had part in your every dispute. Pray together in humility and together meekly present your dispute to me, and if you are contrite before me, I will tell you my part.

...There remains great work yet to be done. Receive my covenant and abide in it, not as in the former time when jarring, jealousy, contention, and backbiting caused anger, broke hearts, and hardened the souls of those claiming to be my saints. But receive it in spirit, in meekness, and in truth. I have given you a former commandment that I, the Lord, will forgive whom I will forgive, but of you it is required to forgive all men. And again, I have taught that if you forgive men their trespasses, your Heavenly Father will also forgive you; but if you forgive not men their trespasses, neither will your Heavenly Father forgive your trespasses. How do I act toward mankind? If men intend no offense, I take no offense, but if they are taught and should have obeyed, then I reprove and correct, and forgive and forget. You cannot be at peace with one another if you take offense when none is intended. But again I say, Judge not others except by the rule you want used to weigh yourself.

[One of the questions that someone asked is, "Why we are admonished to 'pursue judgment'?" The answer are those words I just read to you: "I say, Judge not others except by the rule you want used to weigh yourself." Pursue judgment whenever the opportunity presents itself. Use judgment to evaluate (based upon the standard you want applied to yourself) and pursue judgment.]

...The earth groans under the wickedness of mankind upon her face, and she longs for peace to come. She withholds the abundance of her bounty because of the offenses of men against me, against one another, and against her. But if righteousness returns and my people prove by their actions, words, and thoughts to yield to my spirit and hearken to my commandments, then will the earth rejoice, for the feet of those who cry peace upon her mountains are beautiful indeed, and I, the Lord, will bring again Zion, and the earth will rejoice.

In the world, tares are ripening. And so I ask you, What of the wheat? Let your pride, and your envy, and your fears depart from you. I will come to my tabernacle and dwell with my people in Zion, and none will overtake it.

Cry peace. Proclaim my words. Invite those who will repent to be baptized and forgiven, and they shall obtain my spirit to guide them. (T&C 157:3-6,8-10,17-21,23,48-54,58,63-65)

That excerpt contains nearly 2,200 words of instruction. There is no basis to claim ignorance. Is it possible for people to change their civilization and go from strident, quarrelsome, and pugnacious to loving one another? Perhaps the Book of Mormon contains one account to give us hope.

Following conversion, one group of Lamanites were led by a king who encouraged them to lay down their un-bloodied weapons rather than ever shed blood again. This meant they could not defend themselves. After their king finished his proposal, this took place:

And now it came to pass that when the king had made an end of these sayings, and all the people were assembled together, they took their swords and all the weapons which were used for the shedding of man's blood, and they did bury them up deep in the earth. And this they did, it being in their view a testimony to God, and also to men, that they never would use weapons again for the shedding of man's blood. And this they did vouching and covenanting with God, that rather than shed the blood of their brethren, they would give up their own lives; and rather than take away from a brother, they would give unto him; and rather than spend their days in idleness, they would labor abundantly with their hands. And thus we see that when these Lamanites were brought to believe and to know the truth, they were firm and would suffer, even unto death, rather than commit sin; and thus we see that they buried the weapons of peace, or they buried the weapons of war for peace. (Alma 14:9)

When their resolve was tested, they passed. Rather than take up arms, they laid down their lives.

Now when the people saw that they were coming against them, they went out to meet them and prostrated themselves before them to the earth, and began to call on the name of the Lord; and thus they were in this attitude when the Lamanites began to fall upon them and began to slay them with the sword. And thus without meeting any resistance, they did slay a thousand and five of them; and we know that they are blessed, for they have gone to dwell with their God. Now when the Lamanites saw that their brethren would not flee from the sword, neither would they turn aside to the right hand or to the left, but that they would lie down and perish, and praised God even in the very act of perishing under the sword — now when the Lamanites saw this, they did forbear from slaying them; and there were many whose hearts had swollen in them for those of their brethren who had fallen under the sword, for they repented of the thing which they had done.

And it came to pass that they threw down their weapons of war, and they would not take them again, for they were stung for the murders which they had committed. And they came down even as their brethren, relying upon the mercies of those whose arms were lifted to slay them.

And it came to pass that the people of God were joined that day by more than the number who had been slain.... (Ibid. vs.10-12)

This event is astonishing and many have been shocked by the extreme behavior of these believers. We are not being asked to lay down our weapons and be killed. We are only being asked to lay down [our] hostility, slander, and abuse of one another to become peaceful and loving. This is a good thing that benefits everybody. Despite this, we keep our pride, ambition, jealousy, envy, strife, and lusts. These destructive desires are preferred over forgiving offenses in meekness, love, and kindness. None of us are asked to die for a covenant but are only asked to be more like Christ and forgive and love one another. This seems so difficult a challenge that we quarrel and dispute among ourselves. We remain haughty and self-righteous and fail to realize self-righteousness is a lie, a mirage—utterly untrue. We must trade our pride for humility, or we will never be able to keep the covenant. Remember, it is a group who must keep the covenant, not individuals. Together we must act consistent with the obligation we agreed to perform before God.

Now, I want to be clear about what I am NOT saying. Nothing in what has been said implies that people must be vegan. In the age of the first patriarchs, we learn this about the second generation: *And Abel listened unto the voice of the Lord. And Abel was a keeper of sheep...And Abel, he also brought of the firstlings of his flock and of the fat thereof. And the Lord had respect unto Abel and to his offering...* (Genesis 3:6-7).

There are animals whose lives are given them for the benefit of mankind. Abel raised sheep for the benefit their lives offered in food, clothing, and even company.

I am also NOT suggesting we attempt to domesticate wild animals. Until there is a community that has tamed the wild hearts of human residents and has a land to occupy, animals will remain justifiably fearful of man.[65] Nature will not distinguish between the righteous and the wicked, the hostile and the benign, the people of peace and the people at war with the animal kingdom until there is a "holy mountain." That will be the place made holy by the actions of the people who dwell there. When the Earth sees that righteousness has returned to her face, she will yield her abundance for those whose feet walk in the way that is beautiful.

If we obey the commandments that have been given, we can qualify to inherit a land on which to build a temple. The objective of the covenant was to confer the right to live on the land, surviving the judgments coming upon the wicked. WE need to live up to our end of the covenant. It is clear the Lord is willing to bear with, guide, give commandments to help prepare, and reprove His people when needed. We should not rely on the Lord's patience but should be eager to obey His guiding instruction. His commandments are not to limit us but to increase light and truth. Some intelligence is only gained by obedience to His commandments.

Joseph Smith tried to teach people. They failed to do as they were commanded.[66] They lost the opportunity to have the fullness of the Priesthood restored to them.[67] As a result of their failure, for nearly two centuries institutions have pretended the fullness was restored and they inherited it. Until now, no people have acknowledged the failure, repented, and asked the Lord to restore the fullness of the Priesthood.

Salem was a land filled with abominations. Melchizedek, by faith, obtained the Holy Order, taught repentance, and persuaded them to reform.[68] Nauvoo was a viper's den. It was a place with widespread adultery and conspirators who precipitated the murders of Joseph and Hyrum.

Why (during His mortality) did Jesus Christ not establish a place of peace, a city of Zion? Was not Christ the greatest teacher of all?[69]

Reflect on this, and consider whether the people who were taught by Melchizedek lived with and were taught by Joseph Smith, would they have repented, obeyed, and obtained the fullness?

If Enoch's people lived in Nauvoo, would they have repented? If Joseph, instead of Enoch, taught the people of Enoch, would there have been Zion? Had Joseph (instead of Melchizedek) taught the people of Salem, would they have forsaken their abominations?

Is Zion the result of the teacher or the people?

The people matter more than the teacher. As long as the gospel is taught (including the need for repentance and obedience), any faithful teacher may be enough. But nobody can bring again Zion with people who refuse to repent and obey God's commandments. The teacher is necessary, but only a community of people willing to heed the gospel can fulfill the prophecies.

I have to temper the foregoing by the lesson Alma preserved (I think, perhaps, quoted from writings by Zenos) about Melchizedek:

> *Now this Melchizedek was a king over the land of Salem, and his people had waxed strong in iniquity and abominations — yea, they had all gone astray; they were full of all manner of wickedness. But Melchizedek, having exercised mighty faith and received the office of the High Priesthood according to the Holy Order of God, did preach repentance unto his people. And behold, they did repent. And Melchizedek did establish peace in the land in his days; therefore, he was called the Prince of Peace, for he was the King of Salem; and he did reign under his father. Now there were many before him, and also there were many afterwards, but none were greater.* (Alma 10:2)

If people who had all gone astray and were filled with iniquity and abominations were moved by his message of repentance, could Melchizedek have persuaded Nauvoo to abandon their wickedness, strife, ambition, jealousy, and adultery? There is no answer because of Christ's inability to bring Zion. Christ was greater than Melchizedek, and He could not accomplish with His contemporaries what Melchizedek did with his.

None of us is spared from mutual failure. We are not Zion. We will never be Zion if we do not repent. All of us must repent, turn to face God with full purpose of heart, acting no hypocrisy, or we will not establish godly peace among us.

The Answer to the Prayer for Covenant and the Covenant are the beginning blueprint. That blueprint teaches the need to be better people. Following it is more challenging than reciting it. No one can learn what is required without doing. Working together is the only way a society can grow together. No isolated spiritual mystic is going to be prepared for Zion through his solitary personal devotions. Personal devotion is necessary, of course, but the most pious hermit will collide with the next pious hermit when they are required to share and work together in a society of equals having all things in common. Do not pretend it will be otherwise. Failing to do the hard work outlined in the covenant is failing to prepare for Zion. [It's failing to have oil in the lamp. It's failing to put upon you the wedding garment.]

If you think you are one of the five virgins who will be invited in when the bridegroom arrives and have never attempted to obey the Lord's commandments, you will find yourself left outside when the door is shut. If you come from the highways and byways without a wedding garment because you failed to keep the covenant, you will be excluded.

As aggravating and trying as people are on one another, we need to go through this. There is no magic path to loving one another. Some people refuse and must be left outside. When it comes to loving others, some things must be abandoned, some things must be added, some things must be forgotten, and some things must be ignored. But learning what to abandon, add, forget, or ignore is only through the doing. We chip away at ourselves—and others—by interacting and sharing.

We will learn things about one another that will distress us. And we may well wish we didn't know some things about others. How will the socially-offensive become socially-acceptable without help from a loving society? And how can a society become loving if people are not broadminded enough to figure out that some things just don't matter. Few things are really important. If a man is honest, just, virtuous, and true, should you care if he swears? If a man has a heart of gold and would give you assistance if he thought it was needed, should you care if he is rough or uncouth? The adulterous and predatory will rarely reform and must often be excluded. They will victimize and destroy. We are commanded to cast out those who steal, love and make a lie, commit adultery, and refuse to repent. The instruction we have been given states:

> *You shall not kill; he that kills shall die. You shall not steal, and he that steals and will not repent* **shall be cast out**. *You shall not lie; he that lies and will not repent* **shall be cast out**. *You shall love your wife with all your heart, and shall cleave unto her and none else, and he that looks upon a woman to lust after her shall deny the faith, and shall not have the spirit, and if he repent not he* **shall be cast out**. *You shall not commit adultery, and he that commits adultery and repents not* **shall be cast out**; *and he that commits adultery and repents with all his heart, and forsakes and does it no more, you shall forgive him; but if he does it again,* **he shall not be forgiven**, *but* **shall be cast out**. *You shall not speak evil of your neighbor or do him any harm. You know my laws, they are given in my scriptures.* **He that sins and repents not shall be cast out**. *If you love me, you shall serve me and* **keep all my commandments**. (T&C 26:6, emphasis added)

This teaching is still binding. If your fellowship includes those who ought to be "cast out," you have the obligation to do so rather than encouraging evil. Be patient, but be firm. If a person refuses to repent and forsake sins, you may end fellowship with them and include those who are interested in practicing obedience and love.

There is work to be done. Almost all of it is internal to us. The five prepared virgins and the strangers who brought a wedding garment will be those who keep the covenant. It is designed to give birth to a new society, new culture, and permit a new civilization to be founded.

The Lord's civilization will require His tabernacle at the center. Through it, a recovered religion will be fully developed. God's house will include a higher law; an education about the universe and a Divine university will be established. It will be an Ensign in the mountains, and people from all over the Earth will say, "Come, let us go up to the House of the God of Jacob; He will teach us. We will learn of His paths, to walk in them."[70] That place will house a new civilization. There will be no hermit gurus proud of their enlightenment. No one will offer himself or herself up as some great idol to follow. It will be a place of equality where people are meek and lowly, serving one another without any attempt to compete for "chief seats."

Christ's apostles competed to be greater than one another. In Luke 13:6, Christ's reaction is recorded:

> There was also a strife among them: who of them should be accounted the greatest. And he said unto them, The kings of the gentiles exercise lordship over them, and they who exercise authority upon them are called benefactors; but it ought not to be so with you. But he who is greatest among you, let him be as the younger, and he who is chief, as he who does serve. For which is greater? He who sits at a meal or he who serves? I am not as he who sits at a meal, but I am among you as he who serves.

Christ is the great example. Christ would have fit into Enoch's city, would have been welcomed among Melchizedek's people, and could have dwelt in peace with the Nephites of Fourth Nephi. Has He, as once before (between Jerusalem and Emmaus[71]), walked among them unnoticed to enjoy their peaceful company?[72]

I cannot keep the covenant.

You cannot keep the covenant.

Only we can keep the covenant.

But if we do, God's work will continue and will include the fullness previously offered to the Gentiles[73] and rejected by them.[74] It is impossible to understand the promise that Elijah will turn the hearts of the children to the Fathers[75] unless the fullness is recovered. Joseph Smith cannot fix or finish the Restoration by returning as a resurrected being in the Millennium, as conjectured by Wilford Woodruff. If the necessary rites are not returned before the Lord's return, "the whole earth would be utterly wasted at his coming."[76] There will be a new civilization built around God's tabernacle where He will dwell.[77] We know the purpose of that house will be for the God of Jacob to teach those people to walk in His ways.[78] We know Joseph Smith began adoption sealing as the highest ordinance, and it has now been lost.

We have been given a new revelation that explains resurrection and adoption to the Fathers in heaven are linked together:

> *I was shown that the spirits that rose were limited to a direct line back to Adam, requiring the hearts of the Fathers and the hearts of the children to be bound together by sealing, confirmed by covenant and the Holy Spirit of Promise. This is the reason that Abraham, Isaac, and Jacob have entered into their exaltation according to the promises, and sit upon thrones, and are not angels, but are gods. ([See] T&C 157:42-43)* (T&C 169:3).

The fullness can only be returned through a temple accepted by God as His House. He must return to restore that which has been lost. But ungodly people cannot build an acceptable house for God. There is no commandment to build a temple, because people are not yet qualified to do so. So far, we have been spared the experience in Nauvoo where an abortive attempt to build a temple in which the fullness could be restored resulted in the Lord not performing His oath—nor did the Lord fulfill the promises they expected to receive. Instead of blessings, the people in Nauvoo brought upon themselves cursings, wrath, indignation, and judgments by their follies and abominations.[79] If we are going to receive that same condemnation, it would be better to not begin to build a House of God.

Only **we** can keep the covenant. Only those who keep the covenant together can establish a new civilization, with God's holy House at its center.

In the name of Jesus Christ, Amen.

1 Verbal interjections that were made during the presentation have been added in square brackets.

2 See John 2:1-2. All citations in this talk reference to the Restoration Edition of the Scriptures (RE), unless otherwise noted.

3 See 2 Peter 1:3.

4 "There is no collective salvation. Each person comes to Him one at a time. Even when He redeems a group, He visits with them individually" (www.denversnuffer.com, "3 Nephi 20:23" September 19, 2010). "I doubt there will be collective salvation" (www.denversnuffer.com, "As Soon as Converted" March 19, 2014). "We study, research and ponder this faith individually. For we believe salvation is individual, not collective" (www.denversnuffer.com, "I Am A Mormon, Part 2" May 10, 2012).

5 See T&C 93:8.

6 See, e.g., Joel 1:9; Isaiah 24:1; Revelation 8:8; T&C 123:21.

7 Hugh Nibley, *Temple and Cosmos*, Deseret Book, (Salt Lake: 1992), p.15-25, citations omitted.

8 "…what was the object of Gathering the Jews together or the people of God in any age of the world? The main object was to build unto the Lord an house whereby he Could reveal unto his people the ordinances of his house and glories of his kingdom & teach the people the ways of salvation. For there are certain ordinances & principles that when they are taught and practiced, must be done in a place or house built for that purpose. …If a man gets the fulness of God he has to get [it] in the same way that Jesus Christ obtained it & that was by keeping all the ordinances of the house of the Lord" (*Documentary History of the Church* 5:423-424 [hereafter *DHC*], as quoting from *Wilford Woodruff's Journal, Vol. 2: 1 January 1841 to 31 December 1845*, Signature Books [Midvale: 1983], entry of June 11, 1843, p. 240).

9 See *Wilford Woodruff's Journal*, supra, entry of April 28, 1842, p. 197.

10 "…the land of Egypt being first discovered by a woman, who was the daughter of Ham and the daughter of Zeptah, which, in the Chaldea, signifies Egypt, which signifies that which is forbidden. When this woman discovered the land it was under water, who afterward settled her sons in it" (Abraham 2:2).

11 While this remains a minority view, the most credible proponent is associate-professor of natural science at Boston University, Dr. Robert M. Schoch (see Schoch, Robert M. [1992]. "Redating the Great Sphinx of Giza" in *Circular Times*, ed. Collette M. Dowell. Retrieved 17 December 2008, "Response in Archaeology Magazine to Zahi Hawass and Mark Lehner" in Dowell, Colette M. [ed.]. *Circular Times*; "Geological Evidence pertaining to the Age of the Great Sphinx." Archived 14 April 2009 at the *Wayback Machine*, in Spedicato, Emilio; Notarpietro, Adalberto [ed., 2002]).

12   Joseph Smith composed a talk the day after announcing plans for constructing the Nauvoo Temple, in which he said: "...all the ordinances and duties that ever have been required by the Priesthood under the direction and commandments of the Almighty, in any of the dispensations, shall all be had in the last dispensations. Therefore, all things had under the authority of the Priesthood at any former period shall be had again, bringing to pass the restoration spoken of by the mouth of all the holy prophets..." (T&C 140:17). Joseph's entire talk (T&C 140) is important in order to understand the objective of the final Restoration.

13   This description of the restored temple's significance and role was by revelation on January 19, 1841. Joseph Smith did not petition for membership in the Nauvoo Masonic Lodge until more than 11 months later (on December 30, 1841), and his petition was not acted on until February 3, 1842. He was initiated as an entered apprentice on March 15, 1842. This description was revealed more than a year prior to any Masonic initiation.

14   See Ether 1:13; see also Mormon 4:7.

15   See also Galatians 1:13 and Ephesians 1:2, among other places.

16   See also Mosiah 3:2, Moroni 7:4, and 3 Nephi 4:7 (which contain Christ's words of adoption).

17   The first mention in Joseph's journals states, "...one thing to see the kingdom, & another to be in it, must have a change of heart, to see the kingdom of [God], & subs[c]ribe the articles of adoption to enter therein" (*JS Papers, Journals, Vol. 3*, 15 October 1843, p. 114).

18   *The Complete Discourses of Brigham Young, Vol. 5*, Smith-Pettit (Salt Lake City: 2009), 13 January 1856, Vol. 2, p. 1033-1034.

19   See Abraham 3:1. This is where God's promise is recorded that those who would later receive "this gospel" (meaning the same truths taught to and understood by Abraham) would then receive priesthood that would enable them to become his "seed."

20   See, e.g., First Presidency Secretary L. John Nuttall raised the issue and wanted to be adopted in 1884: "The subject of adoption was presented, Elder L. John Nuttall being desirous to have that ordinance attended to" (*In the President's Office: The Diaries of L. John Nuttall, 1879-1892*, Signature Books [Salt Lake, 2007], p. 147 [May21, 1884]). John Taylor gathered his thoughts and dictated them to Nuttall, which he (Nuttall) referred to many years later: "I conversed with Bro. Lund on the subject of adoption & promised to send him what I wrote as dictated by Prest. John Taylor on that subject" (*Ibid.*, September 22, 1891, p. 471). Those notes have not been published and appear to have been lost.

21   Anderson, Devery, ed., *Salt Lake School of the Prophets: 1867-1883*, Signature Books (Salt Lake: 2018), pp. 11-12; entry of 20 January 1868, quoted as in original.

22   *Ibid.*, p. 12.

23 For example, see Brown, Samuel M., "Early Mormon Adoption Theology and the Mechanics of Salvation," *Journal of Mormon History*, Vol. 37, No. 3, Summer 2011, p. 3; Stapley, Jonathan A., "Adoptive Sealing Ritual in Mormonism," *Ibid.*, p. 53.

24 *Salt Lake School of the Prophets: 1867-1883*, supra, p. 42; December 11, 1869, quoted as in original. The entire quote states: "Man also will have to be sealed to man until the chain is united from Father Adam down to the last Saint. This will be the work of the Millenium and Joseph Smith will be the man to attend to it or dictate it. He will not minister in person, but he will receive his resurrected body and will dictate to those who dwell in the flesh and tell what is to be done, for he is the last Prophet who is called to lay the foundation of the great last dispensation of the fullness of times. Some may think what I have said concerning Adam strange, but the period will come when this people will be willing to adopt Joseph Smith as their Prophet, Seer, Revelator and God, but not the Father of their Spirits, ~~for that was our Father Adam.~~"

25 From *The Diaries of Abraham H. Cannon*: "[December 18, 1890] at 2. p.m. I attended my Quorum meeting. There were present Presdts. Woodruff, Cannon and Smith, F. D. Richards F.M. Lyman and myself. …Thereafter we had a long conversation in regard to sealings and adoptions. …Bro. Joseph F. Smith rather held to the idea that children should be sealed to their parents even when the latter died without a knowledge of the gospel, and thus the connection with our ancestry should be extended as far back as it was possible to each, when the link should be made with the Prophet Joseph who stands at the head of this dispensation and he will form the connecting link with the preceding dispensations. Father [George Q. Cannon] holds that we who live on the earth now and are faithful, will stand at the head of our lineage, and will thus become Saviors as has been promised us. Pres. John Taylor was not sealed to his parents though they died in the Church, as he felt that it was rather lowering himself to be thus sealed when he was an apostle and his father was a high priest; but this is rather a questionable proceeding" (*Candid Insights of a Mormon Apostle: The Diaries of Abraham H. Cannon, 1889-1895*, Edward Leo Lyman, editor, [Signature Books: Salt Lake, 2010], p. 165).

26 *Ibid.*, p. 388.

27 "It is also proper for children to be sealed to their parents, and then have those parents sealed to the Prophet Joseph [Smith]" (*Ibid.*, p. 400).

28 *Ibid.*, p. 488.

29 "Bro. [Samuel] Roskelly of the Logan temple is having a considerable number of persons who are dead sealed and adopted to him. This is right where people request it, but he should not try to induce them to take this course through their surviving relatives, or in their own cases, if alive. Pres. Woodruff will write him to not try to get people to be thus sealed to him, but where they ask if of their own free will it will be proper" (*Ibid.*, p. 466).

30 *Ibid.*, p. 496.

31   "Brother Joseph F. in his remarks to-day bore a wonderful strong testimony...He testified to the eternity of the marriage covenant. Referred to the fact that he looked upon [Heber J. Grant] as his cousin, my mother having been sealed to the Prophet Joseph Smith for eternity" (*The Diaries of Heber J. Grant, 1880-1945 Abridged*, [Privately Published, Salt Lake City, 2010], December 13, 1899, p. 276). At the funeral of Ruben T. Miller, Joseph F. Smith "announced that he looked upon [Heber J. Grant] as being the seed actually of the Prophet Joseph Smith under the new and everlasting covenant, my mother having been sealed to the Prophet for all Eternity, and only married to my father for time" (*Ibid.*, March 29, 1901, p. 281).

32   John M.Whitaker, "Diary, Book No. 4, September 16, 1887 to September 20, 1888," November 16, 1887, MS 0002, Marriott Special Collections; transcription from Pitman shorthand by LaJean Purcell Carruth; as cited by Stapley, Jonathan A., "Adoptive Sealing Ritual in Mormonism," *Journal of Mormon History*, Vol. 37, No. 3, Summer 2011, p. 3; pp. 101-102.

33   *Wilford Woodruff's Journals, Vol. 8: 1 January 1881 to 31 December 1888*, Signature Books (Midvale, Utah: 1985), p. 441.

34   Wilford Woodruff, "Letter to Samuel Roskelley," June 8, 1887, typescript, Samuel Roskelley Collection, Box 2, Book 4, Merrill-Cazier Library; cited in Stapley, Jonathan A., "Adoptive Sealing Ritual in Mormonism," supra, p. 103.

35   Edward Bunker, "Letter to the Bunkerville High Council," April 25, 1891, *Edward Bunker Autobiography* (1894), 37, microfilm of holograph, MS 1581, LDS Church History Library.

36   *Wilford Woodruff's Journal*, supra, 9:203, all as in original.

37   See *In the President's Office: The Diaries of L. John Nuttall, 1879-1892*, Signature Books (Salt Lake, 2007), pp. 73 (November 10, 1881), 80 (November 27, 1881), 129 (April 27, 1884), and 158 (August 24, 1884).

38   "The Law of Adoption: Discourses Delivered at the General Conference of the Church, in the Tabernacle, Salt Lake City, Utah, Sunday, April 18, 1894," *Utah Genealogical and Historical Magazine* (October 1922): 145–58.

39   Clark, James R., *Messages of the First Presidency*, Bookcraft (Salt Lake City: 1966) Vol. 3, pp. 251–60.

40   *The Complete Discourses of Brigham Young, Vol. 5*, Smith-Pettit (Salt Lake City: 2009), 13 January 1856, Vol. 2, p. 1033-1034.

41   On October 9, 1899, Wilford Woodruff, speaking of temple ordinances, said, "There were many things revealed to the Prophet that were not fully understood and that these were changed when there was more light to come" (*Diaries of Heber J. Grant*, supra, p. 101).

42   "No written text of the 1842 or 1843 ritual exists. The first descriptions in any detail date from 1845..." (Buerger, David, *The Mysteries of Godliness*, Smith Research, [San Francisco: 1994], p. 73). This refers to the endowment (1842) and second anointing (1843) rituals.

43   *The Complete Discourses of Brigham Young*, supra, 5:3104.

44   *The Complete Discourses of Brigham Young*, supra, 13 January 1856, 2:1034. This was Wilford Woodruff's report of the talk. Thomas Bullock recorded the same talk a little differently reporting in relevant part, "I tell you there will not be much done until Joseph comes."

45   *Wilford Woodruff's Journals*, supra, 7:322, as in original. "On January 15, 1877, Wilford Woodruff, Brigham Young, Jr., John D. T. McAllister, and L. John Nuttall began writing out the text of the ceremony they had previously retained by memory only. Working laboriously to avoid mistakes, it took them two months to complete the manuscript" (Anderson, Devery S., *The Development of LDS Temple Worship: 1846-2000, A Documentary History*, Signature Books [Salt Lake City: 2011], Introduction, p. xxxi).

46   George Q. Cannon explained to a meeting of the LDS apostles on December 6, 1889, "Father said that he understood when he had his endowments in Nauvoo [Illinois] that he took an oath against the murderers of the Prophet Joseph as well as other prophets, and if he had ever met any of those who had taken a hand in that massacre he would undoubtedly have attempted to avenge the blood of the martyrs. The Prophet charged Stephen Markham to avenge his blood should he be slain; after the Prophet's death Bro. Markham attempted to tell this to an assembly of the Saints, but Willard Richards pulled him down from the stand, as he feared the effect on the enraged people" (*Diaries of Abraham Cannon*, supra, pp. 34-35).

47   *Salt Lake School of the Prophets: 1867-1883*, supra, p. 527; entry of 12 October 1883, quoted as in original.

48   *Ibid.*

49   "Paul said he knew a man who was caught up to the third heaven. But, I know a man who was caught up to the seventh heaven" (*Deseret Weekly*, 38, No. 1, 29 December, 1888; a talk given by Joseph E. Taylor, as quoting Joseph Smith).

50   I commented on changes in a series of posts titled "This and That" on my website, www.denversnuffer.com, January 5th, 7th, 8th, and 9th of 2019.

51   Heber J. Grant referred to a discussion about this in his diary: "President George F. Richards of the Salt Lake Temple called on the Presidency this morning and we discussed the unwritten ceremonies of the temple..." (*The Diaries of Heber J. Grant*, supra, April 14, 1923, p. 323).

52   See Anderson, Devery S., *The Development of LDS Temple Worship: 1846-2000, A Documentary History*, supra. Also note the following:
      -"I spent the day at the Temple where I read carefully all the ordinances used in the temples as changed and corrected and noted 18 times [where there are issues] which I think need changing. It is my intention to present these to the [First] Presidency for their consideration. I also detected 7 errors in copying the ordinances" (*George F. Richards Diary*, September 16, 1922, cited in Anderson at p. 189).
      -"I spent some time with the [First] Presidency and [Presiding] Bishopric considering improvements to be made at the temple" (*Ibid.*, April 19, 1923).
      -"Read aloud for half an hour from temple ordinances to Brother Joseph Fielding Smith and Melvin J. Ballard" (*The Diaries of Heber J. Grant 1880-1945 Abridged*, supra, December 26, 1926, pp. 340-341).
      -"Reached the temple at ten A.M. and were there until five P.M. The regular endowment ceremonies were read over and discussed" (*Ibid.*, December 9, 1926, p. 341).
      -"Attended regular council meeting of the Presidency and Apostles in the Temple at 10:00 A.M. We read over the temple ceremonies and some changes were suggested" (*Ibid.*, December 16, 1923).
      -On April 25, 1933, Grant and George F. Richards "discussed temple matters" (*Ibid.*, p. 382).
      -On April 2, 1936, the Presidency and Twelve met in the temple: "A long report was read at the meeting submitted by a committee of the Twelve, regarding temple ordinances. Some discussion followed the reading of this report" (*Ibid.*, p. 410).
      -All the Twelve and Presidency (with the exception of David O. McKay) met on February 17, 1938, and "we had quite a discussion about the temple ceremonies" (*Ibid.*, p. 420).

53   A book attempting to track the changes made to the temple rites since Joseph's death has been compiled by Devery S. Anderson, editor: *The Development of LDS Temple Worship: 1846 – 2000 A Documentary History* (Salt Lake City: Signature Books, 2011). Changes since 2000 are not included in that book.

54   "And then at that day, before the Son of Man comes, the kingdom of heaven shall be likened unto ten virgins, who took their lamps and went forth to meet the bridegroom. And five of them were wise and five of them were foolish. They that were foolish took their lamps and took no oil with them, but the wise took oil in their vessels with their lamps. While the bridegroom tarried, they all slumbered and slept. And at midnight there was a cry made, Behold, the bridegroom comes, go out to meet him! Then all those virgins arose and trimmed their lamps. And the foolish said unto the wise, Give us of your oil, for our lamps are gone out. But the wise answered, saying, Lest there be not enough for us and you, go rather to them that sell, and buy for yourselves. And while they went to buy, the bridegroom came. And they that were ready went in with him to the marriage, and the door was shut. Afterward came also the other virgins, saying, Lord, Lord, open unto us. But he answered and said, Truly I say unto you, you know me not. Watch therefore, for you know neither the day nor the hour wherein the Son of Man comes." (Matthew 11:15)

55   "And Jesus answered the people again, and spoke unto them in parables, and said, The kingdom of heaven is like unto a certain king, who made a marriage for his son. And when the marriage was ready, he sent forth his servants to call them that were bidden to the wedding, and they would not come. Again, he sent forth other servants, saying, Tell them that are bidden, Behold, I have prepared my oxen, and my fatlings have been killed, and my dinner is ready, and all things are prepared; therefore come unto the marriage. But they made light of the servants and went their ways; one to his farm, and another to his merchandise. And the remnant took his servants, and treated them spitefully, and slew them. But when the king heard that his servants were dead, he was angry. And he sent forth his armies, and destroyed those murderers, and burnt up their city.

"Then he said to his servants, The wedding is ready, but they who were bidden were not worthy. Go you therefore into the highways, and as many as you shall find, bid to the marriage. So those servants went out into the highways and gathered together all, as many as they found, both bad and good, and the wedding was furnished with guests.

"But when the king came in to see the guests, he saw there a man who had not a wedding garment. And he said unto him, Friend, how did you come in here not having a wedding garment? And he was speechless. Then the king said unto his servants, Bind him hand and foot, and take and cast him away into outer darkness. There shall be weeping and gnashing of teeth, for many are called, but few chosen. Wherefore, all do not have on the wedding garment." (Matthew 10:17-19)

56   There must be a purpose for translating or taking people into heaven. Enoch's people, Melchizedek's people, and others—including Moses (see Matthew 9:4 and Mark 5:5) and Elijah (see Malachi 1:12 and T&C 140:19)—were translated to serve as "ministering angels" with specific assignments (see T&C 140:13.) The people of Fourth Nephi attained the status, but having no specific assignment requiring that they be translated, they passed into the spirit world. The coming Zion is intended to welcome the return of Enoch's and Melchizedek's people (see Genesis 4:22). The translated John and Elijah will also be actively involved as this process unfolds.

57   This was a promise in 1831, and when the people failed (by their jarring, contention, and strife), they were driven from the center place dividing the remnant from the Gentiles. Although that moment passed and population shifts removed that center place, the condition for Zion is unchanged. Likewise, the promise to provide needed commandments remains.

58   See 2 Nephi 1:3; 5:11; and 3 Nephi 9:9.

59   "Therefore, all things whatsoever you would that men should do to you, do even so to them, for this is the law and the prophets" (Matthew 3:44).

60   The amount of information contained in the Restoration Archives now requires terabytes of storage.

61   The challenges some faithful people face is daunting. Just getting Scriptures has required them to make great sacrifices.

62   Alfred Lord Tennyson coined this phrase in 1850 in his poem, *In Memoriam A.H.H.* (A.H.H. was his friend, Arthur Henry Hallam.)

63   See also 2 Nephi 12:13, which renders it differently: "And it shall come to pass that the Lord God shall commence his work among all nations, kindreds, tongues, and people, to bring about the restoration of his people upon the earth. And with righteousness shall the Lord God judge the poor and reprove with equity for the meek of the earth. And he shall smite the earth with the rod of his mouth, and with the breath of his lips shall he slay the wicked. For the time speedily cometh that the Lord God shall cause a great division among the people, and the wicked will he destroy. And he will spare his people, yea, even if it so be that he must destroy the wicked by fire. And righteousness shall be the girdle of his loins and faithfulness the girdle of his reins. And then shall the wolf dwell with the lamb, and the leopard shall lie down with the kid, and the calf, and the young lion, and the fatling together, and a little child shall lead them. And the cow and the bear shall feed, their young ones shall lie down together, and the lion shall eat straw like the ox. And the sucking child shall play on the hole of the asp, and the weaned child shall put his hand on the cockatrice's den. They shall not hurt nor destroy in all my holy mountain, for the earth shall be full of the knowledge of the Lord as the waters cover the sea. Wherefore, the things of all nations shall be made known, yea, all things shall be made known unto the children of men. There is nothing which is secret save it shall be revealed, there is no works of darkness save it shall be made manifest in the light, and there is nothing which is sealed upon earth save it shall be loosed. Wherefore, all things which have been revealed unto the children of men shall at that day be revealed, and Satan shall have power over the hearts of the children of men no more for a long time."

64   *DHC* 2:71–72.

65   Timothy Treadwell attempted to live peacefully in nature with grizzly bears in Katmai National Park and succeeded for approximately 5 years. His venture ended when he and a companion were killed and eaten by a bear in 2003. The story is recorded in a 2005 documentary titled *Grizzly Man*.

66   See T&C 141:11.

67   See T&C 141:10.

68   "Now this Melchizedek was a king over the land of Salem, and his people had waxed strong in iniquity and abominations — yea, they had all gone astray; they were full of all manner of wickedness. But Melchizedek, having exercised mighty faith and received the office of the High Priesthood according to the Holy Order of God, did preach repentance unto his people. And behold, they did repent. And Melchizedek did establish peace in the land in his days; therefore, he was called the Prince of Peace, for he was the King of Salem; and he did reign under his father" (Alma 10:2).

69   "And the Lord said unto me, These two facts do exist — that there are two spirits, one being more intelligent than the other; there shall be another more intelligent than they. I am the Lord, thy God; I am more intelligent than they all" (Abraham 5:4).

70   "And it shall come to pass in the last days, when the mountain of the
      Lord's house shall be established in the top of the mountains, and shall
      be exalted above the hills, and all nations shall flow unto it. And many
      people shall go and say, Come and let us go up to the mountain of the
      Lord, to the house of the God of Jacob, and he will teach us of his ways
      and we will walk in his paths. For out of Zion shall go forth the law, and
      the word of the Lord from Jerusalem. And he shall judge among the
      nations and shall rebuke many people. And they shall beat their swords
      into plowshares and their spears into pruning hooks; nation shall not lift
      up sword against nation, neither shall they learn war anymore" (Isaiah
      1:5). "And he shall set up an ensign for the nations, and shall assemble
      the outcasts of Israel, and gather together the dispersed of Judah, from
      the four corners of the earth. The envy also of Ephraim shall depart, and
      the adversaries of Judah shall be cut off. Ephraim shall not envy Judah
      and Judah shall not vex Ephraim. But they shall fly upon the shoulders
      of the Philistines toward the west, they shall spoil them of the east
      together..." (Isaiah 5:4).
71   See Luke 14:2-4.
72   "Let brotherly love continue. Be not forgetful to entertain strangers, for
      thereby some have entertained angels unawares. Remember them that
      are in bonds, as bound with them, and they who suffer adversity as being
      yourselves also of the body" (Hebrews 1:58). Note that Paul's teaching
      on this point couples the ministering of angels with sharing bondage and
      suffering with fellow-believers as if they were all one body.
73   See T&C 156:16.
74   See 3 Nephi 7:5.
75   "Behold, I will send you Elijah the prophet before the coming of the
      great and dreadful day of the Lord. And he shall seal the heart of the
      Fathers to the children and the heart of the children to their Fathers, lest
      I come and smite the earth with a curse" (Malachi 1:12). "Behold, I will
      send you Elijah the prophet before the coming of the great and dreadful
      day of the Lord, and he shall turn the heart of the fathers to the children
      and the heart of the children to their fathers, lest I come and smite the
      earth with a curse" (3 Nephi 11:5). "And again he quoted the fifth verse
      thus: *Behold I will reveal unto you the Priesthood by the hand of Elijah the
      prophet before the coming of the great and dreadful day of the Lord.* He also
      quoted the next verse differently: *And he shall plant in the hearts of the
      children the promises made to the fathers, and the hearts of the children shall
      turn to their fathers; if it were not so, the whole earth would be utterly
      wasted at his coming*" (Joseph Smith History 3:4, italics in original).
76   See Joseph Smith History 3:4.
77   See Genesis 4:22.

78   "And it shall come to pass in the last days, when the mountain of the Lord's house shall be established in the top of the mountains, and shall be exalted above the hills, and all nations shall flow unto it. And many people shall go and say, Come and let us go up to the mountain of the Lord, to the house of the God of Jacob, and he will teach us of his ways and we will walk in his paths. For out of Zion shall go forth the law, and the word of the Lord from Jerusalem" (Isaiah 1:5).

79   See T&C 141:14.

Temple Conference Q&A Session

Transcript from "A Hope in Christ: The Temple" Conference
Grand Junction, CO
April 21, 2019

Apparently our ten minutes are up. And I hate to take away from the 1:00-5:00 lunch hour. I mean, you must be planning on Thanksgiving, Christmas, and Easter dinner all combined for a 1-5 lunch. And I hate to disappoint you, but I've been told that that's a misprint on the schedule and that you will not be given a one o'clock 'til five p.m. lunch break, that things will resume at 2:30 with Rob Adolpho and his wife, Quintina. We call her "Q." It's spelled "Quintina." [Inaudible audience comments.] "That's right?" …says a voice out of the dark that I assume is Q's. We call her Q; Rob calls her, "Yes, ma'am."

Yeah, ten minutes for a bathroom break seems utterly unreasonable; so when they get back and they ask you what they missed, tell 'em, "The most amazing stuff ever! And we've been sworn to not repeat it! …And he told the folks to delete it from the recording." [Audience laughter.]

But I guarantee you, you can't warm coffee with a pillar of fire. (And by the way, that is true.)

Okay, so, [reading off the program] "Q&A with…me." I guess I could ask **myself** questions that I really wanted to answer. This doesn't… I'm not obligated to follow any…

Look, one matter that should not come and go without observation is this date, this day, and this commemoration which, based upon all of our reckoning, is the Eastern Easter Sabbath. It also coincides with the Passover. In one of the groups that we were attending yesterday, the subject of the Passover and the various observances under the Law of Moses were discussed—the Holy Days.

And one observation that I made yesterday (that I want to repeat and maybe expand on) is that there are actually **two Passovers**. The one occurred anciently in Egypt when the blood of the lamb was put on the lintel and posts, and the Destroying Angel passed over those who had been marked by that and preserved all of the firstborn in those households.

There will be a **second** Passover. This one is more expansive and will involve the destruction of all the wicked. It is referred to as part of the covenant that we received (now in the Teachings and Commandments section 158, in ~~verses~~ paragraphs 16-18), it says:

> I will teach you things that have been hidden from the foundation of the world and your understanding will reach unto Heaven. And you shall be called the children of the Most High God, and I will preserve you against the harvest. And the angels sent to harvest the world will gather the wicked into bundles to be burned, but will **pass over you** as my peculiar treasure. (Emphasis added)

So, the Passover—which was instituted as a symbol prior to the Law of Moses—will be one of those observances that will be fully restored in due time because Christ fulfilled the Law of Moses and brought it to an end. But **all** those things that had been instituted by God as an observance prior to the Law of Moses—which **includes** the Passover— **that** will be preserved, even though the Law of Moses was brought to an end and a completion.

So, the Passover, which was instituted before the Law of Moses was established, is one of those observances that was not only relevant at the moment that the children of Israel were saved and freed from their slavery in Egypt anciently, but it is an observance that has relevance also to a **second** promised Passover in which, at some point in the future, the wicked will be gathered into bundles (as the Scriptures describe it) and burned; and the covenant people of the Lord will be passed over, preserved, and allowed to continue safely. Therefore, Passover is relevant to our day as much as it is to them anciently.

All of the things that are most important in Scripture relate to two (and only two) moments in time [and] largely two (and only two) generations of people: the first was that that was here at the time the Lord came into mortality, and the second is the time when the Lord will return again in glory to judge the world.

(I was asked also to announce that one of the organizers of this event, Brian Bowler, and another fellow, Jared Walter, are both celebrating their birthdays today. [Audience applause.] So, happy birthday to both of them—and I'm sorry to impose on you to be here instead of somewhere eating cake.)

The events that occurred on the morning of Easter occurred so early in the morning that the place was still dark when the Lord rose from the tomb.

You have to be on a place where you can see the horizon into the distance (and along the Wasatch Front in Utah, you don't get a chance to see the sun or the moon rise on the horizon until it's up, you know, 30 degrees above the horizon of the Earth because the mountains obstruct your view, and you can't see into that distance). But if you're on the ocean, if you're on a shoreline, if you're in the plains and you can see the horizon (the curvature of the horizon), there's a moment that occurs—and it can be anything from a split second to perhaps as long as a minute—when it arises. (It's the same atmospheric phenomenon as you witness at the poles in the Northern Lights. The Northern Lights are happening because of magnetic and curvature of the atmosphere, trapping of particles, and it sets off these dancing lights that you can see in the Northern Hemisphere.) On the horizon, there comes a moment each day, as the sun and the Earth are moving, that the very first bit of light emerges as this brief, dancing, green light —green flash—on the distant horizon. That moment marks the "new day" anciently. So, when you saw that, it would designate that now the day has arrived. It's dark out. It will remain dark, but that instant, that flash, that atmospheric…

So, if you're charged with being a watchman to designate when a religious observance is going to occur and it is relevant to mark the moment at which the new day arises or arrives, you're watching the horizon, and you're looking for that instant when it occurs. That instant—which is long before the daylight surrounds you, and you have something other than the darkness of night on you—that instant is actually memorialized in one of the titles that's given both to the Lord and to his chief adversary, Lucifer; that's *a Son of the Morning*— because that moment marks the instant that the morning arises.

Christ's resurrection occurred **then**—on whatever the moment was that that occurred, on that morning, on the day of the resurrection—**that** was when the events were set in motion to honor that observance. And so, when they came to the tomb early that morning, it would be based upon **that** appreciation for how holy days (or days themselves) were reckoned and not based upon what we do with our clock and our reckoning. It was… It's tied to nature. It's tied to those circumstances that are built-in as part of this Creation.

And so, when the resurrection occurred, there's only one gospel writer that observes that it was still dark, and that's John; he points it out. It's been in the Bible all along. But in all honesty, to me, "morning" meant "sun's up," daylight, we could see about.

The account that appears in *Come, Let Us Adore Him* (that now will appear as one of the sections in the Teachings and Commandments) was something shown to me that I recorded in my journal—and in fact, the content of that is quoted directly out of my journal.

I do not like the idea that any story/any account is to be trusted to recollection weeks/months/years after the fact. In one of the criticisms that we have about some history involving Joseph Smith is that there are later stories/later developments that got inserted into the narrative, and they weren't contemporaneous with him. So, I don't trust anyone to record anything (or to preserve anything that I consider to be significant) other than myself, and I record it on the date in which it happened at the moment that it occurred. And then if I, as was done with the book *Come, Let Us Adore Him* (or what is now part of the Teachings and Commandments), is later publicly disclosed ('cuz those things were not publicly disclosed for years), then when they are, the only account that gets disclosed publicly are word-for-word—exactly— what got written at the time in which the event took place. So, you're getting the narrative and—verbatim—exactly what was recorded **by the witness** on the day in which that occurred.

Now, when the stuff that just got added was shown to me as something that was proposed to be included, it lifted out a bunch of ellipses—you know, three dots (…). It lifted out a bunch of ellipses from the account that appears in *Come, Let Us Adore Him*. And I said, "For purposes of putting it out there as a…something to be looked at, reviewed, and respected in the future, just drop all the ellipses out." And so, all the ellipses were dropped out. That's because there's a bunch of stuff that went on that's recorded in my journal that is not in that account that draws more attention and distracts away from what was important. What **is important** is in that account. The ellipses represent another moment of profound stupidity/ignorance on my part that is in the journal account. But I thought, "There's no reason at all to focus on that." But I'll tell you about it so that you know what got lifted out. (I'm past the point of being embarrassed about my own stupidity. I acknowledge that all the time—including my wife just a day or so ago, which she reminded me of a couple of times this weekend.)

What happened was: As I was recording the account, at the point in which I'm trying to put into words the joy, the exultation of our Lord —because He had finished the course! He had actually arrived at the point that culminates everything that had been expected of Him, and He'd done it perfectly—at that moment, in the journal, I wrote the words that "the joy that He experienced on that morning made the sufferings in Gethsemane pale in comparison." And as soon as I wrote those words, I felt instantly condemned. In fact, I had an **angry** God on my hands because that was **not appropriate** for me to have recorded. So, it was so abrupt—it was so immediate—that I stopped writing altogether. I just drew a line in the journal, and I left, and I went to work. I was haunted by that all day. And when I got back home, I got the journal out, and I wrote in there that what I wrote before was completely inappropriate because there is **nothing** that can make the suffering in Gethsemane pale by comparison. There simply is no joy, there is no triumph that can make the obliteration of that thing that He endured on our behalf **pale**. It cannot pale. And so, once I confessed that I'd screwed up, then I... The condemnation lifted, and the account then continued and finished up. In between the ellipses is my foolishness, and I saw no reason—in being required to bear testimony of the resurrection of the Lord—to insert into that me running around, ya know, marring the furniture and spilling Coke on the floor. I thought the best thing to do was to keep it focused exclusively...

The Lord did not make me a witness of His resurrection to have you focus any attention on me. It is **all** about Him and only Him; and therefore, the narrative needed to be excised to get the idiot-witness out of view and to put the Lord front and center and squarely within view.

(It's another example, in my view, of just how ill-fitted I am to what's been asked of me. If I could lay hands on someone else's head and say, "There you are; now go get 'em," and drift off into the background and not occupy any public attention again, it would relieve me of an extraordinary amount of anxiety and self-questioning at every turn.)

It's not enough to me to pray and get an answer. For me to pray and get an answer is an easy thing, but **any** answer that I get, I take it, and I scrutinize it for motive, for desire, for my personal potential involvement with the content. I scrutinize it for any weakness of my own that may appear there. Then I take it to the Scriptures, and I look for anything in there that could challenge, contradict, or raise an issue about what is recorded. And then, when I'm satisfied that it is actually pure enough to be regarded as something that I can trust, then I take it back to the Lord to get re-confirmation before I'm willing to do or say anything regarding it. And there are many, many things that I've learned and been exposed to that I don't talk about. It's just not appropriate, and I assume that, at some point, it will be the kind of material that the Lord reveals to each person individually as His (and His prerogative alone) and not something that belongs to us.

I also don't think that rapid-fire inquiries to God are appropriate. It's a fearful thing to approach the Lord, but it's also a fearful thing to then be entrusted with an answer from the Lord and to be accountable to Him for what you do (or you fail to do) with what He has provided. No one of us deserves the kind of responsibility that He alone can impose. No one deserves it. And anyone that feels the burden of it should fear their own weakness above anything and everything else. It's not cause for celebration. It's cause for questioning yourself, questioning your motives, and questioning whether or not—in the wisdom of the Lord—work can and should be done.

————

Now, there were some questions that were provided to me, and some of them were actually answered in the talk, and so, they don't need to be answered again here. But there's one question:

Question 1: "In your opinion are the people ready to have the commandment to build the temple in our day? Are we ready to have the commandment? If not, could you offer suggestions on what more we could do to prepare more completely?"

Answer: Well, my opinion on that really doesn't matter because, unlike some other things, my view on that is that... When you go to D&C section 124 (I don't know what it is in the T&C; I need that set of leather Scriptures so I can learn my new layout—these things are too heavy and bulky to carry around), it's apparent...

They had decided on building a temple. They had chosen a location for the temple. They had begun digging at the spot for the temple **before** there was the inquiry and the commandment given in [section] 124 (the January 1841 revelation). And the wording of the revelation says that "the spot that you have selected is acceptable" (see D&C 124:43-44). K?

If you think carefully about that language from the Lord, what it means is the Lord was willing to permit or entertain the ambition of the people, which doesn't necessarily mean that the people **should** have been doing what they were doing. It doesn't mean that the place was the right place, and it doesn't mean that God was going to protect it. It means that He will **allow** them to do that. And then He warns them that if they **want** Him to come and restore and they **want** Him to come and vindicate and if they **want** Him to protect them so that they cannot be moved out of their place, then they need to **do** things. And the things that they needed to **do** were a list of fairly specific things that they failed, subsequently, **to do.**

So, I think (I'm fairly certain) that I could pray and get permission to build a temple today. I'm not going to do that. I'm not going to inquire. I'm not going to suggest one thing to the Lord about **either** a location for the temple to be built **or** when a temple ought to be commenced in its construction. In my view, "asking and getting permission" are **not** the same thing as the angel Gabriel appearing next to the altar to respond to Zacharias and say, "The Lord is now going to redeem His people Israel, and you shall have a son, and he shall go before Him" (see Luke 1:3 RE). It must—must—be at Heaven's initiative. It must be at Heaven's timing. It must be at the place chosen by the Lord.

Why is it reasonable to expect the Lord to defend—and the Earth to defend—the spot that is **our** choosing? All of these things are a matter of covenant and a matter of prophecy—and their prophecies will be vindicated. The covenants will be fulfilled. God fully intends to do exactly what He has foretold will be done. But for **us** to push the envelope when this is **the** great temple on this hemisphere, this is **the** building to which **His** tabernacle (meaning His **person**) will come and occupy **that** tabernacle (meaning the temple built for the establishment of Zion)—it needs to be entirely entrusted to the care of the Lord and only to the care of the Lord. And so, the issue of what my opinion is, is…

I mean, my opinion was, No, of course not; we're not ready. I sat in on those meetings yesterday and took in things, and I was impressed. I was… We **are** learning how to get along.

In the Scripture committee that I participated in, there are **very strong** personalities holding **very strong** opinions on a variety of **very important** topics, in which it's expected that people with strong personalities and strong opinions would dig their heels in. And I have to tell you, there were **lots** of discussions. There were **lots** of exchanges of points of view.

I don't think there was ever a single dispute. There was **never** a fight. There was never an argument, even when it took time to come together. The process… I think everyone involved grew in ways that were extraordinary over the course of the whole thing.

And there were some people who came very late to the project and who came late after having spent years doing work that explored, more deeply, details that the other people who had been working on it for a couple of years had not plunged to that depth. And so, when he came, you would think people that had spent a couple of years plunging into one level of understanding would sort of resent the newcomer who comes late to the party (and he was one of the younger fellows to participate), and yet, he was openly and warmly accepted, and all of his corrections and additions were welcomed. No one was egotistically involved in trying to get it their way. The only objective was to try to get it **right**. Everyone was keenly aware of how badly things had gone in the handling of the Scriptures in 1833 and 1835, in 1840. Everyone was keenly aware of how mangled the text in places—of all the volumes of Scripture—had become and of how neglected the fullness of the Scriptures (as defined by Joseph Smith) had been treated.

Literally, what is coming out in print is a historical marker, a milestone event in which, for the first time, what God intended to hand to people at the beginning of the Restoration is finally capable of being handed to you. It is an historic moment that literally marks the beginning of a fulsome Restoration. We now have Scriptures upon which everything else will be possible to be built. That hasn't existed until now. It **is** a new beginning, and I'm not sure that what was said made it clear enough, but…

We're accustomed to the print-on-demand publishing industry. You do not make this quality of a publication by printing it on demand. You have to order exactly the number of books that you want printed, and you have to **pay** for every one of them before you receive the delivery of **any** one of them.

Right now the price break is 1,400 copies. The cost of that many books being paid for before we get delivery of any one of them is so great that we're probably going to order 1000 copies in order to eliminate the cost of paying in advance for an extra 400 of them, but it will cost more per copy for the 1000, but in aggregate, it will cost less money to place that order than it will to get to the next price break. And so, the plan right now is to order 1000 copies, and the mechanism for being able to do that is going to be to create a site at which you can purchase and pay for the Scriptures in advance, so that you place the order for whatever volume you want (or volumes you want) printed. There'll be a set of three: a[n] Old Covenants, a New Covenants, and a Teachings and Commandments—"an order" will be for all three volumes. If you want one copy, you buy one. If you want ten, you buy ten. If you want twenty, you buy twenty, but you pay for them in advance, and then it will be months later that they will be delivered.

Unlike what happens with typical book publishing, there's no markup on any of these. They have volunteers that are going to handle them.

They'll have volunteers that will drive copies down to some cities where distribution will be made. All of the costs of handling are gonna be borne by voluntary work. Now, if you're at a location where it has to be mailed, then the price to you will include the price of shipping to you as a direct cost. If these were handled the way books normally are handled in a Scripture setting, the price of these to **you** would be probably double whatever the price is going to be as the order gets placed.

One of the things that we do not know right now is if there is enough demand to take advantage of the price break at 1400 copies (so that we order and pay for 1400 copies to be made) or whether we're going to pay a little more per volume but only incur the total cost for getting a thousand of them printed. But whatever it is in terms of that number, when those are printed and when those are sold, that's the end of printing the leather-bound version of the Scriptures. There will be no plans for **ever** producing them again.

Undoubtedly, there will be a second printing, but that might be five years from now, that might be ten years from now. We don't know when there may be a second printing of the Scriptures. So, the first printing will be an ordered, funded, paid-for, complete first printing, and that's the only one that will exist—at least for some period of time until demand drives a second printing. In the meantime, the way in which the Scriptures will be available will be electronically (in your handheld), electronically (online on your computer), or a print-on-demand source that you can purchase through Amazon.

Yesterday, those who were present heard the report that the print-on-demand in Amazon has been taken down temporarily because all of the layout for the leather-bound Scriptures are now completed. And those are being loaded into the Amazon print-on-demand version so that if you buy a paperback version from Amazon, the page, the layout, the page number, everything about that will be identical with the leather-bound version because the same layout is going to be used for both of them. (I don't know how you are with your Scriptures, but for me, if I want to quote from D&C section 76, beginning with the description of the Telestial, it's on right-side, lower; it's about, beginning verse 99; and it's in your book; it's right there.) Well, the utility of having the same layout for your paperback and for your leather-bound version is the ability to recall the page and the layout on the page from book to book to book so that there's no mistaking what you're trying to find and where you're trying to find it. This version (the print version that I've used), I have not invested the effort to try and know the page number, know the approximate location, know the...where it's gonna be on the page, because I've known that we're gonna get a new layout. But when the leather-bound ones come out, I intend to pore over those to find/to discover the new material that's there and to find the old familiar stuff and relocate it. So, when it becomes available for ordering, keep in mind that if you don't get one of these, it may be many years before it'll be possible to order them again.

Question 2: Okay, there was a question that was posed by Tim Malone about [the] Layton Conference where I said:

> God demands...our hearts turn to the fathers or we will be wasted at His return. This requirement is not to turn to them in just a figurative way, where we do genealogical work to connect ourselves with our recently deceased forbearers. That work is a wrong-headed effort to seal people to those kept in prison. The return of our hearts will require us to have the same religion, and the same beliefs in our hearts that the original fathers had beginning with Adam. Only in that way will our hearts turn to the ~~fullness~~ [fathers].

Then he says, "Given the fact the LDS Church has spent hundreds of millions of dollars building temples specifically for the purpose of sealing individuals to their deceased ancestors, are you advocating that we cease family history research as a waste of time? If so, can you provide some specific counsel how we could better utilize the time?"

Answer: Okay, the answer is: I'm not saying you cease doing genealogical work. When work originally [Denver chuckles]... How to put this...?

The way in which temple work for the dead was intended to be done was that work of baptism for the dead was confined to:

- Only those ancestors you personally knew who you believed would have accepted the gospel with all their heart had they been permitted to tarry and were only kept from accepting the gospel because they died at a time before it was available for them to embrace. That's one category.

- A second category was those ancestors about whom you have enough information from their diaries, their letters, their journals, or accounts of their life so that you believe them to be the kind of people that would have embraced the gospel had they lived at a time when the gospel in its fullness was on the Earth. So, that is a second category.

- And then the third category was those ancestors who appear to you and asked that their temple work be done.

Those were the only ones for whom temple work was supposed to be done, according to the criteria that was established by Joseph Smith at the beginning. It was not a "if you know a name, go get a baptism for 'em." That was never the criteria. The criteria was limited to those three specific categories of people.

The place in which genealogical research for your ancestors becomes **most important** is that second category, in which—through genealogical research—you may be able to locate an ancestor about whom there is enough that you can recover (as information or biography) to know that they were the kind of people who would've embraced the gospel had they been permitted to tarry long enough to have accepted the gospel in its fullness while it was on the Earth. You can't figure that out unless you have genealogical research and something more than just a name on a name-extraction-program. It's gotta be someone about whom you've dug long and hard and deep to find out about them and their lives, to make some kind of an evaluation about them, to make a judgment call. Otherwise, what you're left with are a bunch of names, and the only way to get those names in a position to do work is the third category—in which you know about their existence, but you have no way of telling whether they're suitable for the ordinance; and therefore, **they** must come and request it. They must appear, and they must make the request—and so, they slide into that third category.

The second category can only be achieved through a lot of hard work and genealogical study. The first category you should know from your ancestors that you were familiar with. That probably goes back no further than perhaps a great-grandfather or, more likely, a grandfather or a grandmother. It may go to a great-uncle, a great-aunt. It may go to a deceased aunt. But the criteria was as was outlined, and the second category is where the genealogical work the Church invests money is apt, suitable, just fine.

Question 3: "What words of encouragement can you give to someone whose spouse is not on board with what is happening now?"

Answer: Look—first of all, unlike the Scriptures that other groups of people accept, we actually have an answer to this in our Scriptures. It's in the Teachings and Commandments, [section] 149, verse 3 —it's paragraph 3:

> *Suffer no man to leave his wife because she is an unbeliever, nor no woman to leave her husband because he is an unbeliever. These things are…evil, and must be forbidden by the authorities of the church, or they will come under condemnation, for the gathering is not in haste, nor by flight, but to prepare all things before you, and you know not but that the unbeliever may be converted and the Lord heal him. But let the believers exercise faith in God, and the unbelieving husband shall be sanctified by the believing wife, and the unbelieving wife by the believing husband, and **families are preserved and saved from a great evil**, which we have seen verified before our eyes.* (Emphasis added)

That's one of the sections of the Teachings and Commandments that was from Hyrum Smith (who was, at the time, a president of the Church—co-president, in fact—the prophet to whom Joseph said the Church "should give heed"). That's the instruction.

And I mentioned Tim Malone; he's a great example of this. Tim and Carol Malone are separated, and he talks openly about that in the things he publishes, and he's true and faithful to her. He's doing the right thing. He's the right example. He's doing what Hyrum advised and what the Teachings and Commandments recommend that we do —and continue without haste.

Question 4: And then—oh, some guy named Adrian Larsen. I don't know. Yeah… [Audience laughter.] Shoot—you really wanna go **there**? Okay, I'm… This is decidedly limited in what is appropriate to be said, but the question is about: "Since Christ came to fulfill the law, and the practice of animal sacrifice was done away with, and what we're to offer is a ~~contrite~~ broken heart and a contrite spirit as a sacrifice, and animal sacrifice was a type to teach the people of the coming Messiah —He fulfilled that. Why would animal sacrifice be reinstated?"

Answer: OK, as… I don't want to get out ahead of where we are at this point, but let me say, it will be done for entirely appropriate purposes that will be perfectly satisfactory to the understanding of those that are involved. It's not gonna be some kind of temple-turned-slaughterhouse. It's not gonna be a production line in which the hems of your garments (and the blood shaking from the hems of your garment) becomes a cliché because of the abundance of the flowing of blood in the courtyards of the temple of Solomon (and later the temple of Herod). It will be decidedly confined/limited for purposes that will be adequately understood by those who (on the rare occasions when that practice is reinstated) participate/witness. But I think that's all that can be said. You won't be disappointed.

Question 5: "We're separated from the first Fathers (to whom our hearts must turn) by a vast expanse of time, language, and culture. How can we best reach out in our hearts and our minds to these successful mortals?"

Answer: You know, that's a great question. There is an enormous advantage that you'll find in reading the new Scriptures and all of the things that have been added that focus upon that—both in the Old Covenants and in the Teachings and Commandments (in particular those two) where our knowledge of what the Fathers were up to is **enormously** expanded, and then in parts of the New Covenants that have been added through the Joseph Smith Translation. I think the Scriptures equip us to accomplish something that…

Study them. Look there.

Question 6: "In the 'Elijah' talk, you made reference to the fact that Adam and Eve partook of the fruit out of order—that they were to wait until after the Sabbath; that partaking prior to the Sabbath caused work to be done on the Sabbath. Can you explain/expand on this subject, please?"

Answer: The problem was not that they were never going to be told ~~to partake~~ to not to ever partake of the fruit of the tree of knowledge of good and evil, it's that they were forbidden to partake so that there could be a day of rest—a Sabbath. Everything was supposed to stand down. And then, after they stood down for the day of rest, on the first day of the **next** week, they were then to introduce the knowledge of good and evil in a way that would've been benign, in a way that would've transitioned from the original paradisiacal state into a state in which knowledge of good and evil and mortality itself could enter the world (much as it will be present during the Millennium among the righteous).

But instead, in an act of defiance that resulted in them being kicked out of the Garden because of transgression—and an act that caused labor then to occur on the Sabbath—they partook out of season in obedience to the one who seeks to **always** counsel people to rebel against the order of Heaven, to disobey, and to set at naught the commandments and instructions of the Father, even when doing so means harm to yourself or to others—because the adversary is only interested in the destruction of people, even those who trust and rely upon him. He has no good end in mind for them. And so, they partook out of the ordinary course. As a consequence, there was a fall.

The Fall introduced, on the Sabbath day, the mortal experience. And so, the seventh day—the day of rest—would then require six days of labor to precede their next day of rest, which always put the Sabbath **out of sync** because of the original rebellion, which is why the Lord was resurrected on what they thought was the **first** day of the week. It was, in fact, the "first day of the week" according to **their** reckoning and the "seventh day of the week" according to the **original Creation** (had everything been honored in the original commandment and instruction). And so, the worshippers moved the Sabbath day from Saturday to Sunday (to that first day of the week), which was, in reality, simply restoring back the original violated timeframe—and the early Christians observed (as the seventh day of the week) the correct day of worship, the day that we worship on, which is Sunday and not Saturday, although the tradition of following, in a number of places, remains to do so on Saturday.

It's more important that you keep a day holy—that you set it aside as a day of worship—than it is to figure out the chronology of everything that's gone on. If it was so important for us to get exactly the right day of the week aligned with everything, then we'd all be John Pratt. [Audience laughter.]

Question 7: Oh, man. OK. Wow. "Marriage: one man, one woman. Chastity is important, and there's accommodation going on everywhere to try and allow divergent forms of marriage to be acceptable or tolerated. And some of that is being done as a **desperate** measure to try and reduce suicide rates among young people, where suicide rates in Utah have climbed."

[Full question was as follows: "We are obligated to teach our children that God intended marriage to be between one man and one woman and that chastity is important. As the LDS Church has employed various strategies to promote these values in recent years, suicide rates among the young have climbed in Utah. Do you think this has to do with the way the LDS Church has handled these issues, and if so, do you have any insights into what we might do differently to better help youth who struggle?"]

Answer: Let me, as clearly as I can put it: Wickedness never was and never will be happiness. There is embedded into each of us, as deeply as our DNA itself, a course in life which, if pursued in the proper way, will result in the bearing of children and a fullness of joy, experienced as a consequence of introducing offspring into the world for whom you are granted the challenge, the privilege, and the opportunity of nurturing and caring and teaching. These are things that stretch you beyond your comfort zone. These are things that will tear at your heart. These are challenges that will befuddle you, that will make you question and re-evaluate and reconsider—time and time again—who you are and what you're saying and how you're treating "these" (your children).

The institution of marriage was designed—by its very nature, by that God who created us—to allow us to engage in that **god-like process**. It can be experienced in the way that God intended in one, and only one, way—that is,

- Through the marriage of the man and the woman together,
- Through **their union** that is intended to produce offspring,
- Through **her** struggle to bear and bring forth the child,
- Through **his** protection and providing for **her** during **her** period of inability and **her** period of nursing and caring for the infant (that is utterly dependent upon the body of the mother for its existence).

All of these things are god-like. They are instructions. They are experiences that are intended to convey, through the mortal body and the mortal experience, things that replicate and reflect a divine perspective about life itself, about **who God is**—because God is a male and a female, and they are productive. Their love results in the creation of more life. They experience a fullness of joy. And when you have "all joy in its fullness," the only way in which it is possible to make "more joy" is to create others, in which they too can experience a fullness of joy. And so, that increases through offspring, through family, through progeny.

You will not reduce suicide rates by pursuing a course that says wickedness can be entertained, the purposes of God can be frustrated, the experiences that God intended for us to go through and to have in this life can be set at naught, and you can approach the whole thing in a different mechanism/in a different pretense. Because however deeply you may feel about that structure, at its core, it is defective. It is desolation. It is a practice that if it were universally engaged in, then all who are here today will be the last generation that will ever live, because it produces desolation. And if at the core of the relationship what you have is a desolate future, there is no amount of psychological treatment, anti-depressive medication, or lies you can tell to yourself that will make you say, "What I'm engaged in is not, in the eyes of God, abominable." You cannot destroy that truth. If you want happiness—because of the way we were created by the Creator Himself —it is to be obtained by following the path ordained by the Creator to realize the results that He established in your heart, in your soul, in your spirit, in your body, even in your DNA. [Audience applause.]

Question 8: "Did Emma know the same things that Joseph did? Was she taught from on high as he was? Was he allowed to share everything with her?"

Answer: I would be shocked if Joseph Smith did not share everything with Emma. I would be shocked.

Question 9: [Reading] ...I think I've already covered that.

Question 10: "I noticed a phrase—'pursue judgment'—in both the 'Answer and Covenant' and in our Heavenly Mother's words, quoted in 'Our Divine Parents.'"

Answer: "Pursue judgment" is that you pursue the treatment of others as you would have yourself be treated. You treat them in the same standard.

Question 11: Oh, I love this question: "Share some more of the ways that nature testifies of Christ."

Answer: I hope you garden. If you don't, you should garden in order to experience all the plagues of Egypt [audience laughter], because that's what happens whenever I attempt to garden. There are these loathsome pests that will come along and consume and destroy and invade your garden. (They'll eat everything except zucchini, as it turns out. And zucchini produces in such abundance and so quickly—and ripens so quickly—that all you're left with is a bag of seeds, and they're dreadful.)

But there is a pest that invades the garden (that will eat everything and destroy and wreak havoc) that eventually entombs itself in a chrysalis. And the pest, while it's inside this apparent self-made tomb, has died and gone away. But **eventually**, it will arise from that cocoon—from that tomb—and it will come out, and it has assumed a wholly different form. Unlike that loathsome creature that crawled around ugly and haltingly across your garden, consuming and destroying, once it emerges from the tomb, it now takes flight. It's joined with the sky, with the heavens itself. And it goes about, thereafter, taking pollen and fertilizing the garden and becoming productive. Where before it had destroyed, now it helps create; now it becomes an agent that produces fruit, that produces vegetables.

This little insect is a powerful sermon embedded in nature to testify of who Christ was and, more importantly, to testify of what Christ **did** that will affect **you**, that will turn **you** from what we are now into something glorious, heavenly, and capable of ascending in flight up on high.

Question 12: Oh, "How does equality work when we are all given different gifts, abilities, and levels of understanding, some of which may be more outwardly manifest? Should we encourage one another to use our gifts to benefit all, even though this makes us appear unequal?"

Answer: "Equal" means that you do what you can do, to the best of your ability to do, for the benefit of all that can receive. Not everyone can do what someone with a gift or a talent can accomplish, but all can appreciate the benefits of that gift or talent. We're supposed to find joy, worship God, and bless our fellow man through the gifts that are given. In fact (I don't know what section it is now; I know what the old number was)—but the gifts that are given, the Lord says, specifically are given as a benefit for the church (the definition of the church being all those who repent and are baptized, not some institution). So, the blessing that is given to one has been given in order to bless and benefit the lives of all others. And as a consequence of that, you're depriving the "community of faith" of the gifts when you don't do the best you can with the gifts you've been given. They are intended by you to be a sacrifice by you, for the benefit of others. And if others look on and say, "Gee, I wish I could do that, but I'm not double-jointed, and I'm not interested in riding on one of those things," then, you know… You can admire the X-Games, but you don't have to join 'em.

————

We are going to break for lunch, and lunch will end at 2:30, at which time, Rob and Quintina Adolpho will be giving a presentation on recovering the lost sheep. This is something that both of them are earnestly engaged in and they addressed at a conference over in Hawaii a little while ago. I don't know how much background you have on the two of them, but Quintina is, among other things, a Ph.D. and counselor and Blackfoot (and providing counseling services and care for the Blackfoot people on a reservation). So, it will be more than worth your time, given the fact that the covenant requires that, among other things, we must reach out to recover the lost remnant of people on **this** land. And we have Q from this land and Rob from Hawaii, both of whom identify with native peoples in a way that would be helpful to any who care to come and attend and for **all** who watch the recording of this at a later time.

Thank you.

The Second Annual Joseph Smith Restoration Conference

Transcript of Comments
Boise, ID
June 8, 2019

Clearly…

(I don't know, can you hear me? Is this mic good?)

Clearly, most of you are not familiar with the writings of Hunter S. Thompson, or you would have been a little surprised by him being quoted here: the father of "Gonzo journalism" and the author of *Fear and Loathing in Las Vegas*—a laugh-out-loud funny (but obscene) book. [Audience laughter]

I've enjoyed every talk that has been given today:

- The first one was the recorded testimony of Tony Davis who, essentially, made a plea for us to unite, which has been echoed then in every talk that has been given at the conference this year. This is the second year of this conference. And I have to tell you, last year it felt like we were trying to pull into different camps, and this year it feels very much like we're all trying to pull into one camp. In just one year of reflecting on this subject —remarkable differences. I would suggest all of you go listen to the talks last conference, and then listen again to this conference. There has been **meaningful** progress that has been made.

(Jeremy, you dropped something when you pulled your… Yeah, he's good.)

- I learned something from Neil Simon's talk.

- I noted the omission of Jeremy Hoop's musical number from the schedule. I don't know if that's an answer to prayer—his or ours. [Audience laughter]

- I thought Michael Kelly's comments were, to me, very insightful. I do not know a lot about the Church of Christ and the Temple Lot, and I'm interested now to know if the view expressed by Michael Kelley is a widespread view within that community, or it's his conclusion as a result of the tension that you feel from trying to parse through Mormon history. And I intend to investigate that after today.

- I thought James McKay's reminder about the vigor of the Book of Mormon as a tool for conversion was important.

- Jeremy's talk (delivered much too fast because of the time constraints) contained fabulous information that everyone ought to go back and listen to and look at. ([Speaking to Jeremy] Was that in writing? If it is, can you put the written copy out? That was getting a drink with a fire hose.) [Audience laughter]

- Tausha's "Time to Unify the Branches" was wonderful.

- The music "Come Thou Font"—that song gets to me.

- And Adrian's "Why We Need to be Wrong" was terrific.

I want to go to the Book of Mormon, and I want to look at what it says **as if** the Book of Mormon was only written **to address us**, **to address you**, to speak to people who not only have become believers in the Book of Mormon but who have **read** and are **reading** the Book of Mormon. It does not make much sense to think of the Book of Mormon as a text that's designed to tell you, "Hey, you're okay, but everyone else is screwed up." It makes a whole lot more sense to read the Book of Mormon as if it's saying, "I—God—would really like to save you. But **you** are **so** riddled with error, you are **so** riddled with false tradition, you are **so** riddled with wrong ideas that I'm gonna give you a text in the **desperate hope** that you might take it seriously enough that it **might bring** you a little closer to Me. To the extent that you will accept it faithfully and fully, it will bring you a **lot** closer to Me."

But I'm begging you—

Please give heed to these words, because God wants to bring you, as someone that takes the book seriously, closer to Him.

It was in the same year that the Book of Mormon had been published, a church had been organized (although all it was, was locally gathered believers in a fellowship; no—absolutely no—hierarchy). They held elections to approve people to hold the position of Elder, but that didn't mean anything other than they were elected to a position of Elder. Right now, in any branch of any of the various iterations of the Restoration, people could get together and elect a woman to be an Elder. There's nothing that would prevent that, because the position is not the same thing as priesthood. You do not have to hold priesthood to hold office. You do not have to hold anything but an election to hold an office—in any of the branches. There is no such thing as the "priesthood of Elder"; there is only an office that you can occupy by being elected. You could elect a man to be a Relief Society president if you got enough votes for it. That doesn't mean that he is a female; it means that he is the president of the Relief Society. The same is true of a Sunday School president. There's no such thing as a priesthood office called "Sunday School president," but there's an office within an organization. Most of what we assume to be "priesthood" is simply an **office**.

For many years in The Church of Jesus Christ of Latter-day Saints, the president of that organization, over a two-decade period, took the position that no one needed to have the priesthood conferred upon them. According to Hebrew J. Grant, it was enough simply to set them apart into an office of the Church. And so, for a period of two decades, what people received was ordination (or conferral) of an office within an organization.

Well, there are a lot of things that are peculiar about the history of the various Restoration movements that ought to raise serious questions in your mind about whether or not the traditions of your fathers that have come down to **you really** represent a conferral or a conveyance of what the Restoration commenced as and has been delivered in continuity—that is, preserved/intact/true—and your salvation can be gambled on it.

That first year after the Church existed, after the Book of Mormon had been printed, **speaking to** a revelation given to two members that had been called to the ministry in October of 1830, the Lord said this:

My vineyard has become corrupted every whit, and there is none which does good, save it is a few, and **they** *do err in many instances because of priestcrafts,* **all** *having corrupt minds.* (T&C 16:1; see also D&C 33:4, emphasis added)

Okay? It didn't say, "Fortunate for you two, you belong to a true branch." [Audience laughter] It didn't say, "Now I'm gonna tell you about all those folks out there who were in a state of rapid decomposition, hell-bent for the nether regions of darkness in the afterlife." He's talking to **them** about **them** and everyone else. "My vineyard has become corrupted **every whit**, ...there is none which does good, save it [be] a few, and **they** do err in **many** instances because of priestcrafts, all having corrupt minds." An enemy has snuck in and corrupted your mind—every one of you. You all possess a corrupted mind.

Well, if that weren't good enough to set things on the right course, in September of 1832, not quite two years later (little over a year and a half), another revelation is given. And this one is **specifically** talking **to everyone who**, between 1830 and September of 1832, had become converted/had accepted the Book of Mormon/had been baptized/had joined the organization of a church that existed at that point. So now, you cannot escape these words because they're addressed to the folks from whom **all of you**, one way or another, derive **your tradition**. So, these are those folks from whom **you** spring as a believer:

Your minds in times past have been darkened because of unbelief, and because you have treated lightly the things you have received, which vanity and unbelief have brought the whole church under condemnation. (T&C 82:20; see also D&C 84:54)

We didn't have branches back then. We didn't have Communities of Christ versus LDS versus FLDS versus…

It is one. It's still one; we don't have any break-offs. So, this is the **trunk** from which you all spring. The **whole Church**, all of you, the **whole** of this is under condemnation.

And this condemnation rests upon the children of Zion, even all, and they shall **remain** *under this condemnation until they repent* *and remember the new covenant, **even the Book of Mormon,** and the former commandments which I have given them, not only to **say** but to **do** according to that which I have written, that they may bring forth **fruit** meet for their Father's kingdom. Otherwise, there remains a scourge and a judgment to be poured out upon the children of Zion, for shall the children of the kingdom pollute my holy land? Verily, ...I say unto you, **nay.*** (Ibid.; see also D&C 84:56-59, emphasis added)

Okay? You're not gonna be allowed to do that. So, you're not gonna get possession of a holy land because He's not gonna allow you to pollute it. Because at this point, with our various traditions, if we were to go occupy that land, it would become **instantly** polluted because of what we bring with us, because we are not of one heart, we are not of one mind; and therefore, we can't help but pollute it.

The condemnation that we received... We have learned "[for] not only to say but to do according to that which I have written" did not mean solely that they were **saying** but not **doing**, it meant that they **weren't even saying** what the Lord had written. Hence, the need to go back, repent, and redo the Scriptures from the ground up. Hence, the need for the scriptures.info website that you referred to, because the Scriptures of all the various groups have been corrupted. And all of us remain under condemnation until we stop "not saying" according to what He'd written, and then we begin to **do** according to what He has written. (That project will culminate in the publication of leather-bound versions of those Scriptures within the next few months.)

Well, with that introduction, then—

([Speaking about the AV technology on the podium] You see, I'm afraid I'm gonna touch this, and then some slide is gonna jump up on the screen, and then we'll all be distracted, because if there's a screen to watch—well, we've been conditioned. [Audience laughter])

Okay, so let me then read from the Book of Mormon with that assumption in mind that we began with: that this is talking **to you about you**; to you about your congregation, your denomination, your organization; to you about the whole of this. Okay? And I hope it makes you squirm. "He..." (this is talking about the Lord):

> *He commandeth that there shall be **no priestcrafts**; for behold, priestcrafts are that men preach and **set themselves up** for a light unto the world, that they may get gain and praise of the world, but they seek not the welfare of Zion. Behold, the Lord hath **forbidden** this thing; wherefore, the Lord…hath given a commandment that all men should have charity, which charity is love. And except they should have charity, they were **nothing**; wherefore, if they should have **charity**, they would not suffer the laborer in Zion to perish. But the laborer in Zion shall labor **for Zion**, for if they labor for money, they shall perish…*

So, that's the first part of this. The only reason we should practice our religion is to **sacrifice** for the bringing about of Zion. We're not to be remunerated. We're not to be compensated. If we're not sacrificing, we cannot develop faith. Therefore, sacrifice for your religion is mandatory.

> *And again the Lord hath commanded that men should not murder, that they should not **lie** [great comments about lying made today in Jeremy's talk], that they should not steal, that they should not take the name of the Lord their God in vain…*

That doesn't mean swearing; that means testifying to something as the Lord's doctrine or teaching when it is, in fact, not His. And attributing it to Him, that's taking the name of God in vain.

> *…that they should not **envy**, that they should not have **malice**…*

Envy, malice are particularly relevant when you consider how the various Restoration branches have **regarded** one another, have **condemned** one another, have **competed** with one another, have failed to recognize the goodness that exists within each body of the Restoration congregations.

> *…that they should not contend one with another…*

That's the only thing that has been happening since the various factions have broken up into the Rigdonites and the Josephites and the Brighamites and the Bickertonites and the Strangites and the Hedrickites and "What's-that-guy-in-jail-ites."

> *...that they should not contend [with one]another, that they should not commit whoredoms...that they should do none of these things. For whoso doeth them shall perish...*

"Whoso doeth **them**"—any of them. We're contending with one another? It'll perish.

> *...for **none of these iniquities come of the Lord**. For he doeth that which is good among the children of men, and he doeth nothing save it be plain unto the children of men. And he inviteth them **all** to come unto him and partake of his goodness, and he denieth none that come unto him...*

This is the verse that we got read earlier today by Neil Simons. These are the words that precede what he was talking about—about the absence of divisions.

> *...he denieth none that come unto him, black and white, bond and free, male and female; and he remembereth the heathen, and all are alike unto God, both Jew and gentile. But behold, in the last days, or in the days of the gentiles, yea, behold, all the nations of the gentiles, and also the Jews, both those who shall **come upon this land** and those who shall be upon other lands, yea, even upon all the lands of the earth, behold, **they will be drunken with iniquity** and all manner of abominations.* (2 Nephi 11:17-18 RE; see also 2 Nephi 26:29-33; 27:1 LE, emphasis added)

Just so you know, when these words were written as part of Nephi's valedictory address talking to those who would read the Book of Mormon, he wants it really clear that he's including within this description the Gentiles who shall come upon this (the American) land or **you**—**you** who have a copy of this book to read.

Nephi is trying to summarize what he would like us to get out of his effort in summarizing the vision that he had that he was forbidden from writing. But others had written about the same thing, and so he co-opted the words of Isaiah, put them into his book as **his** testimony —and so that we understood that he was applying the words of Isaiah with his own (Nephi's) message, he gives his valedictory summary of his text in the closing chapters of Second Nephi. This (what I just read and what I'm about to read) comes from that closing summary by Nephi of what he would like the Gentiles to **get** out of this, to **understand** out of his message:

> *For it shall come to pass in that day* [when the Book of Mormon comes forward]…*the churches which are built up, and not unto the Lord, when…one shall say unto the other, Behold, I, I am the Lord's — and the other shall say,* **I, I am the Lord's** *— and thus shall everyone say that hath built up churches and* **not** *unto the Lord…*

I don't have a church. The one I was loyal to kicked me out because I was more loyal to a truthful history than to fairytales. I was still willing to belong to and support with my tithes and with my attendance, but I did not think it had a credible **claim** to be the Lord's—**too many** departures, **too many** failures, **too many** lies, **too many** plain errors. I thought it had value—I think every branch of the Restoration has value, but the Book of Mormon has greater value than **any** of them, greater value than **all** of them collectively.

> *And they shall contend one with another, and their* **priests** *shall contend one with another, and they shall teach with* **their learning**, *and deny the holy ghost which giveth utterance. And they deny the power of God, the Holy One of Israel. And they say unto the people, Hearken unto us and hear ye our precept, for behold, there is no God today, for the Lord and the Redeemer hath done his work, and he hath given his power unto men…*

Hands were laid on heads. Voilá! You are a priest! Not just a priest—a **Melchizedek** priest. And Melchizedek may have done something that was great, but don't worry about it, kid—you're just as great.

> …*because of pride, and because of* **false teachers**, *and* **false doctrine[s]**, *their churches have become corrupted, and their churches are lifted up; because of pride, they are puffed up. They rob the poor because of their fine sanctuaries; they rob the poor because of their fine clothing, and they persecute the meek and the poor in heart because in their pride they are puffed up. They wear stiff necks and high heads…*

See, "stiff necks" means you do not bow in reverence to God's will; you've got another agenda rather than God's, so your neck is stiff because you won't bow to Him. And "high heads" means you're proud of what you know. It's the point Adrian made today: we need to realize, no matter how much we think we know, none of us know that much. None of us ought to hold our heads high. All of us ought to be willing to become as a little child and heed and hearken to the Holy Ghost that giveth utterance. And what is the most often utterance given by the Holy Ghost? "Repent. Repent, forsake your false ideas, forsake your false traditions, return to Me."

> *They wear stiff necks and high heads, yea, and because of pride, and wickedness, and abominations...*

You know, "abominations" is a terrible word; it just sounds bad. But it means that what you're doing is you're celebrating something false as a religious sacrament—that you're treating something that isn't God's (or even approved by Him) as His. It's abominable. It's blasphemy. It's repugnant to God, and it ought to be repugnant to us.

C.S. Lewis wrote a book called *Mere Christianity*. We ought to get back to the **mere-ness** of the Restoration, because in its mere-ness, the Restoration asks us to repent, be baptized, read the words that we get in the Book of Mormon, and then search for and find that God who caused the Restoration to come about to fulfill His purposes. And His purpose is to save us.

> *...abominations, and whoredoms, they have all gone astray, save it be a few who are the humble followers of Christ...*

This sounds very much like that revelation given to the missionaries being sent out during that first year of the Church, "they have all gone astray." Now the words here are slightly different:

> *...they have all gone astray, save it be a few who are the humble followers of Christ. Nevertheless, **they** are led, that in many instances **they** do err because they are taught by the precepts of men. O the wise, and the learned, and the rich, that are puffed up in the pride of their hearts, and all [they that] preach false doctrines, and all [they that] commit whoredoms and pervert the*

> *right way of the Lord,* **Woe, woe, woe** *be unto them, saith the Lord God Almighty, for they shall be thrust down to hell.* (2 Nephi 12:1-3 RE; see also 2 Nephi 28:3-5,12-15 LE, emphasis added)

"Woe, woe, woe" is a three-fold condemnation. You can be condemned with one "woe" or with two, but when you're condemned with three "woes," that follows you on into what comes next. You just don't want to wind up there, particularly when you have the means in your hands to understand how to avoid these kinds of errors and this kind of condemnation.

Well, Michael Kelly (this morning) referred to a statement by Paul in his letter to the Galatians:

> *Though we, or an angel from Heaven, preach any other gospel unto you than that which we have preached unto you, let him be accursed.* (Galatians 1:2 RE; see also Galatians 1:8 LE)

What is that gospel? See, it's almost as if when Christ set up and called twelve apostles to be the ministers He sent into the world to preach repentance unto the world, whom He called and whom He ordained—it's almost as if one of the very first acts of the Lord was to call Paul **outside** of the organization He had set up, **outside** of the group that He had authorized, **outside** of the group that He had ordained. Why would the Lord call Paul on the road to Damascus and give to him a dispensation of the gospel when there was already an **existing** dispensation of the gospel in the hands of the twelve who had been with Him all throughout His ministry? It's almost as if the Lord wanted to make the point from the outset:

Don't ever assume you can rely on a structure.

God will call whom He will call, and Christ made that point with Paul. And so, when Paul writes to the Galatians, "Let anyone that preaches a different gospel than the one I've delivered to you be accursed," we ought to ask ourselves, "Well, what then is the gospel that Paul preaches?" It's a gospel founded upon a man who can bear witness and testimony, like the other twelve could, that Jesus Christ was the resurrected Lord who came and sacrificed, died, and rose from the dead, who will draw all men to Him. And Paul knew that.

That gospel, that same God—who did something very similar with Joseph Smith, who came and delivered to him a dispensation of the gospel in which Joseph could testify—that Lord (who lived, who died, and who rose again) lives and testifies and is the same yesterday, today, and forever. His gospel is unchanging; His act doesn't change. That gospel of ascension in which men are brought up unto Him…

Amos foretold this (and we read these words as if they applied during a 1700/1800 year hiatus between the death of Christ and His Apostles and the opening of the heavens to Joseph Smith; we don't read these words as if anything like this began **again** at the death of Joseph and Hyrum—but I want you to consider that these words may be a description of what began immediately upon the death of Joseph and Hyrum):

> *Behold, the days come, [saith] the Lord God, that I will send a famine in the land — not a famine of bread, nor a thirst for water, but of hearing the words of the Lord. And they shall wander from sea to sea, and from…north even to the east. They shall run to and fro to seek the word of the Lord and* ***shall not find it***. (Amos 1:27 RE: see also Amos 8:11 LE, emphasis added)

Oh, you'll find plenty of:

- *"lo hear"*s and *"lo there"*s,

- *I, I am the Lord's,*

- *God hath **finished** his work* and gave His authority unto me…

You'll find plenty of those. You'll find plenty of preaching involving the traditions of fathers—but you also find a famine. Then, Micah said:

> *Then shall the seers be ashamed and the diviners confounded. Yea, they shall all cover their lips, for there is no answer of God. …The heads thereof judge for reward, and the priests thereof teach for hire, and the prophets thereof divine for money. Yet will they lean upon the Lord and say, Is not the Lord among us? No[ne] evil can come upon us.* (Micah 1:8 RE; see also Micah 3:7 LE)

Evil will come upon them, because Zion is what the Lord intends to preserve. We should be desperately seeking for that. Isaiah said:

> *The land shall be utterly emptied and utterly spoiled, for the Lord ha[th] spoken this word. The earth mourn[eth] and fade[th] away; the world languishe[th] and fade[th] away; the haughty people of the earth do languish. The earth also is defiled under the inhabitants thereof, because they have transgressed the laws, changed the ordinance[s], broken the everlasting covenant. Therefore ha[th] the curse devoured the earth, and they that dwell therein are desolate; therefore, the inhabitants of the earth are burned, and few men left.* (Isaiah 7:1 RE; see also Isaiah 24:3 LE)

Well, that's coming.

Look, whenever the Lord sets about to do a work, vessels are broken, traditions are discarded. **Reform may work to splinter Catholicism, but reform does not work to repair a restoration.** It doesn't, and it can't. You either need a restoration or you're just messing with an old bag that can't take a new patch.

Christ said… This was in a conversation with Nicodemus. Nicodemus was one of the Sanhedrin. He was a member of the Seventy, one of the "presiding authorities," one of those who could speak with authority (with the confidence that he occupied a position approved by God—a governor in the land). Jesus told him, "You're gonna have to get baptized." And Nicodemus, who'd already been baptized…

See, when they came and they questioned John's baptism, they didn't question **baptism**; they questioned the authority of John **to baptize**— because everyone was being baptized. And Nicodemus (who'd been baptized) came to Christ, and Christ told him, "You gotta be baptized again." And Nicodemus' reaction was, "Why do I gotta go do that? I mean, that seems redundant." And Christ's answer to him is the same answer that has to be given to everyone, in every branch, at any time when restoration begins again:

> *No man also seweth a piece of new cloth on an old garment: else the new piece that fille[th] it up taketh away from the old, and the*

rent is made worse [the tear]. *And no man putteth new wine [in]
old bottles: else the new wine doth burst the bottles, and the wine is
spilled, and the bottles will be marred: but new wine must be put
[in] new bottles.* (Mark 2:21-22 LE; see also Mark 2:3 RE)

In other words, any time a restoration begins anew, there has to be
baptism again because you have to acknowledge and accept the fact
that God speaks again.

Well, as was mentioned, a new set of Scriptures has begun the process
of repenting and returning. And those new Scriptures are not the only
thing that is underway. In addition, re-baptism… It doesn't…

You're not joining an organization; we have no organization to join.
The problem with all the Restoration splinters is that they're competing
with one another. We have no interest in providing a competing
organization. We offer baptism. We accept the Book of Mormon not
just as a text, but we accept the Book of Mormon as a covenant.

The early Saints voted to accept Lectures on Faith. They voted to accept
the revelations that were found in the Doctrine and Covenants. They
never accepted the Book of Mormon either as a volume of Scripture
(they just assumed it), and they certainly never accepted the Book of
Mormon as a covenant.

In an effort to undo the condemnation that was given in September of
1832, we've gone back, we've recovered the Scriptures as accurately as it
is possible to do so today—not only to **say** what the Lord wanted said
as accurately as possible but also to **do** according to that which is
written. Once it is **said** correctly, the next thing is to **do** it.

And so, baptism is being offered anew: re-baptism. Most of the
baptisms you read about in the Book of Mormon are re-baptisms.
They'd already been baptized once before, but they had to repent and
return and be re-baptized. All those people that Alma went out in the
wilderness and baptized at the waters of Mormon—those were all re-
baptisms. All the great accounts of conversion in the Book of Mormon
are reconversions/re-baptisms, with the exception of recovering some
particularly militant apostates who had not practiced in faithfulness the
religion that they had been given at the outset.

Look, I hope this conference continues. If as much a difference in spirit can occupy this conference next year as is different from last year to this, then we really are headed towards a greater unity. Tausha lamented all the frustrations she had in trying to get this thing put together. [Speaking to Tausha] Oh, you worry too much; it's that red hair. You just leave it alone. If you're inspired to do it, when it happens, it'll take care of itself, as it has today.

What I saw today (compared to last year) is progress. It's astonishing. It's wonderful. And I feel closer to all of those who have spoken from the various traditions today. I hope we can grow closer again from now until the next of these. And I hope that there is a next of these.

Thank you.

Love Others as Yourself

Transcript of Comments by Denver and Stephanie Snuffer
at a Regional Conference in Sandy, Utah
July 14, 2019

Denver: I wanna thank those that organize this and every other conference—put on by volunteers; facilities are rented by them, at their expense, so that we can come and participate. I don't know how much work or preparation went into this, but 17 days is not inconsequential in terms of the effort that has been required by everyone that has worked on this. Part of what we believe is "to sacrifice" as part of the religion and that putting on a conference requires that, and it requires a lot of hands to make it work.

[Inaudible audience comment]

Is that better? Okay, I lowered my voice when I said, "Is that better?" [Audience laughter.] I would rather be out in the hallway screaming like we heard a little… Better go… Okay, can you hear me? Okay, now that we've got that all figured out…

Since my wife and I are "one," the first part of this talk is gonna be given by her (assuming that she'll actually get up and do this).

All of the best marriages are fiery, and the idea that you somehow failed because you had an argument… What was it? Day four of the marriage? We have this running joke; we keep score. What am I? 12,727 argument wins? And she has four…(or was it five? [audience laughter])…which is a reflection of her charity and generosity. And oh, you just said, "Get the sheep hook out."

She's gonna talk.

Stephanie: Okay, now you have to re-do all this nasty…whatever.

Okay, I've detected a theme—Jennifer, thank you; Tyler, thank you; and some of the others that I have heard—like a genuine, legitimate theme, and I think I'll stick with it, okay? And the good news is, as far as I can tell, there will only be one repeat set of Scriptures from my talk to Jennifer's talk. So…

I've noticed that there are Ten Commandments—ten (oh, someone needs to get me some water, by the way), not 15, not a hundred, and not a thousand, but **ten**. And that doesn't seem like a **lot** to save the entirety of mankind, right? I mean, when I was leaving lists for babysitters, I left more than ten commandments. It takes more than a list of ten things to take care of our dogs when we leave town. So, I find it interesting that there are only ten. But I'm gonna focus on two: the first two.

So, in Mark chapter five, verses 44 and 4̶3̶ [45] (and you have to excuse me; I have had a **terrible** cold, and so forgive whatever comes out):

> *And one of the scribes came, and having heard them reasoning together, and perceiving that he had answered them well, asked him, Which is the first commandment…? And Jesus answered him, The first of all the commandments is: Listen, and hear, O Israel, the Lord our God is one Lord. And you shall love the Lord your God with all your heart, and with all your soul, and with all your mind, and with all your strength. This is the first commandment. And the second is like [unto] this: You shall love your neighbor **as yourself**. There is no other commandment greater than these.*

> *And the scribe said unto Him, Well, Master, you have said the truth; for there is one God, and there is none other but him. And to love him with all the heart, and with all the understanding, and with all the soul, and with all the strength, and to love his neighbor **as himself**, is more than all whole burnt offerings and sacrifices.* (Mark 5:44-45 RE, emphasis added)

So, the question is, What is this thing about loving yourself, k? I'm not sure, but let's take a look at it.

So, I'm wondering if God gives "love your neighbor as yourself" as the second great commandment because He thinks we're all ego-maniacal narcissists, and the only possible way we're able to love **other people** is if we love them as much as we love **ourselves**? Yep? No, I don't think so, because there are plenty of examples of people who are literally selfless people and who give up their lives and everything they have for other people. So, that can't be it.

So, let's start with Romans [1:]65 [RE],

> *Therefore, owe no man anything but to love one another, for he that loves another has fulfilled the law for this: You shall not commit adultery, You shall not kill, You shall not steal, You shall not bear false witness, You shall not covet; and if there is any other commandment, it is briefly comprehended in this saying — namely, You shall love your neighbor as yourself (love works no ill to his neighbor; therefore, love is the fulfilling of the law), and that, knowing the time — that now it is high time to awake out of sleep, for now is our salvation nearer than when we believed.*

Did you all catch that? If there is any other commandment, it is briefly comprehended in the command to **love your neighbor as yourself**. If you love God and your neighbor, the other eight commandments take care of themselves—because people who love each other work no ill to their neighbor. Therefore, love is the fulfilling of the law, and our salvation is nearer than when we believed. So, it is—quite literally—time to wake up.

Galatians 1:19 [RE],

> *I wish they were even cut off who trouble you; for, brethren, you have been called unto liberty. Only use not liberty for an opportunity to the flesh, but by love serve one another; for all the law is fulfilled in one word, even…this: You shall love your neighbor as yourself. But if you bite and devour one another, take heed that you be not consumed one of another.*

So, here are a few interesting commentaries on that "bite and devour" thing:

- In the Weymouth New Testament, it says, *But if you are perpetually snarling and snapping at one another, beware lest you are destroyed by one another* (Galatians 5:15 WNT).

- The Contemporary English Version says, *But if you keep attacking each other like wild animals, you had better watch out or you will destroy yourselves* (Galatians 5:15 CEV). Okay?

- God's Word Translation says, *But if you criticize and attack each other, be careful that you don't destroy each other* (Galatians 5:15 GWT).

So, how do these words apply to you? And me? Because they do—that's why they're part of the Scriptures. I just described **us**; that is us. So, let's ask it again: What's up with loving our neighbors as ourselves?

So, Luke 8:7 [RE] says: *And he answering said, You shall love the Lord your God with all your heart, and with all your soul, and with all your strength, and with all your mind, and **your neighbor** as yourself. …But he* [the man asking the question], *willing to justify himself, said unto Jesus, And who is my neighbor?*

Well, we're not gonna do that, are we? We're not gonna try and justify who our neighbor is. Okay? So, who are our neighbors, and what does it mean to love them?

In this context, I can tell you what love **doesn't** mean:

- It is not necessarily an intense feeling of deep affection;
- It is not necessarily a great interest and pleasure in something; and
- It is not necessarily to feel a deep romantic or sexual attachment to something.

~~Enos 2~~ Enos [1:] 2 & 3 [RE] says:

> *Now it came to pass that when I had heard these words, I began to feel a desire for the welfare of my brethren the Nephites; wherefore, I did pour out my whole soul unto God for them. And while I was…struggling in the spirit, behold, the voice of the Lord came into my mind again, saying, I will visit thy brethren according to their diligence in keeping my commandments. I have given unto them this land, and it is a holy land; and I curse it not, save it be for the cause of iniquity. Wherefore, I will visit thy brethren according as I have said, and their transgressions will I bring down with sorrow upon their own heads. And after I, Enos, had heard these words, my faith began to be unshaken in the Lord. And I prayed unto him with many long struggling[s] for my brethren the Lamanites.*

And it came to pass that after I had prayed and labored with all diligence, the Lord said unto me, I will grant unto thee according to thy desires because of thy faith. And now behold, this was the desire which I desired of him: that if it should [be] so…that my people the Nephites should fall into transgression, and by any means be destroyed, and the Lamanites should not be destroyed, that the Lord God would preserve a record of my people [that] the Nephites, even if it so be by the power of his holy arm, that it might be brought forth some future day unto the Lamanites, that perhaps **they** *might be brought unto salvation. For at the present, our strugglings were vain in restoring them to the true faith. And they swore in their wrath that if it were possible, they would destroy our records, and us, and also [our] traditions of our fathers.* (Emphasis added)

In Helaman 4:2 [RE], it says:

And it came to pass that in this year Nephi did cry unto the Lord, saying, O Lord, do not suffer that this people shall be destroyed by the sword, but O Lord, rather let there be a famine in the land to stir them up in remembrance of the Lord their God, and perhaps they will repent and turn unto thee. And so it was done according to the words of Nephi, and there was a great famine upon the land, among all the people of Nephi. And thus in the seventy and fourth year the famine did continue, and the work of destruction did cease by the sword, but became sore by famine. And this work of destruction did also continue in the seventy and fifth year. For the earth was smitten, that it was dry and did not yield forth grain in the season of grain; and the whole earth was smitten, even among the Lamanites as well as among the Nephites, so that they were smitten that they did perish by thousands in the more wicked parts of the land.

And then we move on to Nephi. (And just as a side note, I'm pretty sure Nephi did not love his brothers, k? I just don't think he did. They were abusive; they were violent; and they were fratricidal, okay?) But this is what he does—[1] Nephi 2:4 [RE]:

And it came to pass that when I, Nephi, had spoken these words unto my brethren, they were angry with me. [Yeah, so what's new?

They were always angry with him.] …*But it came to pass that I prayed unto the Lord, saying, O Lord, according to my faith which is in thee, wilt thou deliver me from the hands of my brethren? … And it came to pass that when I said these words, behold, the bands were loosed from off my hands and feet, and I stood before my brethren and I spake unto them again. …And it came to pass that* **I did frankly forgive them** *all that they had done, and I did exhort them that they would pray unto the Lord their God for forgiveness. …And after they had done praying unto the Lord, we did again [a] travel on our journey towards the tent of our father.* (Emphasis added)

Genesis 11:4-9—again, another story of fratricide, k? Pretty sure Joseph didn't love his brothers, and his brothers certainly didn't love him—because 4 thru 9, *And a cert...*

Genesis 11:4-9 [RE]:

> *And a certain man found him, and behold, he was wandering in the field. And the man asked him, saying, What do you seek? And he said, I seek my [brothers]; tell me, I pray you, where they feed their flocks. And the man said, They are departed from here, for I heard them say, Let us go to Dothan. And Joseph went after his brethren and found them….*

And when he comes, they see him, and they conspire against to slay him.

> *And they said one to another, Behold, this* **dreamer** *comes….*

They don't even call him by name, okay? They have so much contempt for Joseph that they just call him "the dreamer."

> *Come now therefore and let us slay him and cast him into [the] pit, and we will say some evil beast has devoured him, and we shall see what will become of his dreams.*
>
> *And Reuben heard it, and he delivered him out of their hands and said, [Let's] not kill him. And Reuben said…Shed no blood, but cast him into this pit…*

That's great—we'll just cast him in this pit....Verse 7:

> *And it came to pass when Joseph had come unto his brethren...they stripped Joseph out of his coat, his coat of many colors that was on him, ...they took him and cast him into a pit. And the pit was empty, [and] there was no water....*

> *And they sat down to eat... [And lo and behold, they see] a company of Ishmaelites coming from Gilead with their camels bearing spicery, and balm, and myrrh, going to carry it down to Egypt. And Judah said... [Hey,] What profit [it is] if we slay...and conceal his blood? Come...let us sell him to the Ishmaelites...let not our hand be upon him, for he is our brother and our flesh...*

Well, that's nice. We don't hate him enough to kill him, but we just sell him to this band of Ishmaelites.

> *And his brethren were content.*

So, they sell him for 20 pieces of silver. Reuben went back to the pit; Joseph wasn't in it.

> *...he rent his clothes. And he returned [to] his brethren and said, The child is not; and I, where shall I go? And they took Joseph's coat, ...killed...the [goat], ...dipped the coat in...blood. And they sent the coat of many colors, and they brought it to their father and [they] said, [Oh, oh, oh, it's so terrible!]*

Okay, so you know the story. Lots of stuff happens, and then this—Genesis 11:39 & 40 [RE]:

> *Then Joseph could not refrain himself before all them that stood by him, and he cried, Cause every man to go out from me! And there stood no man with him while Joseph made himself known unto his brethren. And he wept aloud, and the Egyptians and the house of Pharaoh heard. And Joseph said unto his brethren, I am Joseph. Does my father yet live? And his brethren could not answer him, for they were troubled at his presence [because, yeah, what happened to you?]. And Joseph said unto his brethren, Come near to me, I pray you. And they came near. And he said, I am Joseph, your brother whom you sold into Egypt. Now therefore be not*

grieved nor angry with yourselves that you sold me here, for God did send me before you to preserve life. For these two years has the famine been in the land, and yet there are five years in which there shall neither be plowing nor harvest. And God sent me before you to preserve [your] posterity in the earth and to save your lives by a great deliverance. So now it was not you that sent me here, but God. And he has made me a father to Pharaoh, and [a] lord of all his house, and a ruler throughout all the land[s] of Egypt.

And more happens and more happens…

And he fell upon his brother Benjamin's neck and wept. And Benjamin wept upon his neck. [And] he kissed all his brethren and [he] wept upon them. And after that, his brethren talked with him.

Wow. The forgoing Scriptures illustrate that forgiveness, intercession, and relationships do **not** have to be based on "love" as we culturally define it here.

So, let's get back to who our neighbors are. We're gonna start with the most intimate relationships and work out from there:

- At the top should be my relationship with the gods (which is not always my focus, but ideally, it should be).
- And then we go partner/spouse,
- Family/children,
- Extended family (aunts, uncles, in-laws),
- Friends, co-workers, religious community, work community, neighborhood (blah, blah, blah…),
- Until we get down to our enemies.

The makeup of these relationships might look different for everyone. Some of us may have all of them, and some of us may have only a few. But we all have intimate and significant associations or relationships, and we all have enemies.

So, how do we do it? How do we love them?

So, as a side note, I would like to make a distinction here—**service is not love**. It can be **motivated** by love, but there's a difference, because serving is actually quite easy—dropping off my gently-used clothes, tithing, dollar bills, blankets, granola, water bottles, taking my old "but I'm getting a new washer or dryer" to someone in need, plant a garden, make a casserole, take a salad or a dessert—don't get me wrong; these are great. We should engage in these. These are really nice things to do. However, they **can** be done at an arm's length—no conversation, no association, no relationship, no love, no risk. Relationships are where the real work takes place. Relationships are difficult **and** effortless. They are risky, and they are safe. They are uncomfortable, and they are comfortable. They are rich and rewarding. And they ebb, and they flow. They are **the** vehicle wherein we move through and into love, charity, sanctification, and ultimately, salvation. To be a part of the family of God up there requires us to **create** a family of God down here.

So, moving back into "How we justify who our neighbors are, and why we think we don't need to love them," I've got some hypothetical scenarios—completely made-up (except I have heard variations on themes):

- Example one: "My best friend doesn't go to church anymore. She believes some strange things that I'm having a hard time understanding. Our religious beliefs were a pretty significant part of our relationship, and I don't believe we have much in common anymore. She is willing to talk to me about some of this stuff…" (Excuse me) "…and I do listen, but because I know she's wrong about her new beliefs, I think I should just stop being friends with her. I'm really torn. I'm worried about how this will affect what kind of person she is, and I don't want her wacky ideas influencing my family."

- Example two: "My daughter has confided in me about some frustration and hurt she's been dealing with because of the way her husband (my son-in-law) is treating her. I am resentful and holding a grudge. I treat him fine in public—and I do love him —but I can't help thinking negative things about him because of what I know. When I express my frustration to my friend, she commiserates with me and agrees that I am justified in resenting him."

- Example three: "My sister borrowed a significant amount of money from me a few years back with a promise that she'll pay it back. I don't ask her for it because I don't really need it, and I'm okay with my financial circumstances, and I really do wanna be charitable. The problem is: every time I see her buying something or spending money, I judge her based on her promise to pay me back. When I talk to my husband about it, he says I should ask her to start a payment plan and get it back. We could use it for a vacation or something. And she **did** say she would pay it back."

- Example four: "My mother-in-law is not very nice. She's critical and unkind. I feel really insecure when I'm around her, and it's exhausting. For the sake of my relationship with my husband, I let her come over; and we ~~associate her with as much as reason~~ associate with her as much ~~as reason~~ as is reasonable, but I stew and grumble about it for days before and after. My sister thinks I should just explain to my husband how difficult this is for me and suggest that he can see his mom without me."

When I read an article or hear a news story about some tremendous act of forgiveness on the part of someone who has given absolution to another person for some grievous offense, I think, "So what?" The dad who forgives the drunk driver who killed his entire family; the woman who forgives the man who raped her; the elderly man who doesn't hold a grudge against the businessman who conned him and stole all his money—so what? We treat these instances as though they are great acts of emotional heroism. We heap praise and adulation upon the people who are so magnanimous that they forgave the horrible bastard who grieved or assaulted or offended them. It's ridiculous! We **lie** to ourselves when and if we think we are **ever** justified in resentment, grudges, judgments, or accusations. We are not, **ever**.

The Lord's standard is pretty clear, and there's not much wiggle room. You want Heavenly Father to forgive **you**? You forgive each other. That sounds like a really good way of **loving yourself**. Forgiveness is a **requirement**—it is a condition—and the Lord has this to say about it. 3 Nephi 5:34 [RE], *And forgive us our debts as we forgive our debtors. … For if ye forgive men their trespasses, your Heavenly Father will also forgive you, but if [you] forgive not men their trespasses, neither will your Father forgive your trespasses.*

Colossians 1:13 [RE]:

> *Put on therefore as the elect of God, holy and beloved, hearts of mercies, kindness, humility of mind, meekness, long-suffering, bearing with one another and forgiving one another. If any man have a quarrel against any, even as Christ forgave you, so also do you; and above all these things put on charity, which is the bond of perfectness. …Let the word of Christ dwell in you richly, in all wisdom, teaching and admonishing one another in psalms, and hymns, and spiritual songs, singing with grace in your hearts to the Lord. And whatever you do in word or deed, do all in the name of the Lord Jesus, giving thanks to God and the Father by him.*

This sounds like loving yourself. Teaching[s] and Commandments section 157:58:

> *I have given you a former commandment that I, the Lord, will forgive whom I will forgive, but of you it is required to forgive all men. And again, I have taught that if you forgive men their trespasses, your Heavenly Father will also forgive you; but if you forgive not men their trespasses, neither will your Heavenly Father forgive your trespasses. …If men intend no offense, I take no offense, but if they are taught and should have obeyed, then I reprove and correct, and forgive and forget.*

God is the **only** one who judges correctly. He is the only one who can decide whether an offense was intended or not, and then **He** reproves, corrects, **forgives**, and **forgets**. We are rarely worthy to judge, and we are only able to reprove and correct people we have a relationship with —and we are **always** expected to forgive and forget.

So, the real question comes down to this: Do we believe these words? It's pretty much that simple. Relationships with spouses, children, co-workers, parents, siblings, friends, enemies require vulnerability, work, and a deliberate effort to see the good and **be** the good. Relationships (excuse me)… Relationships are emotionally fulfilling. People who have community live longer and healthier lives. Working on those relationships and having them be positive and uplifting for **your** benefit sounds like **loving yourself**.

(Excuse me.)

I have a simple formula that works for me, and I'll share it with you. I figure that every single interaction I have with another human being will achieve one of three things:

- The experience will either build our relationship with a positive interaction,
- It will leave it unchanged or status quo, or
- It will tear down the relationship with a negative interaction.

Grocery store clerks, gas station attendants, students, teachers, husbands, children—doesn't matter. The good news about this formula for me is that I get to choose, **every single time** with **every single person**. It's **never** out of my control. There is no love for others **or yourself** if your time's spent focusing on flaws, criticizing, imputing intent, or taking offense for no good reason.

Here's what the Lord says about judgment, flaws, criticism, ascribing motive, offense, and intent—and it's time we start taking Him seriously. So, He moves on from the Ten Commandments to the Sermon on the Mount.

In Matthew 3:40 [RE], He says:

> Now these are the words which Jesus taught his disciples that they should say unto the people: Judge not unrighteously, that you be not judged, but judge righteous judgment; for with what judgment you [shall] judge, you shall be judged, and with what measure you mete, it shall be measured to you again.

(It's like a person with a cold's worst nightmare [audience laughter].)

The difference it here that I see between the "no judging" and the "righteous judgment" is likely related to Final Judgment, as opposed to all those in-between judgments that we can do if we **think** we have the Lord on our side, in terms of righteous judgment.

And then moving from Matthew into Third Nephi—3 Nephi 6:6 [RE]:

And why beholdest thou the mote that is in thy brother's eye, but considerest not the beam that is in thine own eye? Or how wilt thou say to thy brother, Let me pull [that] mote out of thine eye, and behold, a beam is in thine own eye? Thou hypocrite, first cast out the beam...of thine own eye, and then shalt thou see clearly to cast out the mote out of thy brother's eye. Give not that which is holy unto the dogs, neither cast ye your pearls before swine, lest they trample them under their feet, and turn again, and rend you.

And so, I say to that: What the heck does that have to do with anything? So, on the assumption that it is actually related to what came before that, I spent a reasonable amount of time contemplating it, and this is my version of pearls and swine and dogs and whatever. (It's a strange ending to this particular thought.) So, what if it means that **we** are the dogs and the swine, and judging is a holy and precious act— one that we don't have anywhere near the godliness to engage in, at least without seriously pursuing God's help—and we will get out of the attempt (and **all** we will get out of the attempt) at that kind of judging is trampling and rending. So, that's my take; and so, let's not do it. Okay? Let's just not do it.

In the forgoing Scriptures, we are being told to worry about ourselves **first** (and **that** should take a long, long, long time). And then, if we need to, we can worry about other people after that. So, in theory, if we're as critical towards ourselves as we are others, we should be doing a lot of repenting, improving, growing in love and charity and empathy —as we make ourselves better; because it's just about beams and motes, people. That's it—just don't do it.

When it comes to our interpersonal life, knowing how to make yourself better takes a lot of courage and introspection; you have to be willing to be clear on what's wrong with **you**. It's a lot easier to think about what's wrong with other people. So, asking questions like:

- How did I make **that** better or worse?
- What did I do or say to make them react that way?
- What did I say or do to cause their defensiveness? or
- Why did I do or say what I did or said, and how and what could I have done differently?

...are absolutely necessary in order to become more Christ-like. However, if focusing on other people is your jam, then do it charitably; impute the highest motive and best motive to other people; assume their best intentions; engage in empathy and perspective-taking. **These** are godly acts. They make **your** life better. They wash away the bitterness, anger, hurt, and unhappiness **you** feel when you're focused on the negative. This sounds like loving yourself.

Ephesians [1:]12&16 [RE]:

> *I, therefore, the prisoner of the Lord, implore you that you walk worthy of the vocation with which you are called, [and] with all lowliness and meekness, with long-suffering, bearing with one another in love, endeavoring to keep the unity of the spirit in the bond of peace, in one body [in] one spirit, even as you are called in one hope of your calling — one Lord, one faith, one baptism, one God and Father of all, who is above all, and through all, and in you all.*

> *...Wherefore, putting away lying, speak every man truth with his neighbor, for we are members one of another. Can you be angry and sin not? Let not the sun go down upon your wrath, neither give place to the Devil. Let him that stole steal no more, but rather let him labor, working with his hands for the things which are good, that he may have to give to him that needs. Let no corrupt communication proceed out of your mouth, but that which is good to...use of edifying, that it may minister grace unto the hearers. And grieve not the holy spirit of God whereby you are sealed unto the day of redemption. Let all bitterness, ...wrath, and anger, and clamor, and evil speaking be put away from you with all malice. And be kind one to another, tenderhearted, forgiving one another, even as God for Christ's sake has forgiven you. Be therefore followers of God, as dear children, and walk in love, as Christ [has also] loved us and has given himself for us, an offering and a sacrifice to God for a sweet-smelling savor.*

So, it still comes down to one simple question: Do I believe the words of God?

And then He raises the standard again—3 Nephi 5:24-26, 30, and 31 [RE].

[24] *Ye have heard that it hath been said by them of old time, and it is also written before you, that thou shalt not kill, and whosoever shall kill shall be in danger of the judgment of God. But I say unto you that whosoever is angry with his brother shall be in danger of his judgment. And whosoever shall say to his brother, Raca, shall be in danger of the council, and whosoever shall say, Thou fool, shall be in danger of hellfire.*

[25] *Therefore, if ye shall come unto me, or shall desire to come unto me, and rememberest that thy brother hath aught against thee, go thy way unto thy brother and first be reconciled to thy brother, and then come unto me with full purpose of heart and I will receive you.*

[26] *Agree with thine adversary quickly while thou art in the way with him, lest at any time he shall get thee and thou shalt be cast into prison. Verily I say unto thee, thou shalt by no means come out thence until thou hast paid the uttermost senine. And while ye are in prison, can ye pay even one senine? Verily, verily I say unto you, nay.*

[30] *...And behold, it is written, An eye for an eye and a tooth for a tooth; but I say unto you that ye shall not resist evil, but whosoever shall smite thee on thy right cheek, turn to him the other also. And if any man will sue thee at the law and take away thy coat, let him have thy cloak also. And whosoever shall [compare] thee to go a mile, go with him twain. Give to him that asketh thee, and to him that would borrow of thee, turn thou not away.*

[31] *And behold, it is written also that thou shalt love thy neighbour and hate thine enemy; but behold, I say unto you, love your enemies, bless them that curse you, [and] do good to them that hate you, and pray for them who despitefully use you and persecute you, that ye may be the children of your Father who is in Heaven, for he maketh his sun to rise on the evil and...the good. Therefore, those things which were of old time, which were under the law, in me*

are all fulfilled. Old things are done away and all things have become new.

These admonitions are designed to make **your life better.** Much like the other eight commandments, the first two are so that we can (and will) live loving, Christ-like lives, being obedient to God's instructions, which we **really** need to take seriously.

Having said all that, I don't believe we can actually **do** any of this. Down here, the natural man takes over, and we're pretty much **incapable** of living the standard—at least on our own. **We need God.** We need God to change us. Inter-personally speaking, most of us aren't capable (or even willing) to do the hard work of evaluating ourselves, of checking our own "beams," of considering our own motives, of loving ourselves enough to become godly. We need to be willing to let God change us, mold us, and make us into something **He can use** to further **His** kingdom.

I had an experience several years ago that really opened my eyes and helped me see clearly some things that were seriously wrong with me. Some of you have heard this story, and I'm gonna tell it again because it illustrates why I feel so passionately about this subject:

Years ago, we took the family down to "Circus Circus" in Las Vegas for a softball tournament. And the team was in the arcade, Denver was in the hotel room, the girls were swimming, and it was my job to just be the "mother" down at Circus Circus. But there were so many parents there, I didn't have to be in the arcade. So, I was reading—and I remember the book I was reading; it was called *The Element* by Sir ~~Ken Wade~~ Ken Robinson. And I was sitting outside on a marble platform, outside of Circus Circus. And I was watching **loads** of people just walking by—back and forth, back and forth—and I was having a **heyday** judging these people. Ya ever been to "Circus Circus"? Okay, I… I mean, I can't even… I had thoughts going in my mind, things like, "Oh my gosh, I would hide my children from that person." (I would literally put them behind my legs and hide them from people.)

And I was just (in my mind, obviously; I wasn't talking to anybody; no one was there)—but I was on a rant, put my book down, people-watching. And as clear as… I don't know—it was in my mind; it wasn't an audible voice. But as clear as day, I hear, "How dare you. These are My people! And at the moment, I love them more than you." No, that wasn't it—but the fact was, I was suitably chastised for what I was doing. And I thought, "Oh, I mean…and I…" It didn't take me… I mean I didn't need anything more than that. It was instant. It was like, "Oh, my gosh. That is 100% true."

So, as I thought about it (over the next few months and whatever), I came to two conclusions:

- One, I am literally, figuratively, theoretically (and every other adverb word)… I am no better than anyone. Period. End of story. That's it.

- Conversely, nobody is better than me. K? So there is no—like Jennifer said—there are no "subs" this, or I am **not** "sub" to anyone, people are not "sub" to me.

And so, as I contemplated this and have tried to incorporate this into my life over the past several years, I see it everywhere. I see it in books I read. I see it in the Scriptures I read. I am looking for it because I am truly, truly trying to change me. This was one of those moments in my life where God literally transformed me. He woke me up, and He completely altered the way I see my neighbor. And I've had several more of those experiences, but it's probably because I'm looking for 'em. So, start looking for 'em.

So, in addition to "start looking for 'em," start asking the question, "What lack I yet?" And then **listen** to the answer. Start seeing people the way God sees them and then engaging with them in a way that reflects that. Start asking God to take the scales from **your** eyes, so that you are no longer deceived into thinking whatever is untrue for you. Start wanting to change you, and start taking the things God says seriously.

Now, you might think I'm being too absolute or too literal, and that's fine. You might even be right. However, ask yourself this:

Was Jesus absolute and literal when He ended verse 31 with this?
Therefore, I would that ye should be perfect, even as I or your Father who is in Heaven is perfect (3 Nephi 5:31 RE).

Authority, Keys, and Kingdom

Comments delivered at a Regional Conference in Sandy, Utah
July 14, 2019

See, when they told me about the theme of this conference, I thought, "Well, it's right down her alley. Why would I talk about that when she's spent years thinking about the very topic?" So, I'm not gonna talk about that; she covered the subject, and I'm gonna talk about something else.

There are three ideas that create a lot of problems, a lot of tension, a lot of conflict and discussion—and I want to address those three subjects here with you today: authority, keys, and the Kingdom of God.

On the subject of "authority," the Scriptures draw a contrast between two kinds of authority. One kind involves preaching, teaching, or statements holding self-evident or compelling truth that convicts or convinces the hearers of the truth. There's some examples of this.

Matthew 3:49 [RE]: *And it came to pass, when Jesus had ended these sayings with his disciples, the people were astonished at his teachings, for he taught them as one having authority from God and not as having authority from the scribes.* **The authority was resident inside the message—** didn't have to be borrowed from somewhere, didn't require a badge, didn't require a collar, didn't require a mitre; it simply held compelling truth that, in the ears of the listener, convicted them.

When they asked Jesus where He got authority from, they might just as well have posed the question, "How do you preach with such persuasive conviction?" Because **Christ had moral authority**. It was that same moral authority that caused the guards—who came at night to arrest Him in Gethsemane with their swords and with their armaments—to stumble backwards and fall down when He identified Himself, "I am the man" (see Testimony of St. John 11:2). This is the **prophetic form of authority**.

Another form of authority involves the right to exercise control or demand obedience that is obeyed because of fear of the one holding that authority. There are examples of that in Scripture. *Jesus called them and said, You know that the princes of the gentiles exercise dominion over them, and they that are great exercise authority upon them* (Matthew 10:3 RE). He's explaining to His disciples another form of authority.

The Apostle Paul held this second kind of authority before his conversion. He said: *And many of the saints did I shut up in prison, having received authority from the chief priests; and when they were put to death, I gave my voice against them* (Acts 12:40 RE). This kind of authority is a **priestly form of authority**.

Priests deal with rites, ordinances, commandments, and procedures. This **durable** approach to preserving a belief system allows a dispensation of the gospel to continue **long after** the prophetic founder has died. Moses, for example, established a system of rites and observances that then became the religious fare of priests who perpetuated the system from the time of Moses until the coming of Jesus Christ.

Prophets deal with God and angels. They receive new insight, promises, and covenants. Their conduct can even appear to violate the tradition of the religion they follow, but that is only because they are not bound to the **tradition** as practiced by the priests. Instead, they have penetrated into the underlying meaning the original power—the **purpose** of the rites. They express the **original view from heaven** that motivated the founding prophet.

The *prophetic* form is rarely present, even among the people of God. It comes to restore and refresh, to call to repentance, and to move God's work along. The *priestly* operates for centuries trying to perpetuate the founding prophet's restoration, but once the religion falls exclusively into the hands of the priests, traditions always creep in that stray from the original and keep **forms** intact without maintaining the spiritual substance.

It's been the history of God's people that those who are raised at a time of only the *priestly* form will **always** assume they are guided by God's messengers holding God's authority, and therefore, the *prophetic* is alien to their thinking. This is the condition Nephi foretold would happen after the Book of Mormon came forth.

They shall teach with their learning, and deny the holy ghost which giveth utterance. And they deny the power of God, the Holy One of Israel. And they say unto the people, Hearken unto us and hear ye our precept, for behold, there is no God today, for the Lord and the Redeemer hath done his work, and he hath given his power unto men. Behold, hearken ye unto my precept. (2 Nephi 12:1 RE)

Nephi teaches: Believers in our day will eventually choose the *priestly* over the *prophetic.* But Nephi counsels us to, instead, always choose the *prophetic* over the *priestly.* People accept priestly authority over the prophetic word of God because of false traditions. Those who arrive late at the scene—in the generation after God's voice has become quiet —then start traditions to explain away that silence. Generations that follow them do not even **notice** "there is no God today" **because** "he hath given his power unto men."

In the present circumstances of the Restoration, when the priestly authorities speak, **all** of the Restoration traditions (from the LDS to the FLDS) claim that **is** the voice of God. The tradition of priestly authority in Christ's day justified the guard in striking Jesus.

*The high priest then asked Jesus of his disciples and of his doctrine. Jesus answered him, I spoke openly to the world. I ever taught in the synagogue and in the temple where the Jews always assemble, and in secret have I said nothing. Why do you ask **me**? Ask **them** who heard me what I have said unto them. Behold, they know what I [have] said. And when he had thus spoken, [behold,] one of the officers who stood by struck Jesus with the palm of his hand, saying, **Do you answer the high priest so?** Jesus answered him, If I have spoken evil, bear witness of…evil, but if well, [then] why do you smite me?* (John 10:4 RE, emphasis added)

The officer was so subject to the priestly tradition that he was only able to conceive of the high priest as God's representative. It made him blind to the Son of God because he could not imagine something greater than the established and trusted priestly tradition.

It was that same priestly tradition that made Ananias think he had the **right** to have the Apostle Paul struck on the mouth for testifying of Christ. Ananias, no doubt, thought of himself as the authorized and empowered priest who spoke for God. Culturally, and according to their traditions, Ananias was correct.

> *On the next day, because he desired to have known with certainty why he was accused of the Jews, he commanded the chief priests and all their council to appear, and brought Paul down and set him before them. And Paul, earnestly beholding the council, said, Men and brethren, I have lived in all good conscience before God until this day. And the high priest Ananias commanded them that stood by...to smite him on the mouth. Then said Paul unto him, God shall smite* **you**, *you whitewashed wall, for do you sit to judge me after the law, and command that I be smitten contrary to the law? And they that stood by [him],* **Do you revile God's high priest?** (Acts 12:20 RE, emphasis added)

Ananias was defending his **role** and his **office**. He was the anointed high priest and, therefore, believed he deserved, even required, respect. He believed that if you disrespect the high priest of God, then you likewise disrespect God. The officers who received this command likewise thought everything was as it should be—Paul had no right to disrupt the priestly tradition. But the priestly tradition must always give way to the prophetic. The priestly tradition has **no right** to judge the prophetic, but the prophetic has **every right**, and invariably the **duty**, to judge the priestly.

Then there is the concept of "keys." The best way to conceive of a "key" is as knowledge or understanding; it means something that unlocks the hidden truths you did not previously comprehend. A new, true concept that acts like a catalyst to solidify an idea that eluded you is a "key." When the term "eternal punishment" was defined as God's punishment (because God is eternal, and punishment for Him is "eternal punishment"), we had a new key given to us.

Prophets hold keys because they unlock understanding:

- *And this greater Priesthood administers the gospel and holds the key of the mysteries of the kingdom, even the key of the knowledge of God* (T&C 82:12).

- *This, therefore, is the sealing and binding power, and in one sense of the word the keys of the Kingdom, which consists in the key of knowledge* (T&C 151:12).

- And then we have in Proverbs: *It is the glory of God to conceal a thing, but the honor of kings to search out a matter* (Proverbs 4:1 RE).

It's an important thought. We'll return to that when we get to the Kingdom of God.

Joseph Smith taught, "Salvation cannot come without revelation; it is in vain for anyone to minister without it" (*Teachings of the Prophet Joseph Smith [TPJS]*, p.160). Joseph taught, "Where there is a prophet, a priest, or a righteous man unto whom God gives his oracles; there is the kingdom of God and where the oracles of God are not, there the kingdom of God is not" (*TPJS*, p. 272). Joseph Smith could ask and get an answer from God. Because of this, he held the keys of the kingdom—**because God presided**. God is the King of His Kingdom. When His voice is silent, you have **no kingdom** because **the King is not speaking**. When we cannot have an answer from God, there is no Kingdom of God—because the King's voice is silent.

A key concept is one that solves the riddle, answers the question, or clears up the controversy. A key removes ignorance. When God explains something to improve man's understanding, He provides us keys or knowledge.

The Book of Mormon is filled with keys, including giving us answers to:

- Who (at least one of) the other sheep were that Christ mentioned to His disciples in Jerusalem. When you explore that topic and you go into the closing comments of Nephi, you find a bit more about the other sheep because they've been divided, they've kept records, and they will be visited. When you go to the allegory in Jacob chapter 5 [LE; see also Jacob 3 RE], you learn yet more about the other sheep and how the vineyard has been populated with His sheep worldwide.

- One of the other keys of the Book of Mormon is what Christ did following His ascension into heaven. That same Jesus, two angels standing by, "that same Jesus whom you saw ascend unto heaven, shall in likewise return" (see Acts 1:3 RE). Well, He did that; He's gonna do it in glory to judge the world in the future, but He did that again in order to visit with the Nephites—because the description of the ascension to the Nephites in Third Nephi mirrors the description of the ascension in the book of Acts. It's symmetrical.

- Book of Mormon has keys to tell us what happened to other Israelites who were led away from Jerusalem.

- It explains and defines what it means to be redeemed from the fall.

- It explains and clarifies—in a way that the entire Christian and Jewish world could never understand—how pre-Babylonian Judaism really was practiced.

- It explains and clarifies that many Israelites were divided from the land of Jerusalem and continued as organized bodies in scattered parts of the world.

- It explains that many prophets wrote Scriptures that we know nothing about.

- It tells us and promises that a great body of Scripture exists, which God intends to gather into one.

There are many other keys or insights that have been kept from our knowledge, and the Book of Mormon reveals **some** of them.

"Keys" and the "Kingdom of God" are necessarily linked together. Because Samuel could obtain the voice of God, Samuel held the keys of the Kingdom of God. When the people of Israel demanded a mortal king, God explained to Samuel what their request really meant.

> But the thing displeased Samuel when they said, Give us a king to judge us. And Samuel prayed unto the Lord. And the Lord said unto Samuel, Listen unto the voice of the people in all that they say

unto you; for they have not rejected you, but they have rejected me, that I should not reign over them...

Reigning is what a king does. Reigning is what God, through Samuel, was doing **for** the people of Israel. They were rejecting their Heavenly King because they wanted a mortal king in His stead.

According to all the works which they have done, since the day that I brought them up out of Egypt even unto this day, in which they have forsaken me and served other gods, so do they also unto you. Now therefore listen unto their voice. Nevertheless, yet protest solemnly unto them, and show them the manner of the king that shall reign over them...

Now, I want you to listen carefully to what Samuel does with that commission to warn the people about what happens when you displace God as the king and you put a man in the place of God. What will happen to you:

*...This will be the manner of the king that shall reign over you: he will take your sons and appoint them for himself, for his chariots and to be his horsemen; and some shall run before his chariots. And he will appoint him captains over thousands and captains over fift[y], and will set them to plow his ground and to reap his harvest, and to make his instruments of war and instruments of his chariots. And he will take your daughters to be compounders, and to be cooks, and to be bakers. And he will take your fields, and your vineyards, and your oliveyards, even the best of them, and give them [un]to his servants. And he will take the tenth of your seed [out] of your vineyards, and give to his officers and to his servants. And he will take your menservants and your maidservants, and your **best young men**, and your asses, and put them to **his** work. [And] he will take the tenth of your sheep, and you shall be his servants. And you shall cry out in that day because of your king whom you shall have chosen you, and **the Lord will not hear you in that day**.* (1 Samuel 4:2-3 RE, emphasis added)

This is how the Kingdom of God is evicted from Earth. Prophets fall silent, and priests overtake the kingdom to make it **theirs**. Then, possessing the kingdom, they take a tenth of all the people earn and divert it to their captains, to their appointed authorities—and they require the young men and daughters to serve as servants in the kingdom of the supplanters.

Emma Smith, Sidney Rigdon, and William Marks all said that without Joseph Smith there was no longer a Kingdom of God on Earth.

Dispensations are founded by prophets who establish practices and forms of worship to be administered by priests. In the moment a dispensation is founded, both the prophet **and** the priest are present. Moses was a prophet and established priestly rites. Christ was a prophet (and more), and He also established priestly rites. Similarly, Joseph Smith was an authentic dispensation head who was both a prophet and established priestly rites. **We** expect to have added to the prophetic voice heard among us an additional priestly set of rites in a temple founded by God. We await commands to identify the location and to begin construction. We've been told to expect that command will come.

The reason an apostasy can be concealed from the view of the religious believers is because the presence of continuing priestly tradition conceals the absence of the prophetic tradition. Concealing the fact that the prophetic is gone happens so easily because priests focus on **authority** and move the idea of authority into the **central (even controlling)** issue for salvation.

Catholics held a monopoly for a thousand years, using the idea of keys from Saint Peter as the foundation upon which the religion was built. It was not until the Eastern Orthodox faith departed there was any choice to be made between keys. Only then could people choose between claims of keys in Rome and keys in ~~Constinople~~ [Constantinople]. It took Martin Luther to finally peel away the fraud of keys held by wicked men, independent from righteousness. His expositions on the priesthood of faith allowed a divorce between claims of priestly keys and faith in God. It took Martin Luther's revolution in thinking to spread for several hundred years to create a religious landscape where Joseph Smith and a new dispensation of the gospel could be introduced.

These things move slowly because mankind is generally imprisoned by their traditions and are incapable of seeing the difference between the *priestly* and the *prophetic*. This **blindness** becomes the **tool** through which the priestly tradition controls mankind.

- *Priestly tradition* is stable, authoritarian, controlling; focused on outward conduct; amasses wealth, power, and prestige. Priestly tradition can continue in the absence of spirit, revelation, or even godliness. Priestly tradition can become the friend of government, business, and empires and can work hand in hand with the powers of this world.

- *Prophetic tradition* is unruly, unpredictable, and challenges the god of this world. It **cannot work** with the powers of this world but **strikes** at its authority. It cannot exist without the direct involvement of God and angels, and it cannot be divorced from continuing revelation.

You can have *both* traditions without an apostasy. You can have the *prophetic* without an apostasy. You can even have a *priestly* tradition without an apostasy, but that is **much less likely**. In any complete apostasy, the presence of the priestly tradition is **essential** to be able to accomplish the **trick** of an unacknowledged apostasy. The trick to successfully substituting apostasy for the Kingdom of God is to distract people into thinking there hasn't been any change. The believers need to think everything remains intact. Apostate priests always claim there has been a perfect continuity and preservation of the keys.

So, the idea of apostasy changes in the hands of the apostates. Instead of focusing on the silence of God in absence of the prophetic, apostasy is **redefined** to require individual conformity to the group. Only **individuals** become apostate, **not the group**. This allows claims of apostasy to be discussed under the watchful eye of the priests without anyone ever searching into the overall condition of a **fallen people**.

The Jews mocked efforts to tell them they were apostate. They thought it was humorous when Lehi preached the idea—because they were so very religious, so devout, so unassailably active in following God. The idea was absolutely laughable that **they** were apostate.

The Apostle Paul said the problem would begin at the top with the shepherds who would teach them falsehoods as truth. *For I know this: that after my departing shall grievous wolves enter in among you, not sparing the flock. Also, of your own selves shall men arise, speaking perverse things to draw away disciples after them* (Acts 12:4 RE). These new leaders would have only a form of godliness without any real power to save.

Paul wrote:

> *This know also: that in the last days, perilous times shall come; for men shall be lovers of their own selves, covetous...*

—covetous of their authority, covetous of their status, covetous of their rank, covetous of the priestHOOD and of their priestly position—

> *...boasters, proud, blasphemers...*

It's blasphemy to attribute to God what **God did not authorize**. It's not merely bearing false witness, it's also blasphemy. You hear blasphemy from the religious leaders who, speaking and pretending to act in the name of God, have no authority or permission from Him to do as they claim.

> *...unthankful, unholy, without natural affection, trucebreakers, false accusers, without self-control, fierce, despisers of those that are good, traitors, headstrong, haughty, lovers of pleasures more than lovers of God, having a form of godliness but denying the power thereof.* (2 Timothy 1:8 RE)

The Christian world adopted another false replacement of the original church. It became so universal it was hailed as the Universal (or Catholic) Church. It "rule[d] from the rivers to the ends of the Earth" as the only official form of the faith established by Christ. To accomplish this, Satan was concerned with the macro-institutional failure, not just individuals falling away. That's always **his objective**! If the religion becomes corrupt, then devotion **for even the best of people** is meaningless. They cannot achieve salvation because the Kingdom of God has departed.

Satan is involved in **strategic** defeat of mankind. The small tactical battles between people is the concern of lesser fallen spirits. It's the small, minor spirits who follow Lucifer who tempt individuals to commit sin. Success for the adversary is not accomplished in petty enterprises. He wants "failure for the whole" so **none** can be saved. For that, **apostasy must be universal.** He has never succeeded by admitting there has been a failure—the trick is always to have the apostasy come unnoticed, unacknowledged, and from within.

Christ quoted the Father as He foretold what would happen:

> At that day when the gentiles shall sin against my gospel, and shall reject the fullness of my gospel, and shall be lifted up in the pride of their hearts above all nations and above all the people of the whole earth, and shall be filled with all manner of lyings, and of deceits, and of mischiefs, and all manner of hypocrisy, and murders, and priestcrafts, and whoredoms, and of secret abominations, and if they shall do all these things, and shall reject the fullness of my gospel, Behold, saith the Father, I will bring the fullness of my gospel from among them. (3 Nephi 7:5 RE)

Apostasy must first be noticed, acknowledged, and exposed before it is possible to repent and return. Until then, it progresses a-pace, discarding and rejecting what might have been given, all the while being happily ignored by the believers whose devotion will not save. The enemy succeeds when he manages to get us **not** to **reject** ordinances but to **change** them. As soon as they are changed, they are broken.

> The earth also is defiled under the inhabitants thereof, because they have transgressed the laws, changed the ordinance, broken the everlasting covenant. (Isaiah 7:1 RE)

> And the day comes that they who will not hear the voice of the Lord, neither his servants, neither give heed to the words of the prophets and apostles, shall be cut off from among the people, for they have strayed from [mine] ordinances and have broken my everlasting covenant. They seek not the Lord to establish his righteousness, but every man walks in his own way and after the image of his own god, whose image is in the likeness of the world,

*and whose substance is that of an idol which waxes old and shall
perish....* (T&C 54:3)

Those two statements about changing the ordinances and breaking the
covenant are: first, a quote from Isaiah who prophesied about it
happening; and second, a revelation through the Prophet Joseph Smith
saying it **was** happening.

Changing the ordinances has always been an important step because
then even people who believe there was a restoration through Joseph
Smith can continue to claim they follow a true religion, while
practicing one that has been broken. These practitioners become like
the ancient Jews who mocked Lehi because they knew they were still
righteous; they knew Lehi was foolish, even fraudulent. They still had
the truth, the ordinances, the temple, and the priesthood. Lehi was
thought to be merely a mistaken crank.

The Kingdom of God is with **us**, and for the present, we are still left
among people who have not awakened to their awful situation. We
should warn them and seek to recover as many as will listen. If you're
awakened, warn your neighbor. We have a work to do among others
before the Lord will have us depart from people He still loves and
hopes to save.

I've seen and read of prayers and fasting by those among us who want a
temple. Why do you think the Lord hesitates in giving the command?
When He answers and says for us to remain and labor among other
people He hopes to save, do you think we can neglect that obligation
and still hasten His command to build a temple? I leave it to you to
answer those questions.

Now, I want to clarify a point, because Joseph Smith actually knew
what he was doing and—had he been around long enough—would
have accomplished a work that was still at its very incipient stage at the
time that he was slain. In the Council of Fifty, which he called the
Kingdom of God (which was nondenominational because members of
other religious beliefs were invited into the Kingdom of God)...

The Kingdom of God was not the Church. The Church was simply a
mechanism for promulgating the gospel, disseminating the Book of

Mormon, and accomplishing a certain work. But the Kingdom of God was something different.

Inside that Kingdom of God, Joseph Smith had himself anointed a king (and Emma, a queen). Hold that thought for one moment, because there's a statement made in Second Nephi. These things need to be understood.

> But behold, this land, saith God, shall be a land of thine inheritance, and the gentiles shall be blessed upon the land. And this land shall be a land of liberty unto the gentiles, and there shall be no kings upon the land who shall [rise] up unto the gentiles, and I will fortify this land against all other nations. And he that fighteth against Zion shall perish, saith God, for he that raiseth up a king against me shall perish. For I the Lord, the King of Heaven, will be their king, and I will be a light unto them for ever that hear my words. (2 Nephi 7:2 RE)

Joseph Smith knew exactly what he was doing. He intended to be a king, **subordinate to** the King of Heaven. He intended to create **other** kings, subordinate to **him, all of them** subordinate to God—because the God of this land and the King that will rule over this land is Christ. "He that raiseth up a king **against me** shall perish." Joseph Smith was not seeking to establish a kingdom **against** God. He was seeking to establish a kingdom **subordinate to** and **obedient to** the overall King of Heaven—as a subordinate to Him. Joseph Smith intended to establish the Kingdom of God and to be a king because that is what the Kingdom of God consists of.

Look, I read it just a moment ago. *It is the glory of God to conceal a thing, but the honor of **kings** to search out a matter* (Proverbs 4:1 RE). Joseph Smith was **always** searching out and revealing new things to the people. It was his **honor** as the **king** to do that: "…the glory of God to conceal a thing but the honor of kings to search out a matter"—and who is the **king** that allowed the earthly man to search the matter out? It is the King of Heaven; it is Christ. The one who conceals is also the one that can reveal. Joseph Smith was fitting the pattern.

And then, this last thought, and we'll end, and you can socialize or fight among yourselves or…or she and I can go argue in the hallway about something.

Joseph Smith wrote a letter that was never canonized (an excerpt from it—altered in **its** form even—got published in the LDS canon of Scriptures), but the entire letter that he wrote is now in the Teachings and Commandments, section 146. And there's a statement that gets made that I want to make sure, as part of this talk, I clarify or give a key (yeah, there's one), so you can comprehend **this** thing.

The standard of truth has been erected. The "standard of truth" is the Book of Mormon. It's been erected because it's been put into print. It's been in print, albeit in an altered form, until we fixed that with the latest set of Scriptures; it goes back to manuscripts and tries to fix as much of that as possible. Nevertheless:

> *The standard of truth* [that is, the Book of Mormon] *has been erected. No unhallowed hand can stop the work from progressing: persecutions may rage, mobs may combine, armies may assemble, calumny may defame, but the truth of God will go forth boldly, nobly, and independent, till it has penetrated every continent, visited every clime, swept every country, and sounded in every ear, till the purposes of God shall [have been] accomplished and the great Jehovah shall say, The work is done.* (T&C 146:20)

This prophecy is not about an institution. This prophecy is about the "standard of truth" going forward. And while the "standard of truth" has gone forward primarily in the hands of missionaries belonging to The Church of Jesus Christ of Latter-day Saints (to whom credit should be given for all of that good work), it is going to go forth **independent**, meaning no one is going to own and control and have the institutional right to profit from the "standard of truth" going forward. It will sweep the Earth, and right now, one of the biggest challenges of getting the Book of Mormon to be taken seriously by people is the apparent coupling of the Book of Mormon **to** The Church of Jesus Christ of Latter-day Saints. There are people out there who have great offense, umbrage, and opposition to the LDS Church who, for that reason alone, will not consider reading the Book of

Mormon. But it is another testament, and it was always intended that it go forth **independent** of everything else.

I've spent a great deal of time and effort, including just within the last few months, traveling around the country, attending conferences in Tennessee with evangelicals, speaking to a group in Montgomery, Alabama that included Catholics and Baptists and others, attempting to get them to take seriously the Book of Mormon as an authentic Christian message, separate and apart from any institution. I would hope Presbyterians and Lutherans… I would hope that people that belong to the Church of England would all be willing to look at the Book of Mormon and see what it adds to their Christian faith. I've said before and I'll repeat it again: We can baptize anyone who is willing to accept the doctrine of Christ. You don't have to swear allegiance to the Southern Baptist Convention in order to be saved. You don't have to pledge allegiance to the Pope or kneel to the president of any of the various Restoration groups.

Accept the doctrine of Christ. There are those who, free of charge, will baptize you. They expect nothing from you. They intend to sacrifice their time, their means, and their effort in order to perform the ordinance. No one is profiting. None of you who are practicing the faith in the form that it is presently being practiced should profit from that. We gather tithes, and we use that tithe to help those among us who need assistance—and there are presently some people among us who **need** assistance. And the glory of God is manifest in their life by the outpouring of your generosity. You're going to help them. You're giving of funds to help them defray their indebtedness, answering their medical needs. **Those** are the kinds of things that knit hearts together. **That's** what the religion was intended to accomplish. It was not intended to buy the minister a house or to pay to fly a church official with his bodyguards in first-class to Europe to attend area conferences. It was not intended to build ornate marble floors and statuary, in order to prop up the claim of priests who know not God.

Well, I've enjoyed everything that I've seen and heard in this conference. There was a mom who had a little baby a couple rows in front of us during the opening prayer, and the baby, during the prayer, lost all patience with the length of our opening prayer and began to offer a petition of her own. And I really enjoyed that! And to my dismay, mom got up and took the child out. I was trying to figure out what the child was praying for 'cuz I was thinking, "I might want some of that too, if I could…." Babies don't have words yet; they have noises. And a lot of time the noise sounds like a cry when, in fact, they could be communicating phenomenal things to us, their tongues not being loosed for our sake because if we heard what they had to say…

Perhaps they're announcing the judgment of angels upon our poor assembly. Perhaps they're celebrating in what way they can. I love it when the kids are around, and that noise, to me, is a delight, not an irritant.

Let me end by bearing testimony to you that all of the good things that you do, all of the faith that you have, all of the labors that you do for Christ's sake, in seeking after Him with a pure and unworldly "unprofitable in this world" motivation, all of that cleanses your soul and brings you closer to Heaven. You want to know how to get angels to pay attention to you? Sacrifice for the benefit of others.

In the name of Jesus Christ, Amen.

Man: Denver, can you take some questions?

Denver: I'll take one question. It's gotta be a good one. Does anyone got a good question? Yeah, oh, okay…

Man: So, you mentioned one thing. So, one thing that's been on my mind is, as a group, what lack we yet? You've got to admit, you've been kind of pessimistic about our prospects for Zion. And you mentioned one thing during this talk and that was about opening our mouth to those who the Lord loves. Anything else you want to say?

Denver: Yeah, I want to…

Man: Can you justify your pessimism?

Denver: Yeah, okay. So, the question was premised on my pessimism that I've expressed before, and I want to challenge the premise because I thought something happened over at the conference in Grand Junction—last conference we had—that was… There was a real different look and feel to what went on over there. And to me, it was like we had turned a corner.

We have been a really rancorous group of people who are strongly opinionated. It's like we're refugees from an abusive experience in a hierarchical religion that, as soon as we are set at liberty, everyone wants to pick at the slightest hint that you're aspiring to be the next Relief Society president or the next bishop or—just all of that. There's a decompression, there's a "post-religious trauma syndrome" that was really evident. Everyone was walking around saying, more or less, "I've been abused. Religion has been a source of anxiety and trouble in my life, and you're practicing religion—but by damn, you're not gonna practice your religion on me! I mean, I want to have the liberty with which Christ has made me free. I do not want to have that experience repeat itself. I want nothing of that." And that... We were wearing that, and probably every one of us were wearing that chip on all of our shoulders.

I didn't see that over at Grand Junction. I didn't see people worried about the motivations of one another. I didn't see them looking for cause to complain or cause to take offense at what someone else was saying. I thought we turned a corner, and something happened. And maybe we needed a little while to decompress. Maybe we needed a little while to—

And as other people come in, they're probably gonna walk in with exactly the same attitude that many of us had for the first several years because of our prior experience. We're just going to have to bear with that. And they need to get over that, because there's a lot of personal intrusiveness and personal abuse that goes on in the name of the Restoration. It's worse among the fundamentalist group. It's worse among the people that have come out from that tradition to say, "Let us join in here." All of them have suffered from religious abuse.

But I am not as pessimistic as I was. I really...

I was authentically down, and now I'm saying, "Ah, this may happen." In fact, at this point...

Man: But don't you think that's a minority? As I look around at the fellowships, and I don't see that clamor, and that— and I have maybe just a little...

Denver: No, but it dominated the dialogue; the conflict dominated the dialogue. And that's one of the tools that get used. You can have ten good people, and if you have two of them (or two others, so there's a total of 12), if two of the 12 are willing to be rancorous and complaining and upsetting, that spirit will invade the other ten. The problem is not just aggregating good people, the problem is also knowing how to not take offense from the people that are still running around pecking on one another. We're gonna have those people, and more of that attitude will come as people say, "I can no longer uphold this tradition. I respect Joseph; I respect the Restoration; I accept the Book of Mormon; I believe that God intends to bring back Zion—I believe all those things." But they come among us with this trauma, and they need a while to decompress. We're still gonna have that. What we need to do is to become adult enough to do the kinds of things that Jennifer Willis and my wife were talking about earlier today—about not taking those offenses—and letting them vent. Maybe what they're talking about is absolutely therapeutic and healthy for them, and they need to vent. Just don't join in; just don't encourage it. Let 'em know you understand. Put an arm around them and say, "I've been there," and then move on. "Hey, let's go help weed a garden."

There was an occasion when a son and I (he was a teenager, at the time) were really at odds—I mean, a pretty sharp conflict—and he and I about came to blows with one another. And I didn't like the way that left, and I didn't like the way that unfolded. So, the next day, I got him up early (it was on a weekend), and he and I went out and worked in the yard. There was a project that needed to be doing, and we did the project together. It involved shovels and a lot of hard work. And both of us, for about, I don't know, a couple of hours, we dug like angry men. After two hours of digging and taking it out on the project that needed to be done, we didn't have the energy left to fight anymore. It... We... "You thirsty? You wanna run down to McDonald's and get something?" And it was over; the conflict was over because the backyard took the anger, and we got over it.

People act rationally; people don't vent without a cause. For the most part, when it comes to religious anxieties, what motivates them can be very deep, can be very troubled, can be very sincere. And if you extend empathy and sympathy and hear 'em out, you may find that underlying all of that is not aggression, underlying all of that is a broken heart and disappointment with what their fellow man has done.

I mean, one of the things that Christ—in the Sermon on the Mount—tells people to do is to bless those that curse you. Every one of us have seen the religious phony, the hypocrite, the pretentious religious character who comes along, portraying themself as something that they're really not. The reason Christ in the Sermon on the Mount says to bless the people that are despitefully using you or abusing you and to do good that treat you evil for His namesake is because they're doing that to you, initially, because they think you're one of those hypocrites. They think you're one of those false religionists. They believe you, too, are nothing more than the last guy who abused someone on the mission, who took advantage of their position of authority, who exploited (maybe in a way that was felonious, and they ought to be in jail) victims—and they're angry about that, and they're taking it out on you. But if you really are a disciple of Christ, you will turn the other cheek; you will return kindness for goodness; you will ask them, even as they crucify you, "Father, forgive them, for they know not what they do." Many times they literally do not know what they're doing. They've got in their mind a monster, and they react to that monster. And it takes a while before they begin to recognize the image of Christ in the countenance of the kindly and the forgiving. You have to be the kindly and the forgiving. And there are a lot... In fact, the whole theme of this conference is devoted to that very issue.

How do we get along better with one another? Start assuming that underlying much of the anger and hostility and friction is a broken heart and a legitimate reason for their anger and their fear and their troubled heart. And soothe that troubled heart.

That is a good question. Thank you.

The Book of Mormon Holds the Covenant Pattern for the Full Restoration

A Lecture delivered at the "Keeping the Covenant" Conference
Caldwell, Idaho
September 22, 2019

That was lovely. I contrast that with Bart Simpson sneaking in the In-A-Gadda-Da-Vida soundtrack for the church lady to play that resulted in near collapse.

I want to thank the organizers that have put this conference together and have spent the time and the effort and the resources to make all of this available. Unlike other groups of believers that associate together, we don't own any buildings; we don't have any facilities; no one gets paid to do any of the things that have to be done in order to put together a conference. And so, what we see and what we experience when we come to one of these conferences is the result of volunteer effort, volunteer sacrifices, voluntary contributions. All of the costs are borne by the folks that put a conference together. And I want to thank all those that are involved in getting this event to take place. I also want to thank the organizers for inviting me to come and speak, because those who organize a conference are entitled to ask who they will and see who they can get to voluntarily contribute.

Beginning in 2013, I spoke for a year in what's called the Mormon Corridor, giving a series of talks. I've since traveled to Los Angeles, Dallas, and Atlanta to present talks to Christians. All of that (in the talks to the Christians) were done with the aid of volunteer technical support. I've also had, with the aid of volunteer technical support, a website devoted to the Restoration, another devoted to the Christian Reformation—that website is now being turned into a site for general Christianity, with the help of volunteers. I've been able to produce, with a lot of help, a series of videos about historic Christianity, about the Reformation, and about the Restoration, also requiring a lot of voluntary technical assistance.

In just this last year:

- In January, I was in Twin Falls for a meeting with folks. I attended a South Carolina conference, and then I met with a delegation of remnant folks (I call them "remnant folks" because I don't know what else to call it—people that believe as we do) who are undertaking an effort to try and approach the Jewish remnant.

- In February, I spoke at a meeting in Syracuse and attended appointments with several people that are doing and volunteering to do work.

- In March, I gave a talk in Centerville, and later that month, I flew to Houston and met with a group of people in a fellowship there.

- In April, I spoke at a fireside in Independence, Missouri during the World Conference of the Community of Christ. The Community of Christ World Conference only occurs every four years, and I went back during their World Conference and spoke to a number of those that were interested in hearing something. Then I attended a conference and spoke in Colorado, and later that month, I flew out to Tennessee and attended a three-day conference in Tennessee involving Evangelicals.

- In May, I met with (and spoke with) a group, and then I traveled to Alabama to speak with a group of Christian folks about Christianity and about the Restoration.

- In June, there was a Restoration conference held in Boise, Idaho that brought together various factions that believe in the mission of Joseph Smith but have divided into separate groups, and I spoke at that Restoration conference. I also attended meetings with small groups in Utah during that month.

- In July, I spoke at a conference in Sandy, Utah that had been organized.

- Last month, in August, I went to Sandpoint, Idaho, and I visited with Rock and Connie Waterman. (Rock intends to write again, particularly after his work slows down this winter, and he wanted me to give his regards to all of you.)

- And I'm attending this conference this month.

- Next month there is a… Shawn McCraney (I think) is a former Mormon. He's doing a podcast called *Heart of the Matter* that I've agreed, at Rock Waterman's urging, to go ahead and participate in.

There are those who are working directly to try and reach a hand out to invite and present information to the remnant of the Lamanite/Nephite group, and there are those that are working on trying to complete several projects that will attempt to introduce the Restoration to Jewish communities and in Israel itself.

I'm doing what I can. All of that travel comes at a sacrifice. No one pays me to go anywhere or do anything; no one reimburses me for the cost of doing so, and very often, in order to be able to have the venue available, others have to contribute as well, in order to sacrifice their means to advance what's going on.

An issue was recently raised about how one harmonizes when they are contributing: contributing to a temple fund or contributing to those who may be in need? And I thought that was a good point to start with because I assume since the issue came up that it's an issue for more than one person.

In the Scriptures, we have little to guide us about conflicts, but we have lots to inform us about the issues that then leave it our responsibility to resolve the conflict.

There was an incident that occurred **just before** the Savior went in on the triumphant entry into Jerusalem, where he was greeted with people shouting, "Hosanna, Hosanna," spreading out their cloaks or palm branches for Him to ride in upon the colt/the foal. That incident is covered in these words:

> *Then took Mary a pound of ointment of spikenard, very costly, and anointed the feet of Jesus, and wiped his feet with her hair; and the house was filled with the odor of the ointment. Then says one of his disciples (Judas Iscariot, Simon's son who should betray him), Why was not this ointment sold for three hundred pence and given to the poor? This he said, not that he cared for the poor, but because he*

*was a thief, and had the money bag, and stole from what was put
therein. Then said Jesus, Let her alone, for she has preserved this
ointment until now, that she might anoint me in token of my
burial. For the poor always you have with you, but me you have
not always.* (John 7:9 RE)

So, here is an incident in which something in the form of an ordinance
that is necessary to prepare the Savior for His burial (about which the
Scriptures don't say enough) is taken care of at an **extraordinary**
expense. It was an **extravagance** to perform the ordinance, and the
Savior, in response to the criticism about the apparent financial waste,
says, "Don't criticize her; this has been kept in place and prepared until
now *that she might anoint me in token of my burial.*" She and He both
knew that this needed to be attended to, and it was; and it was essential
and extravagant. When the issue of "What about the poor?" comes up,
the Savior I don't think was being dismissive; I think He was being
rather lamenting about the condition. "The poor always you have with
you, but me you have not always." The time for taking care of what
needed to be taken care of had a limited opportunity associated with it,
and if it were not performed within that limited opportunity, then the
time would come and the time would go, and the event would not
have occurred.

It's very often the case with assignments or opportunities that are
presented to mankind that the opportunity is extended and the time
has to be taken advantage of, but if not, then the opportunity comes,
and the opportunity goes. And in this case, the principle that I would
say relates to what we are concerned with and the question that was
asked to me is that when we're given an opportunity, even though it
may seem extravagant, if we don't take or avail ourselves of that
opportunity, it will come, and it will go, and that will be that.

But you have to juxtapose that issue about the propriety of sacred
things (even when they involve cost) being attended to, on the one
hand, with another event involving the Savior, in which He told, in
response to the query, "Who's my neighbor?" this account:

*A certain man went down from Jerusalem to Jericho, and fell
among thieves who stripped him of his raiment, and wounded
him, and departed, leaving him half dead. And by chance, there*

came down a certain priest that way, and when he saw him, he passed by on the other side of the way. And likewise a Levite, when he was at the place, came and looked upon him, and passed…on the other side of the way — for they desired in their hearts that it might not be known that they had seen him. But a certain Samaritan, as he journeyed, came where he was. And when he saw him, he had compassion on him, and went to him and bound up his wounds, pouring in oil and wine, and set him on his own beast, and brought him to an inn, and took care of him. And on the next day, when he departed, he took money and gave to the host, and said unto him, Take care of him, and whatever you spend more, when I come again, I will repay you. Who now of these three do you think was neighbor unto him who fell among the thieves? [And the person who had posed the question to the Savior responded] *…He who showed mercy on him. Then said Jesus unto him, Go and do likewise.* (Luke 8:8 RE)

Those words, "go and do likewise," echo down through the corridors of time into our own ears and remind us of the obligation not only to be neighborly to each other but to be neighborly to all mankind. See, when he was on the road from Jerusalem to Jericho and fell among thieves, that was not his fault. It was a well-traveled road and should have been safe. (It's two places at which sacred events had and **would** take place.) He was on familiar, even sacred, terrain, and he fell into misfortune through no fault of his own; others came and perpetrated it. So, what I take from that (as a principle for us) is that we ought not be judging those who fall into bad circumstances, nor should we be hesitant about putting them on our own beast to be transported, paying the innkeeper, binding up the wounds, doing everything we can —**not** to say, "How might I conserve resources in the process of giving aid?"

Everything you do for the benefit of another, as a neighbor, is a good thing. Don't question whether or not your contribution to help someone else is extravagant or could be better used (…or you could find a cheaper house to rent in which to house the injured man or, perhaps, a less demanding innkeeper to pay). Don't… Your contribution is good. It's right. And your assistance helps those in need.

When you give, give with gratitude, and then take no more thought about it. And if you choose to donate to the temple, take no more thought about it. Don't go about always doubting and second-guessing. No matter how you reconcile the conflict between the principle that "supporting and providing the means for ordinance work to take place is extravagant" or "there's a way to help and give less"—how you divide up the resources and how you contribute, you decide how you resolve the conflict. Do what you think best, and don't question yourself after you've done that. Be at peace. Christ's example covers **both**, and there are conflicts—**deliberately**. The gospel is full of dilemmas that require us to act and to choose and to resolve limited means, limited time, limited strength, limited resources, and how you apportion them. But when you make the choice and you do the apportionment, be at peace.

I mention the temple funds, and I can give you the following information because I met with the people involved this last week. Not one cent of the temple funds have been spent, nor are there, at present, any plans to spend any of the funds until we have some direction from the Lord.

Every name and every amount that is contributed is being maintained. There are those who contribute… A handful of people have contributed in very small amounts who have chosen to remain anonymous. We know the date of the contribution, we know the amount of the contribution, but we don't know the name for that. But for almost all the funds that have been contributed, the person who made the contribution is known. When the temple is completed, a complete accounting will be available for anyone to review. However, most of those who have donated, to this point, wish to remain anonymous; therefore, the accounting will only show the names of those who consent to having their names disclosed. And for the others, the donations that they made will be disclosed and the dates on which the contributions were made—but their names will be withheld. Also, all the costs associated with the building will be provided. But donors who wish to remain unnamed will have their identities withheld.

The path to Zion is so far beyond the reach of mankind that we know of only two successful times in Scripture where Heaven and Earth united in Zion. One was at the time of Enoch; the other, the city of

Melchizedek. In Eden, Heaven and Earth were united—but Eden fell. Following the visit of Christ to the Nephites, there were several hundred years of peace. But Christ's visit was temporary, and they did not reunite with Heaven as a people.

We face a challenge to become something very rare, godly, even holy. It's perplexing how people were able to lay aside all envy, strife, ambition, selfishness, and enmity between one another—yet that is exactly what **we** are asked to do.

We cannot obtain land without purchasing it. We have revelations that command us:

> *Behold, the land of Zion; I, the Lord, hold it in [mine] own hands. Nevertheless, I, the Lord, render unto Caesar the things which are Caesar's. Wherefore, I, the Lord, will that you should purchase the lands, that you may have advantage of the world, that you may have claim on the world, that they may not be stirred up unto anger. For Satan puts it into their hearts to anger against you and to the shedding of blood. Wherefore, the land of Zion shall not be obtained but by* **purchase** *or by blood; otherwise, there is no inheritance for you. And if by* **purchase**, *behold, you are blessed, and if by blood, as you are forbidden to shed blood, lo, your enemies are upon you and you shall be scourged from city to city, and from synagogue to synagogue, and but few shall stand to receive an inheritance.* (T&C 50:7, emphasis added)

The saints in Joseph Smith's day failed. The Lord, speaking of that, said:

> *Behold, I say unto you, were it not for the transgressions of my people, speaking concerning the church and not individuals, they might have been redeemed, even now. But behold, they have not learned to be obedient to the things which I require at their hands, but are full of all manner of evil, and do not impart of their substance, as becomes saints, to the poor and afflicted among them, and are not united according to the union required by the law of the Celestial Kingdom. And Zion cannot be built up unless it is by the principles of the law of the Celestial Kingdom, otherwise I cannot receive her unto myself. And my people must needs be*

chastened until they learn obedience, if it must needs be by the things which they suffer. (T&C 107:1)

This building up of Zion, according to the principles of the law of the Celestial Kingdom, does not initially involve the law of consecration. Joseph Smith ended that practice. He said, "...that the law of consecration could not be kept here and that it was the will of the Lord that we should desist from trying to keep it, and if persisted in, it would produce a perfect abortion, and that he assumed the whole responsibility of not keeping it until proposed by himself" (*History of the Church*, 4:93; cf. 105:34). And Joseph died, of course, without ever proposing again the keeping of that law, although there were subsequent attempts made which proved to be a perfect abortion.

Consecration will eventually follow, but like everything that is distant and above this fallen world, it is not a single step. It is a stepped-process and cannot be done in haste nor in a single instant. We have to grow, degree by degree, measure by measure, in order to attempt.

This is another revelation:

> *Therefore, in consequence of the transgression of my people, it is expedient in me that my elders should wait for a little season for the redemption of Zion that they themselves may be prepared, and that my people may be taught more perfectly, and have experience, and* **know** *more perfectly concerning their* **duty** *and the things which I require at their hands. And this cannot be brought to pass until my elders are endowed with power from on high, for behold, I have prepared a great endowment and [the] blessing to be poured out upon them, inasmuch as they are faithful and continue in humility before me. Therefore, it is expedient in me that my elders should wait a little season for the redemption of Zion.* (T&C 107:3, emphasis added)

It is clear, at least to me, that the temple is where the Lord intends for people to be taught more perfectly and have experience and know more perfectly concerning their duty and the things which He requires at our hands. He calls that an endowment with power. Knowledge is power, but to qualify to receive that endowment, we're required to be like Abraham, who described himself in these words:

Having been myself a follower of righteousness, desiring also to be one who possessed great knowledge, and to be a greater follower of righteousness, and to possess a greater knowledge...

All of those things go together. These are not disconnected thoughts. They are also not thoughts that are unrelated to "returning knowledge and understanding that reaches back into the creation itself, and before the creation," and then goes forward to the end of this cycle of creation. So, he desired to possess:

...great knowledge...to be a greater follower of righteousness, and to possess a greater knowledge...

Those things go together.

...to be a Father of many nations...

He was situated at a time where that was **necessarily** one of the things that followed from obtaining what he sought after.

...a prince of peace, and desiring to **receive instructions** *and to keep the commandments of God...*

We tend to think that instructions and commandments from God can be burdensome. Abraham viewed it as an opportunity to gain greater knowledge, greater understanding, and therefore, with a better perspective and understanding of what God expected of us, to be a greater follower of righteousness, to fit into a pattern.

...I became a rightful heir, a high priest, holding the right belonging to the Fathers. It was conferred upon me from the fathers: it came down from the fathers, from the beginning of time, yea, even from the beginning (or before the foundations of the earth) to the present time, even the right of the firstborn (or the first man — who is Adam — or [the] first Father) through the Fathers unto me. (Abraham 1:1 RE)

This is what God has in mind for the Restoration to be completed. This is what God intended for us to inherit as our endowment, as our greater knowledge, and enabling us to be greater followers of righteousness.

Now, for purposes of the discussion today, I want to redefine the term "Mormon." I thought it was gonna be an orphaned term, but apparently, that has proven to be very problematic for another institution. But today, I want to redefine the term "Mormon" for purposes of my comments to mean "those who accept the Book of Mormon as a covenant," so that they become those who are Mormons, of which I speak.

There's… In this restoration process, there's an obligation we have to reach out to Lamanites and to the remnant of the Jews and to seek to recover and reclaim them. We do not need to turn ourselves into Jews, nor do we need to turn Jews away from the things that they prize in order to have them accept the Restoration. But **everyone** needs to understand what the **objective** of the Restoration is, because it's going to reach back into something that is altogether earlier and more complete than anything presently in the possession of Mormons or Jews or Lamanites. We need to have a greater understanding of God's covenants with **all** of Israel.

The Torah is part of the Old Covenants. It is important for us to preserve and to understand the Torah. It testifies throughout of Christ. Studying the Torah has value, but that is not the objective of the Restoration. A religion much older is to be restored. The gospel, as it was taught to and understood by Adam and the Patriarchs (or the fathers that Malachi refers to), is the gospel that God wants and we seek to have restored. Turning the hearts of the children to the Fathers is turning the hearts to the faith that they believed and practiced.

Joseph Smith taught this:

> *Jehovah…continued to [Noah] the keys, the covenants, the power, and the glory with which he blessed **Adam** at the beginning, and the offering of sacrifice which also shall be continued at the last time.*

> *For all the ordinances and duties that ever have been required [of] the Priesthood under the directions and commandments of the Almighty, in any of the dispensations, shall all be had in the last [dispensation]. Therefore, all things had under the authority of the Priesthood at any former period shall be had again, bringing to*

pass the restoration spoken of by the mouth of all the holy prophets, then shall the sons of Levi offer an acceptable [offering] to the Lord. And he shall sit as a refiner and purifier of silver; and he shall purify the sons of Levi, and purge them as gold and silver, that they may offer unto the Lord…

It will be necessary here to make a few observations on the doctrine set forth in the above quotation, [and] it is generally supposed that [the] sacrifice was entirely done away when the great sacrifice [that is, the sacrifice of the Lord Jesus] was offered up, and that there will be no necessity for the ordinance of sacrifice in [the] future, but those who assert this are certainly not acquainted with the duties, privileges, and authority of the Priesthood or with the prophets…

These sacrifices, as well as every ordinance belonging to the Priesthood will, when the temple of the Lord shall be built and the sons of Levi be purified, be fully restored and attended to: [in] all their powers, ramifications, and blessings. This ever did and [ever] will exist when the powers of the Melchizedek Priesthood are sufficiently manifest. Else, how can the restitution of all things spoken of by…the holy prophets be brought to pass?

It is not to be understood that the Law of Moses *will be established again, with all its rites and variety of ceremonies. This has **never been spoken** of by the prophets, **but** those things which existed prior to Moses' day, namely sacrifice, **will** be continued.* (T&C 140:16-18,20-21, emphasis added; see also *History of the Church* 4:211-212)

The Old Covenants <u>now</u> explain how the law given through Moses was an altered and lesser law intended to **prevent those under it from entering into God's presence**.

*Hew [thee] two other tablets of [stone], like unto the first… But it shall not be according to the first, for I will take away the Priesthood out of their midst. Therefore, my Holy Order and the ordinances thereof shall not go before them… But I will give unto them the law as at…first; but it shall be after the law of a carnal commandment, for I have sworn in my wrath that **they shall not enter into my presence**, into my rest, in the days of their* *pilgrimage.* (Exodus 18:5 RE, emphasis added; compare Exodus 34:1-3 LE)

The Book of Mormon clarifies that the Law of Moses was both temporary, incomplete, and intended to come to an end. Abinadi declared:

> *And now ye have said that salvation cometh by the law of Moses. I say unto you that it is expedient that ye should keep the law of Moses as yet; but I say unto you that the time shall come when it shall no more be expedient to keep the law of Moses. And moreover, I say unto you that **salvation doth not come** by the law alone; and were it not for the atonement which God himself shall make for the sins and [the] iniquities of his people, that they must unavoidably perish, **notwithstanding** the law of Moses. And now I say unto you that it was expedient that there should be a law given [unto] the children of Israel, yea, even a very strict law. For they were a stiffnecked people, quick to do iniquity and slow to remember the Lord their God. Therefore there was a law given them, yea, a law of performances and of ordinances, a law which they were to observe strictly from day to day, to keep them in remembrance of God and their duty towards him.* (Mosiah 8:1 RE, emphasis added)

Paul explains essentially the same thing to the Galatians in his letter to them:

> *Now to Abraham and his seed were the promises made. He says not, And to [the] seeds (as of many), but as of one: And to **your** seed — who is **Christ**. And this I say, that the covenant that was confirmed before God in **Christ**, the law (which was four hundred thirty years **after**) cannot disannul, that it should make the promise of no effect. For if the inheritance is of the law, then no more of promise; but **God gave it to Abraham** by promise.*
>
> *Wherefore...**the law** was added because of transgressions, until the seed should come to whom the promise was made in the law given to Moses, who was ordained by the hand of angels to be a mediator of this first covenant (the law). Now this mediator was not a mediator of the **new covenant,** but there is one mediator of the*

*new covenant, who is Christ, as it is written in the law concerning the promises made to **Abraham and his seed**. Now Christ is the mediator of life, for this is the promise which God made unto Abraham.*

*Is the law then against the promises of God? God forbid. For if there had been a law given which could have given life, truly righteousness should have been by the law. But the scripture has consigned all under sin, that the promise by faith of Jesus Christ might be given to them that believe. But before faith came, we were kept under the law, **shut up** unto the faith which should afterwards be revealed. Wherefore, **the law was our schoolmaster** until Christ, that we might be justified by faith; but after faith has come, **we are no longer under a schoolmaster**.* (Galatians 1:9-11 RE, emphasis added)

We study the Torah to learn what the schoolmaster was instructing for generations about the Savior who would come. We don't study it to practice it (although I see no harm if someone wants to engage in that, so long as they understand the ends of the law were fulfilled in Christ and that they are no longer under the schoolmaster—or at least under **that** schoolmaster).

The Lord declared in April of 1830: *You cannot enter in at the strait gate by the law of Moses…* (Joseph Smith History 18:8 RE).

If the law of Moses were salvific, then we would still be under the obligation of following it—but we are not. We seek the Restoration of the first, original gospel, as Paul wrote also in Galatians: *And the scripture, foreseeing that God would justify the heathen through faith, preached before the gospel unto Abraham, saying, In you shall all [the] nations be blessed* (Galatians 1:7 RE).

That is the gospel **we** seek to have restored—not the one added 430 years later at the time of Moses, but the one that existed at the time that it was preached unto Abraham. Abraham explains:

But the records of the Fathers, even the Patriarchs, concerning the right of Priesthood, the Lord, my God, preserved in my own hands. Therefore, a knowledge of the beginning of the creation, and also of

> *the planets and of the stars, as they were made known unto the Fathers, have I kept even unto this day, and I shall endeavor to write some of these things upon this record for the benefit of my posterity that shall come after me.* (Abraham 2:4 RE)

This is an English version of whatever it was that Abraham wrote, and we're familiar with the word "planets" in the present meaning of that sense. But the original word that got used (that is translated now as the word "planets") was a word that meant "wandering stars." So, at the beginning, knowledge of the beginning of the Creation and knowledge about the wandering stars and the fixed stars were made known to Abraham. These are topics that belong squarely and comfortably within the gospel that was known to Abraham because all things testify of Christ. And Abraham attempts to write some of them upon his record to give a clue of what it was that that original gospel included.

All volumes of Scripture refer to the Restoration as having the effect of turning the hearts of the children to the Fathers and the hearts of the Fathers to the children, which is not genealogical work. It's... Genealogical work has a place in the grand scheme of things, but the Fathers to whom the hearts are to turn are the Fathers that were in possession of the original gospel in its completeness, the original patriarchs. Because they were entitled to come forth out of the grave (and did so at the time of the resurrection of Christ), they then assumed positions back in the heavens. Joseph Smith refers to *turn[ing] the hearts of the children to [the] Fathers* (T&C 98:3), as turning our hearts to the "Fathers in heaven."

Because the first general resurrection occurred at the time of Christ (and because the second installment of that general resurrection is going to occur at His Second Coming), none of your ancestors who died after the resurrection of Christ until this day are among those who are the Fathers in heaven. Rather, they are imprisoned in the spirit world, awaiting the opportunity to be resurrected at the Lord's return (or some time following that). Turning the hearts of the children to the dead is not the objective of the promise that is made about the Restoration of the gospel having the effect of turning the hearts of the children to the Fathers.

Is it your ambition to join your kindred dead? Well, you're going to do that. Why is it not your ambition to join the **Fathers of whom Malachi spoke**, who were the first Fathers, who are the Fathers now in Heaven, having returned back in a resurrected and glorified form to dwell in the Heavens? **Those** are the ones about whom the promise is made. You're one motorcycle accident away from your dead kindred. You're one bout of some nasty, infectious disease from joining them. There's no great accomplishment to be spoken of by dying and going into the world of the spirits. The promises are more glorious, but they are also about something **far more ancient**.

> *Behold, I will send you Elijah the prophet before the coming of the great and dreadful day of the Lord. And he shall seal the heart of the Fathers to the children and the heart of the children to their Fathers, lest I come and smite the earth with a curse.* (Malachi 1:12 RE)

That is how the prophecy of Malachi is worded in the Old Covenants (in the Scriptures that are being published now that include Joseph Smith's interpretation or inspired rendering of the text). "He shall **seal** the heart of the Fathers to the children and the heart of the children to the Fathers." That's not there in the typical rendering and not in the King James Version, because there it says, "He'll **turn** the hearts of the children to the fathers" (see Malachi 4:6 LE).

This is referred to, also, in the New Covenants: *And he shall go before the Lord in the spirit and power of Elijah, to turn the hearts of the fathers to the children, and the disobedient to the wisdom of the just, to make ready a people prepared for the Lord* (Luke 1:3 RE) is how it's rendered in Luke.

In Third Nephi, the Lord quotes Malachi to have this information added to the record in possession of the Nephites. This is how the Lord rendered it:

> *Behold, I will send you Elijah the prophet before the coming of the great and dreadful day of the Lord, and he shall turn the heart of the fathers to the children and the heart of the children to [the] fathers, lest I come and smite the earth with a curse.* (3 Nephi 11:5 RE)

In the Joseph Smith History, when he was visited by the angelic visitor Nephi, he quoted the prophecy in these words:

> *And he shall plant in the hearts of the children the promises made to the fathers, and the hearts of the children shall turn to their fathers; if it were not so, the whole earth would be utterly wasted at his coming.* (Joseph Smith History 3:4 RE)

So, now we have (in various renderings of this) something that is referred to as "**sealing** hearts, Fathers to children, children to Fathers," something that is called "**turning** the hearts," and something that is called "**promises made** to the fathers."

"Promises made to the fathers" are covenants that God made with them concerning the last-days' work, in which there would again be on the Earth those who are connected to the Fathers in a way that avoids the Earth becoming utterly wasted at His coming. This is something that has to be attended to through the restoration and construction of an authentic temple conforming to the pattern of heaven, in which these things can be attended to and the knowledge and understanding imputed in order for people to comprehend what it means to be a "greater follower of righteousness."

This was a revelation given in March 2015: "Hence, the great need to turn the hearts of the children to the fathers and the fathers to the children—and this too by covenant and sealing through the Holy Spirit of Promise" (*Plural Marriage*, Denver C. Snuffer, Jr., March 22, 2015). This is to restore **us**—as God restored Abraham— to the original religion.

Abraham came into this world uniquely different from the Fathers that had gone before. There was an unbroken chain that continued from father to son and father to son from the time of Adam down through the generations until the time of Melchizedek. All of them were participants in an unbroken familial line. Abraham came into an apostate family in which ~~they~~ his father worshipped—indeed made— dumb idols as the god to be worshipped. Therefore, Abraham is the first one that will join this line who emerges from apostasy into possession of the original holy order. In that sense, Abraham is representative of **all** who would follow after that seek after righteousness in a world that is **constantly** overcome by apostasy.

Apostasy exists the **instant** that God ceases to talk, the instant that God ceases to **restore**, the instant that further light and knowledge by conversing with the Lord through the veil comes to an end. Abraham —**because** he came at a time of apostasy and **because** his father had turned to the worshipping of dumb idols—could not inherit that same standing as the first uninterrupted period unless it were possible for that to be accomplished through adoption. Therefore, Abraham represents the revolutionary idea that one can emerge out of a state of apostasy back into (and be adopted into) the line that is in possession of the fullness of the gospel and to be one equal with them. Abraham represents an astonishing revolutionary moment in the history of God's dealing with mankind, and he also represents the opportunity for redemption for others at remote times/in remote places who dwell among people who are apostate. It represents hope for **us**. And so, when the hearts of the children are turned to the Fathers, that hope is verified and confirmed **primarily** through God's covenant with Abraham. Abraham inherited the promises that had been given to the first Fathers, to be sure, but Abraham represents **hope for us**. He represents **our** opportunity to, likewise, obtain that same hope, which was given to Abraham 430 years before the law was added through Moses.

Now, at the time of the founding of Egypt, the original Pharaoh of Egypt was a righteous man who sought earnestly to imitate the order that began with the first Fathers. The government of Egypt was an attempt to imitate Adam and imitate a family order that came down from the beginning. That founding occurred at a period that is referred to as Predynastic; and the Early Dynastic Period also is plagued with some lack of records, some destruction of material. The Old Kingdom really begins with the Fourth Dynasty, and it's **after** the Eighth Dynasty that (what is referred to in Egyptian history as) the First Intermediate Period took place.

The First Intermediate Period represented a radical period of apostasy from what had gone on before. While there had been an effort to preserve the order that came down from the beginning in Egypt, the

First Intermediate Period represented something very much akin to what would take place in the Jewish Kingdom at the time of the bickering and the fighting and the strife of the Deuteronomists, when the Southern Kingdom was taken captive into Babylon. And then a remnant of the Southern Kingdom returned back to rebuild the temple, at which point the religion had been remarkably revised and the content changed to reflect the kind of strife that was taking place just a few years before the "migration out" of Lehi and his family (that we read in the first chapters of the Book of Mormon—where the idea of the Messiah was trying to be suppressed, trying to be altered). One of the reasons why Zenos was dropped out of the record of the Old Testament is because it's **filled** with Christological content that they intended to suppress.

Well, the kingdom of Egypt was going through something similar, and in the First Intermediate Period, they were forsaking things that had come down from the beginning. What is remarkable is that **Abraham entered Egypt to *teach the Pharaoh* immediately following the First Intermediate Period**. Now, the right that Pharaoh claimed was not his; indeed, when Abraham went into Egypt, Abraham entered possessing that right. (I don't know that he claimed that in the presence of Pharaoh; that might have been fatal.) But he came to **teach**, and he came to **restore**, and he came to reinvigorate the understanding of the Egyptians concerning that first order that came down from the beginning. Therefore, when Abraham came, he came not merely as evidence that you can emerge from apostasy and inherit the rights that belong to the first Fathers by adoption, he also came as a messenger and a restorer to provide such light and knowledge as those who were his contemporaries were willing to receive.

In many respects, **you** are now in possession of a great body of knowledge—much of it originally established through Joseph Smith but neglected or misunderstood or misapplied or currently being opposed—that the people among whom **you** live would benefit by having that knowledge restored to them.

The works of Abraham are not limited to taking a son out and attempting to sacrifice him. The works of Abraham include all of these things:

- The seeking after righteousness,

- The willingness—indeed, the desire—to receive commandments and to obey instructions, so that he might become a greater follower of righteousness, and then

- To go among those who were fallen and apostate (but who were attempting to mirror something they simply did not possess) and to bring to them news and light and truth and knowledge that could benefit them, so that what they were willing to receive, they could receive, but what they were not willing to receive did not need to be imposed upon them to their condemnation.

We have a delicate balance that we're trying to achieve.

I mentioned all of the folks to whom I have presently spent my time attempting to persuade to accept greater light and truth. It's a daunting effort. I began among the people that should **welcome** the idea that the Restoration (which is, obviously, incomplete) can and should move forward; and that if the original failure provoked divine ire for three and four generations, that they had now passed, and the time had arrived in which it's possible to now move forward. I went on from there to the Christians, and we're now making efforts (me, primarily, behind the scenes) to reach out to the Lamanites (the remnant of Lehi) and to the Jews (the remnant that still identifies themselves with Israel). Don't spare your own effort in that regard—because only a handful are laboring to accomplish what needs to be accomplished to fulfill the covenant.

The Book of Mormon makes this subject a major theme of the Book of Mormon text. On the title page of the Book of Mormon, it says the purpose of Mormon's work in this book: *...which is to shew unto the remnant of the house of Israel how great things the Lord hath done for their fathers, ...that they may know the covenants of the Lord, that they are not cast off for ever.* It's the intent of the book to bring people to understand concerning the covenants that were made to the Fathers.

After Nephi finishes his testimony that Christ will visit all of scattered Israel, he then uses Isaiah to show Christ's ministry and that He will visit Israel and keep His word that He gave. Then Nephi explains how God's work will take place after Israel has been scattered among all the nations. He writes:

> After [they've] been nursed by the gentiles, and the Lord has lifted up his hand upon the gentiles, and set them up for a standard, and their children have been carried in their arms, and their daughters have been carried [on] their shoulders — behold, these things... which are spoken [of] are temporal, for thus **is** the covenants of the Lord with our fathers...[Then] the Lord God will proceed to do a marvelous work among the gentiles...**unto the making known of the covenants of the Father of Heaven unto Abraham**, saying, In thy seed shall all the kindreds of the earth be blessed...

And he goes on to say:

> They shall be brought out of obscurity and out of darkness. (1 Nephi 7:3 RE, emphasis added)

That's the whole purpose of the Restoration—to bring further light and knowledge.

Lehi gave a final blessing to his son Joseph, the younger twin of Jacob, born in the wilderness. In his blessing to his son Joseph, he refers to and commends Joseph to the example of their ancestor, Joseph of Egypt. He says:

> I am a descendant of Joseph who was carried captive into Egypt. And great were the covenants of the Lord which he made unto Joseph. Wherefore, Joseph truly saw our day. And he obtained a promise of the Lord that, out of the fruit of his loins, the Lord God would raise up a righteous branch unto the house of Israel, not the Messiah, but a **branch** which was to be broken off, nevertheless to be remembered in the covenants of the Lord, ...bringing...them out of darkness unto light, yea, out of hidden darkness and out of captivity unto freedom...

Freedom, in the sense used by prophets, does not mean that you're not captive by a corrupt culture and subject to a corrupt government. Freedom means that you have the ability to escape sin in your life because you know enough to understand the will of God, and you're devoted, and you fulfill it. He goes on that...

Father Joseph of Egypt testified:

> *A seer shall the Lord my God raise up, who shall be a choice seer unto the fruit of my loins...*

And then he says,

> *He* [that choice seer, Joseph Smith,] *shall do a work...which shall be of great worth unto them, even to the bringing of them to the knowledge of the covenants which I have made with thy fathers. ...I will make him great in mine eyes, for he shall do my work.* (2 Nephi 2:2-3 RE)

In the grand scheme of things, Joseph Smith came here to do the work that God assigned to him to accomplish, and he did that against the resistance and opposition of people who were **internal** to his followers.

In the book *A Man Without Doubt*, I took the three longest things written by Joseph Smith, and in order to understand the heart of the man, I gave a brief historical context so that you could see the opposition or the failure or the trouble that produced the document that Joseph Smith wrote. Out of what should inspire bitterness and rancor, anger, frustration, and disappointment, what you get are three remarkably cheerful, upbeat, hopeful, encouraging, lovely documents that testify of truth. The hope that I had in writing *A Man Without Doubt* ([cough] excuse me) was to put people in possession of something Joseph wrote, so you could see the heart, you could see the mind of the man through his own words—but then you could understand him within a context that had extraordinary opposition.

Joseph Smith was, perhaps, least understood and least respected by the people who were closest to him because they tended, invariably, to assume that he was a man of like-passions with them. Joseph Smith was different than his contemporaries. In many respects, his contemporaries **could not** understand him because they made the wrong assumptions in contextualizing him. As a consequence, when Joseph was nearing the end of his life and speaking to the audience in Nauvoo (that would subsequently write the history), he said, "You don't know me; you never knew me." And yet, they would be the ones to compose the history and then take over the legacy—and then figure out that the legacy that he left behind was susceptible of aggregating social and monetary and political power. And then what Joseph Smith founded became a great institution—which, incidentally, has preserved much of Joseph Smith's teachings that are of value to us.

I don't begrudge them the accumulation of wealth and the satisfaction of self-interest. If they had not been able to monetize Mormonism, we might not have the Book of Mormon today. I'm grateful for all that they've done. (And there have always been among them sincere believers, devoted people who believe in and accept the work of Joseph and of the Book of Mormon and the revelations and teachings that came through him.)

But they've never done enough. Almost immediately after the process began, they fell under condemnation because they failed not only to say but to do the things that had been revealed in the Book of Mormon and in the former commandments, which is why—as an act of collective repentance, as an act of the desire to repent and return—one of the very first things that has been accomplished is for a group of people to go out and do the research necessary to try and find, as close as we can, the original text of the Book of Mormon, together with such alterations as Joseph Smith had made or authorized or clearly intended to have take place.

Now, you may have all heard this story, but the original transcript of the Book of Mormon is one long sentence from beginning to end with no punctuation. That original manuscript was copied by hand, and then the **copy** was taken to E.B. Grandin, and E.B. Grandin put the Book of Mormon into print. The **copy** made from the original still exists in its entirety. The original was put into the cornerstone of the Nauvoo House, and the cornerstone leaked. We only have about 22% of the **original** manuscript, but we have 100% of the **copy** of the printer's manuscript. Therefore, we can make a comparison between the two, and we know that (on average) mistakes were made throughout the copying. Then E.B. Grandin punctuated it; and E.B. Grandin's punctuation reflects **his** understanding.

One of the first acts of repentance was to go back and to look at everything that is available, to try and sort through, and to get the Book of Mormon in as close a way to mirror what was intended to be handed to us as the text. Sadly, we **know** that the Book of Mormon that we have today—even though what we have put together in the research effort is the closest to anything that Joseph Smith endowed us with—it nevertheless, invariably, necessarily must contain mistakes. But as an act of penitence, we've gone as far as we can. We've done the same thing with the revelations that came through Joseph Smith, and we did the same thing with the Joseph Smith translation of the Bible, which is his inspired revision of the Bible. **The Scriptures are not perfect**, but they were presented to the Lord as our best (though inadequate) effort, and they were **accepted** by the Lord. And He said that they were **adequate for His purpose**. Therefore, we have the confidence that for the work that we are to perform in the process of completing the Restoration and getting us in a position to emerge from under the condemnation for failing not only to say but to do, we have the confidence that we can now rely upon something that the Lord has identified and clarified is sufficient or adequate, in order for the tasks that we've been handed to be accomplished. Or in other words, while they may not be perfect, they are **enough** for God to labor with us to continue the Restoration. Therefore, our act of collective repentance to return again has pleased the Lord enough that He's given us acceptance and extended to us the opportunity to enter into a covenant.

Jacob (Nephi's brother) delivered a sermon that Nephi records in his second book. In his second book, after Jacob had read from Isaiah to teach his brethren that were interested in learning about things, he then elaborates or explains the prophecy given by Isaiah:

> *And now my beloved brethren, I have read these things that ye might know concerning the covenants of the Lord, that he has covenanted with **all the house of Israel**...*

That's important—because "all the house of Israel" is greater than those that they left behind at Jerusalem. "All the house of Israel" is greater even than the Nephites plus those left at Jerusalem. The Ten Tribes had left the Northern Kingdom. They had migrated away years before Lehi left Jerusalem. Therefore, "all the house of Israel" (which includes those scattered on the isles of the sea, as the Nephites were) were remembered, and Jacob wants his brethren to understand that God's plan is all-inclusive, wherever they are, in whatever scattered condition. Even if they've altogether lost their identity as members of the house of Israel, yet they are remembered in the covenants of the Lord.

> *...[he's] spoken unto the Jews by the mouth of his holy [prophet], even from the beginning, down from generation to generation, until the time cometh that they shall be restored to the true church and fold of God, when they shall be gathered home [into] the lands of their inheritance* [lands—plural, not singular] *and shall be established in **all their lands** of promise.* (2 Nephi 6:1 RE, emphasis added)

What Jacob is teaching to his brethren is that there are those who have received (who belong to the house of Israel) covenants that have handed to them—by covenant—**lands**, plural:

- This land has people upon it today who have entered into a covenant (with the Lord today) that has made this land a place of their inheritance.

- The descendants of the Lamanites likewise descend from fathers with whom a covenant was made that **they** inherit this land.

- The Jews in Israel have a promise given them: That land is theirs by divine decree—God gave it to them; it is their land.

- And there are **other** broken branches from the house of Israel living on lands (their descendants today) that they possess by right.

Jacob continued his sermon over a second day; and in the sermon the second day, this is the second part of Jacob's teaching concerning the covenants:

> *Wherefore, for this cause, that my covenants may be fulfilled which I have made unto the children of men, that I will do unto them while they are **in the flesh**, I must needs destroy the secret works of darkness, and of murders, and of abominations. Wherefore, he that fighteth against Zion, both Jew and Gentile, both bond and free,*

*both male and female, **shall perish**; for they are they who are the whore of all the earth. For they who are not **for** me are against me, saith our God. For I will fulfill my promises which I have made unto the children of men that I will do unto them **while they are in the flesh**.* (2 Nephi 7:3 RE, emphasis added)

This isn't some dreamy, distant, other-worldly event. He says He is going to establish, in the flesh, a people that will become Zion; and He will defend those people who are His Zion.

As Nephi closes his record, he explains plainly what he wants **us** (the Gentiles) to understand from his record:

Woe...unto him that shall say, We have received the word of God, and we need no more of the word of God, for we have enough. ... unto him that receiveth I will give more; and from them [which] say, We have enough — shall be taken away even that which they have.

...I will be merciful unto them, saith the Lord God, if they will repent and come unto me...

...there shall be many at that day when I shall proceed to do a marvelous work among them, that I...remember my covenants which I have made unto the children of men, ...that I may remember the promises which I have made unto thee, Nephi, and also unto thy father, that...shall say, A bible, a bible, [we've] got a bible, ...there cannot be any more bible. But thus saith the [Lord]: O fools, [that] shall have a bible...

O ye gentiles, have ye remembered the Jews, mine ancient covenant people? Nay, but [you've] cursed them, [you've] hated them, and have not sought to recover them... Thou fool that shall say, A bible, [we've] got a bible and we need no more bible. Have ye obtained a bible, save it were by the Jews? Know ye not that there are more nations than one? ...I, the Lord your God, have created all men, and...I remember those [that] are upon the isles of the sea? ...I rule in the heavens above and [I rule] in the earth beneath... Wherefore murmur ye because...ye shall receive more of my word?...

That was the very objective that Abraham sought: to **get more** of God's word. He wanted to know more; he wanted to receive commandments; he wanted to receive instructions.

> *Because that I have spoken one word, ye need not suppose that I cannot speak another... The Jews shall have the words of the Nephites, and the Nephites shall have the words of the Jews, and the Nephites and the Jews shall have the words of the lost tribes of Israel, and the lost tribes of Israel shall have the words of the Nephites and the Jews. ...my people which are of the house of Israel shall be gathered home [into] the **lands** of their [possession], and my word also shall be gathered in one. ...I am God, and...I covenanted with Abraham that I would remember his seed for ever...*

That includes those portions of the family of Abraham that migrated out of the view of the Scriptures we presently possess, so that when they drop out of the biblical narrative (or they drop out of the Book of Mormon narrative), God was still with them; He was still doing with them; He was still leading them and teaching them; and ultimately, He visited them. All of them kept records. Those are all to be restored.

> *Ye need not suppose that the gentiles are utterly destroyed. For behold, I say unto you, as many of the gentiles as will repent are the covenant people of the Lord... For the Lord covenanteth with none save it be with them that repent and believe in his Son, who is the Holy One of Israel.* (2 Nephi 12:6-11 RE, emphasis added)

Therefore, the covenant people of the Lord (according to the Book of Mormon) who will inherit the promises of Abraham necessarily include those Gentiles who are willing to covenant with Him to allow Him to labor through them to restore things that will bring the remainder of the house of Israel back to the knowledge of their God.

Mormon interrupts his narrative summary of events by an observation he makes about the work of the Lord (inserted into his account just prior to the final round of apostasy, violence, and the great tempest that destroyed the wicked—and then Christ's visit to the other sheep that are covered in the Book of Mormon). This is Mormon's insertion into the record:

Surely shall he again bring a remnant of the seed of Joseph to the knowledge of the Lord their God. And as surely as the Lord liveth [he will] gather in from the four quarters of the earth all the remnant of the seed of Jacob.... He hath covenanted with all the house of Jacob, even so shall the covenant wherewith he hath covenanted with the house of Jacob be fulfilled, in his own due time, unto the restoring all the house of Jacob unto the knowledge of the covenant [which] he hath covenanted with them. ...then shall they know their Redeemer, who is Jesus Christ, the Son of God... (3 Nephi 2:18 RE)

In Christ's teachings to the Nephites (after He had been resurrected, appeared to them, had them come and be in contact and witness of His death and resurrection), He delivered to them the Sermon on the Mount in a slightly different form: the Sermon at Bountiful. And after He had taught that sermon, He commanded that they write down and preserve **these** teachings that He's going to give:

(Hmm... Someone wrote in the margin of my book. It looks like my handwriting, so I wanted to read that [laughter].)

The remnant of their seed, who [should] be scattered forth upon the face of the earth because of their unbelief, may be brought in...

Okay, He's now talking to the Nephite believers about the descendants of the Nephite believers, and He's telling them, "You have to write this down." And He tells them what they're to write down is that eventually their descendants are gonna be scattered upon the face of the Earth because of their **unbelief**, but those descendants may be brought in. The note I wrote in the margin is that even the Lamanite remnant, who are the target of the covenant, **have to be reclaimed**, have to be brought in, have to **know** of their inheritance in order to take advantage **of** it. If **they're** not brought in, then they still suffer under the plague of unbelief.

...because of their unbelief, may be brought in, or may be brought to a knowledge of me.... I [will] gather them in.... I [will] fulfill the covenant which the Father hath made unto all the people of the house of Israel. ...in the latter day shall the truth come unto the

> gentiles, that the fullness of these things shall be made known unto **them**...

In other words, He's promising to the Nephites... Their descendants are going to fall away, but He promises their descendants will be gathered back in. In order to bring the descendants back in, He's promising them that the Gentiles shall receive **this knowledge**—the truth shall come unto the ~~knowledge~~ [Gentiles],

> ...that the fullness of these things shall be made known unto them...

> I will remember my covenant unto you, O house of Israel, and ye shall come unto the knowledge of the fullness of my gospel. But if the gentiles will repent and return unto me, saith the Father, behold, they shall be numbered among my people, O house of Israel. (3 Nephi 7:4-5 RE, emphasis added)

When the Gentiles repent and they return, then they're numbered back —just like the descendants of the Nephites—when they are awakened and repent and are taught the truth and return unto God, **all** become one house, one fold, one people.

Then, after Christ had introduced the sacrament and had commanded that Isaiah's words be searched because they tell of fulfilling of God's covenant, Christ then teaches:

> This people will I establish in this land unto the fulfilling of the covenant which I made with your father Jacob, and it shall be a New Jerusalem. And the Powers of Heaven shall be in the midst of this people, yea, even I will be in the midst of you...

Christ is reiterating to this group, in this setting, promises directly to them that He had **previously given to Enoch** about what would happen in the last days. When He told Enoch about it, He said that there would come a point at which righteousness and truth would spring forth; it would be upon the Earth; there would be a tabernacle or a temple there; and that He, along with Enoch's people, would return and fall upon and kiss the necks of those who gather there. This is the same prophecy that was given to Enoch (one of those first Fathers in that first direct descent)—this is a covenant that Christ is reiterating, but it goes back to the first Fathers. Indeed, if we had a full restoration of all that had been given, we would know that the gospel in its fullness was understood far better by the first generations—or the original Fathers—than it is understood by us today. He says to the people gathered there (this is Christ, same talk):

> *...ye are of the covenant which the Father made with your fathers, saying unto Abraham, And in thy seed shall all the kindreds of the earth be blessed, the Father having raised me up unto you first, and sent me to bless you in turning away every one of you from his iniquities — and this because ye are the children of the covenant. And after...ye were blessed, then fulfilleth the Father the covenant which he made with Abraham, saying, In thy seed shall all the kindreds of the earth be blessed, unto the pouring out of the holy ghost through me upon the gentiles...*

In genealogical research, what you find is that if you start with yourself and you go backwards—generations—for about 500 years, your genealogy chart expands and expands and expands. And at about the 500-year-mark, it begins to contract and contract and contract, so that the genetic spread of the blood of Abraham throughout the world is so far and so wide that you practically can't find people anywhere on the Earth that don't have some of the blood of Abraham, to whom He said, "**all** the kindreds of the earth will be blessed in thy seed."

> *If they shall harden their hearts against me, I will return their iniquities upon their own heads, saith the Father. And I will remember the covenant which I have made with my people, and I have covenanted with them that I would gather them together in mine own due time, that I would give unto them again the land of their fathers for their inheritance...*

So, it should begin to emerge into your view that physical descendancy is one thing to open up an opportunity—but covenanting, remembering, repenting, returning, accepting what God has to offer is the component in the last days that distinguishes whether or not they are **redeemed**, whether or not they are to be **gathered**, whether or not they are to be **recognized** in the own due time of the Lord as His, to be protected and to be preserved against the harvest. It's not enough merely to have genealogical connection back to some remnant of Father Abraham.

I can trace my genealogy back to Jewish ancestry, to Native American ancestry. That doesn't mean a thing if I don't repent and return. I remain on the outside. I remain a Gentile. I remain a disbeliever unworthy to be gathered. I suspect everyone in this room has a direct genealogical connection, probably, not only to Abraham but also Joseph—and perhaps eleven out of the twelve tribes of Israel. It's just the way that descendancy works.

Christ continues:

> Then shall this covenant which the Father hath covenanted with his people be fulfilled; …then shall Jerusalem be inhabited again with my people, and it shall be the land of their inheritance.
>
> …when these things which I declare unto you — and which I shall declare unto you hereafter of myself and by the power of the holy ghost…shall be made known unto the gentiles, that they may know concerning this people who are a remnant of the house of Jacob…it shall be a sign unto them that they may know that the work of the Father hath already commenced unto the fulfilling of the covenant which he hath made unto the people who are of the house of Israel. (3 Nephi 9:8,10-11 RE)

The gentiles, if they will not harden their hearts, that they may repent, and come unto me, and be baptized in my name, and know of the true points of my doctrine, that they may be numbered among my people, O house of Israel (Ibid., emphasis added) means that it was always the design that the Gentiles should also be gathered in—or that what is, in all likelihood, an unsavory, bitter-fruit-producing branch of the original tree should be taken and gathered back to the original root and gather nourishment from that original root, that they may come in and be numbered among the house of Israel. It's always been the intention of the Lord to restore the Gentiles and to make them the means through which the last-days' work would become accomplished.

As Mormon completed the record of Christ's visit to the Nephites, he provided this description of the Book of Mormon's purpose:

*When the Lord shall see fit in his wisdom that these sayings shall come unto the gentiles according to his word, then ye may know that the covenant which the Father hath made with the children of Israel concerning their restoration to the **lands** of their inheritance is already beginning to be fulfilled. And ye may know that the words of the Lord which have been spoken by the holy prophets **shall all be fulfilled**. ...the Lord will remember his covenant which he hath made unto his people of the house of Israel.* (3 Nephi 13:7 RE, emphasis added)

And as Moroni concluded the record, he inserted some final words of instruction for the people who would receive the Book of Mormon in the last days. These words were taught to him by his father. He says:

*Hath miracles ceased? ...I say unto you, nay; neither have angels ceased to minister unto the children of men. For...they are subject unto him, to minister according to the word of his command, shewing themselves unto them of strong faith and a firm mind in every form of godliness. And the office of their ministry is to call men unto repentance, and to fulfill and to do the work of the **covenants** of the Father which he hath made unto the children of men...declaring the word of Christ unto the chosen vessels of the Lord, that they may bear testimony of him; and by so doing, the Lord God prepareth the way that the residue of men may have faith in Christ, that the holy ghost may have place in their hearts, according to the power thereof; and after this manner bringeth to pass the Father the **covenants** which he hath made unto the children of men.* (Moroni 7:6 RE, emphasis added)

There are numerous other passages in the Book of Mormon that speak to the same thing. The Book of Mormon is a forerunner—a harbinger —that was intended to say to the people who receive it:

There are covenants that go back to the very beginning, to the original Fathers. Those covenants got renewed/they got restored/they got continued in the form of Abraham (who received all that had been there originally) coming out of apostasy and being adopted back into that line of Patriarchs. That original covenant material provoked the creation of the Book of Mormon, and it is one of the major testimonies that is given to us by the Book of Mormon about the work that God intends to do in the last days. You can believe in the Bible; you can accept Jesus as your Savior; you can be (in the words of the Evangelical community) "born again." You can be (in the words of Latter-day Saints) someone whose calling and election is made sure. But the work of God, at this point, is not about, merely, individual salvation; it is the work of fulfilling the covenants that were made with the Fathers. It is the work of restoring again that original gospel (of which the law given to Moses pointed forward to but did not comprehend).

We tend to view priesthood in institutional ways. And it's hard to be terribly critical of misunderstandings because, quite frankly, priestly authority (following the success of the Petrine branch of original Christianity and its triumph, with emphasis on authority and priesthood and keys) predisposed the entire Christian world. Even the Christian world, after the Protestant Reformation succeeded in finally breaking off areas in which a different form of protest Christianity could be practiced that was not subservient to the Roman "See" and papal decree, they still had this misapprehension about priesthood. So, when Joseph Smith began to talk about priesthood and to begin the process of restoring it, he gave a new kind of vocabulary. But possession of a vocabulary does not mean possession of the thing.

When Abraham talks about becoming a rightful heir and becoming a high priest, it would be best if you threw out everything that you have heard or learned or understood about the concept of priesthood. Priesthood includes the prerogative, the right, the obligation, or the duty to go out and perform ordinances that are effective, that God will recognize to be sure—and that's part of it, and it's a true principle.

However, priesthood in the original sense was something far more vast. It included an understanding of things that relate back all the way to the beginning—or before the world was—and goes forward through all periods of time until the end. It includes a basis of knowledge. So, when you read Abraham's description of what it was he looked for and he mentions priesthood, you have to merge that into the entirety of what he's talking about: knowledge, understanding, commandments, instructions; having the capacity to see things in their correctly-ordered fashion, similarly to how God originally intended that it be ordered— so that you are no longer out-of-sync with this Creation and doing your best to "reign with blood and horror" by subduing nature with the iron plow and gunpowder and lead—but instead you find yourself situated in a place that Eden itself can be renewed, and harmony can be achieved between man and the Earth.

The Book of Mormon is talking about something vast, but it continually points back to Abraham. And I do not care what arguments can be made or what a pitiful effort has been put together to defend the Book of Abraham that Joseph Smith provided us. It was essential to the Restoration that the Book of Abraham be given to us, because without it, we would not understand a great deal about the Restoration and what the final objective of the Restoration was to achieve.

If you're going to please God, you don't please Him by having your "born again" experience (or having your "calling and election made sure" experience) if the result of that is to make you proud, conceited, self-assured, and arrogant, and to disconnect you from the restoration process that was begun through Joseph Smith (and has yet a greater work to be done than was achieved at the time of Joseph Smith). Go off and be saved, but you will not fulfill the work of the covenants that God intends to achieve. He has committed Himself to that end.

Those who will labor alongside Him—whether they be Gentile or Lamanite or Jew, it does not matter—if they will repent and accept the process of the Restoration, as it began through Joseph Smith, not only to say it correctly but to do what it tells us needs to be done, then you will be numbered among those people that God has covenanted to gather against the coming harvest.

But if you want to be the lone guru whose commentaries fill pages of blogging and hours of pontification but you're going to labor at odds, I read you the warning: All that fight against Zion are going to perish. So, you can shout your hallelujahs in the spirit world, and you can proclaim your calling and election guarantees you something, but quite frankly, practically everyone's calling and election can be made sure. You get to continue progress. You get to continue to repent. God's not gonna terminate you at the end of this cycle of Creation, but you're gonna be allowed to go on—and upward—if you'll continue to repent.

You will always be free to choose, but the work of the covenants that the Book of Mormon foretell are to be accomplished through the reclaiming (by repentance and returning to Him) of Gentiles that will, ultimately, reach out to (and include) restoring the Lamanites/restoring the Jews to a knowledge of the works of the Father, that—**that**—is what is on the mind of God today. **That** is the purpose of the covenant that was given unto us in Boise just a few years ago—two years ago. **That** is what fulfilling the covenant ultimately requires that **we** labor to achieve.

That effort began in earnest with the reclaiming of the Scriptures and the presenting of those to the Lord for His acceptance—and the marvelous news that God accepted them as adequate for His purpose for us—and the commitment that He would labor with us to go forward.

Anyone can join the party. Anyone can come into this work. Anyone can remain a Catholic or a Presbyterian, a Catholic or a Latter-day Saint. It doesn't matter. Those things are more like civic clubs. I don't care if you're a Rotarian or a Kiwanis Club member—means about the same thing as belonging to any of those organizations. Associate with whoever you like to associate with, but you **must** accept baptism. You **must** accept the Book of Mormon. It **is** a **covenant**. The covenant must be accepted, and you **must** help labor alongside those who seek to return Zion.

Now, just a couple of short comments.

(Wow, I took more time than I thought I was gonna take. I know they gave you a schedule, but whatever I'm gonna cover, I'm gonna cover—and then we'll sing or whatever comes next.)

In September of 2014… I want to remind you of something. This was the talk given down in Phoenix, September 14, 2014:

> Last general conference the entire First Presidency, the 12, the 70, and all other general authorities and auxiliaries, voted to sustain those who abused their authority in casting me out of the church. At that moment, the Lord ended all claims of the Church of Jesus Christ of Latter-day Saints, to **claim it is led**

by the priesthood [meaning the leaders who exercise control, compulsion, and dominion, and not the powerless who had no part in the affair]. They have not practiced what He requires. The Lord has brought about His purposes. This has been [done] in His heart all along. He has chosen to use small means to accomplish it, but He always uses the smallest of means to fulfill His purposes. (*40 Years in Mormonism*, Talk 10, "Preserving the Restoration," page 8 of the paper, emphasis added)

If you will take a moment to consider the path that has been taken by that church's leaders since April of 2014, you can see how (in only five years) they have shown, by their decisions, the lack of heavenly guidance. Their trajectory will continue to arc downward. If you doubted my declaration in Phoenix in September 2014, then do not doubt the course taken by those church leaders since then.

Then I gave some closing remarks in the September 3, 2017 conference that I want to read to you:

> Those who have entered faithfully into the covenant this day are going to notice some things. The spirit of God is withdrawing from the world. Men are increasingly more angry without good cause. The hearts of men are waxing cold. There is increasing anger and resentment of gentiles. In political terms, it's rejection of white privilege.
>
> Language of scripture gives a description of the events now underway and calls it the end of the times of the gentiles. This process, with the spirit withdrawing, will end on this continent as it did with two prior civilizations in fratricidal and genocidal warfare. For the rest of the world, it will be as in the days of Noah in which, as that light becomes eclipsed, the coldness of men's hearts is going to result in a constant scene of violence and bloodshed. The wicked will destroy the wicked.
>
> The covenant, if it is kept, will prevent you from losing light and warmth of heart as the spirit now steadily recedes from the world. The time will come when you will be astonished at the gulf between the light and truth you will comprehend and the

darkness of mind of the world. (*Closing Remarks*, Covenant of Christ Conference, 3 September 2017, pg. 1)

And I ended by saying:

> May God bless you and send to each of you a growing light and warmth. As the spirit withdraws from the world may it continually shine un-eclipsed on each of you to enlighten your minds and warm your hearts. (*Ibid.*, pg. 2)

In the Answer that we received, there was an explanation given to us. It says:

> *In your language you use the name Lucifer for an angel who was in authority before God, who rebelled, fought against the work of the Father and was cast down to the earth. His name means holder of light, or light bearer, for he had gathered light by his heed and diligence before he rebelled. He has become a vessel containing only wrath and seeks to destroy all who will hearken to him. He is now enslaved to his own hatred.*
>
> *Satan is a title, and means accuser, opponent and adversary; hence once he fell, Lucifer became, or in other words was called, Satan, because he accuses others and opposes the Father.*
>
> *…there are those who have been Satan, accusing one another, wounding hearts and causing jarring, contention, and strife by their accusations. Rather than loving one another, even among you who desire a good thing, some have dealt unkindly as if they were opponents, accusers and adversaries. In this they were wrong.*
>
> *You have sought to recover the scriptures because you hope to obtain the covenant for my protective hand to be over you, but you cannot be Satan and be mine.* (T&C 157:7-10)

I read those excerpts from the talk in Phoenix and from the Covenant Conference in Boise to remind you about what was described in both of those events. There **is** a process that **is** underway. People are increasingly accusing, opposing, and fighting with one another without good cause. It is as if they are submitting themselves to listen to obey the spirit of Satan (or the spirit of strife, envy, jarring, accusing). That course is not going to change. I hope it may plateau for a season. There are things we have to do, and we need something other than chaos and warfare in order to accomplish the things that we need to achieve. But I believe when the command is given that we're going to have to act with alacrity if we are going to be able to fulfill the covenants and the obligations that have been promised by God and handed to us to do.

But don't expect the world to get better, and don't expect organized religions to get better. But hopefully, there will be more and more who come to take refuge among a band of believers who have no hierarchy, office, position, who have only ourselves to fellowship with informally, gathering at one another's homes, renting (on occasion) facilities like these to meet in larger groups.

I intend to continue my efforts among all of those people that I have been working with up to this point. I will continue that labor for so long as I am allowed to participate in any of this. But each of us, similarly, have the same kind of obligation to spread the truth and the knowledge and the Scriptures (that we now have) that more accurately recover. We have to go back to what was given to us through Joseph Smith as the foundation in order to qualify to be able to move forward.

The new Scriptures are a **vital** part of the Restoration process. And I want to thank all of those who participated in that recovery effort—because it was not easy, and it wasn't just one or two people. There was a great number of people, ultimately, who were necessary, in order to get the work accomplished. But as the Lord labored with the group and opened doors, there literally were computer programs that were essential to the collaborative process that were not available. There were resource materials that were essential to the collaborative process that came out (either online or in print) just in time to be available so that the work could be accomplished. The timing, the serendipitous occurrence that coincided with the Scripture effort was remarkable. And all that were involved realized that this was not a work that could have been done ten years ago, let alone attempted last century. This is a work that only could be done at the time that it took place because the doors opened and the materials became available.

So with that, there's a musical number and then an intermission. And so, we can shout, Hallelujah, indeed! And then, I'm supposed to come back here and answer questions. Someone handed me a bag of questions. I'll come back.

OK, I'll be back at twelve. The musical number is next—if they want to come up. You know, why don't we resume at ten to twelve. Is everyone okay with that? Let's do that. Let's do that.

Keeping the Covenant Conference Q&A Session

Transcript from the "Keeping the Covenant" Conference
Caldwell, Idaho
September 22, 2019

Hah! I guess it's "ten to" [the hour], and the blessed moment has arrived. That was a great musical number, and both ~~Sarah~~ [Sariah] and Doug did a remarkable job with that. And I'm led to believe that there's yet another great musical number coming up to conclude this.

I was handed some questions, and some of 'em are pretty good, and let me see what good I can do.

Question 1: "How can you know if the boils you receive in life are due to being like unto Job or because you are more akin to Pharaoh?"

Answer: It's a great question; I love the question. First, there's an interesting exercise that I would commend to any of you. Go to the account of Exodus, the early events, and only read the words of Moses. Just read Moses' responses, his reactions, his complaints, his fear, his doubts. And what you will realize is that it doesn't matter if someone occupies a great position (as Moses did) or the lives that each of us are now living. No one fits easily or comfortably or without anxiety into the work of the Lord. There's a measure that you take of yourself in which you look inward and say, "I'm not adequate to what needs to be done; I don't have the faith required." And you'll see that that's exactly what Moses was telling God—that looking inward, he did not think himself equal to it.

In the Book of Mormon, Nephi gives us an account of their journey. After they had been delivered from ~~Israel~~ Jerusalem, which was about to be destroyed, and they were migrating, here are some comments that he makes about their experience:

- *We have suffered much afflictions, hunger, thirst, and fatigue* (1 Nephi 5:10 RE).
- *We did travel and wade through much affliction in the wilderness* (vs. 11).
- *We had suffered many afflictions and much difficulty, yea even so much that we cannot write them all* (vs. 14).

This is Nephi explaining his experience in the wilderness: afflictions, hunger, thirst, fatigue—so many afflictions that they can't even talk about 'em. We don't **look** at those words; we pass over them as if Nephi were somehow being modest, or Nephi were being self-deprecating. We pass over what Moses says when he's getting the responsibilities imposed upon him by the Lord as if it's just common sense that he's heroic and larger than life and greater than the common man. But when you read his reaction, he sounds like us: he sounds common; he sounds ordinary. And when you read the lamentation... We suffer because we **are**, because we're **mortal**, because we're **here**, because that's the common lot that is designed to be experienced as a consequence of the fall. And there's no escaping that.

The question isn't: Are we going to suffer while we are here? The only question is: To what degree do we bear up under the troubles of this life, graciously and humbly and acknowledging that God rules in the Heavens above, He rules in the Earth beneath, and He rules in your life, too. And that everything that you experience is designed to make you be added upon by the things that you suffer and the things that you experience here.

Question 2: I was asked, verbally, if I would comment on some of the challenges that people of faith have in defending the Book of Abraham.

Answer: And that's probably a subject that's worth writing about, rather than just talking off the cuff, but here's, generally, my observation.

The people want to know what Joseph did and how he did it in order for them to understand (maybe) how **they** can do it. So there's this relentless inquiry into: "How did that process take place? What went on?" When, in fact, the gifts of God are almost entirely incapable of being transferred from one to another. Each person has to come to God on their own.

Oliver Cowdery was a man of faith, and he believed in Christ and the possibility of the Second Coming of Christ being proximate (or in close proximity) to his life. He believed in and he got answers from God; and then he hears about what Joseph is doing, and he goes to become his scribe.

One of the early revelations that were given to Oliver talked about his own (Oliver's own) gift—that he had this gift in which Oliver could get yes or no answers by using the (what we would call a) "divining rod" (or a stick) that would respond positively or negatively to inquiry. And so, he had this... And the revelation does not call it anything other than "a gift." It may seem like a peculiar gift to you and I; but it's, nevertheless, a gift, and it came from God.

Joseph had a gift in which he was capable of receiving revelation—sometimes through instrumentalities, sometimes by study, sometimes simply by God speaking through him in the first person in a spontaneous way. How he went about doing that is unique to him. The way in which you relate to God is unique to you. Running out and trying to replicate something—in order for you to know the process by which God involved Himself in revelation in Joseph Smith's experience—is not gonna teach you what Joseph Smith experienced. In the same fashion, those that would like to anchor the process of restoring the Book of Abraham to the surviving remnant of the Joseph Smith papyri and to say that that is the source material from which the Book of Abraham was derived are neglecting the bigger part of the process.

Can God use a bird in flight to answer a prayer? Can God use a billboard to convey a truth or an idea? Can God use a song to inspire you? Can God use the words of a poet, speaking about something entirely different, to convey to the mind, inspired by the light of Heaven, to see those words in a context that speaks directly and immediately to what it is that they're searching for?

There's a line in one of the Indigo Girls' songs: "The less I seek my source for some definitive, the closer I am to fine." It's a beautiful song. It's about the frustration that they have with gurus, generally, and the notion that you really need to divorce yourself—

> There's more than one answer to these questions,
> Pointing me in a crooked line...

is part of that same song.

> I spent four years prostrate to the higher mind,
> Got my paper and I was free...

The less I seek my source for some definitive,
The closer I am to fine.
(*Closer to Fine*, Indigo Girls)

…because the answers that you get from most of the authoritative sources will always point you in a crooked line, but the paths of God are straight—which is one of the reasons why I juxtaposed those two issues involving "sacrificing for the sacred" and "sacrificing for the benefit of man," which, if you adopt in an absolute sense, point you in a crooked line. And yet, it's incumbent upon you to find the harmony, to find the middle road, to find the path that reflects the graciousness of Christ's walk while He was down here in this troubled sphere dealing with all of the troubling issues in which we find ourselves.

In one of the very earliest meetings that we have a report of, Hyrum Smith got up to introduce his brother, Joseph, and he introduced him by saying, "And Joseph will now explain to you the process by which the Book of Mormon was translated." And Joseph got up and said, "It's not needful for that to be explained." The person who understood the process of translating the Book of Mormon was Joseph Smith. Even the scribes who were in the immediate area don't know the process by which the Book of Mormon was translated.

The reason for settling upon the Book of Abraham (and the remnant or relic of the Book of Abraham) as a basis for criticizing Joseph Smith is to enable them (who desire to discredit Joseph) to then extend the argument from the translation of the papyri to the translation of the Book of Mormon—so that they can dismiss the work of Joseph Smith altogether and not have to trouble themselves with the heavy, unnerving obligation that devolves upon the shoulders of every person who finds out that God sent a prophet (in the form of Joseph Smith) in order to begin anew and complete the process of preparing mankind for the Second Coming of the Lord.

And so, criticisms directed at the Book of Abraham and that translation process are surrogate for criticism, ultimately, intended to be aimed at the Book of Mormon—in order that Joseph might be *diminished* as a authoritative figure, on the one hand, to equip you to *dismiss* him as authoritative figure, on the other hand. People want a much smaller, more cunning, more contriving, less virtuous Joseph

Smith because then it justifies **them** in their smallness and cunningness and treachery in dealing with their fellow man.

One of the reasons why I mentioned, earlier, *A Man Without Doubt* is because it's impossible (in my view) for a small, cunning man to write the things that Joseph Smith wrote in the three transcripts of his three longest writings (apart from the Book of Mormon) that are put into *A Man Without Doubt*—particularly given the graciousness with which Joseph Smith endured the circumstances he was put into by the betrayal of people who should have been his friends and who should have endeavored, in a kindly manner, to reclaim him if they thought he were deluded. That's a quote from what Joseph Smith wrote about his history in the Joseph Smith History that he was recreating in 1838 after being betrayed by John Whitmer (the Church Historian who took all of the history) and his brother (one of the Three Witnesses). They betrayed him, and they took it.

So, when Joseph was writing in 1838, and he was reflecting back upon how he was treated when he had mentioned (to a handful of people) the first vision—when that had happened (in 1820, as he dates it in that history), he wasn't really talking about the persecution that he had received when he was a child; he was commenting to the people of his day who, if they had thought him to be deluded, ought to have endeavored in a kind and affectionate manner to have reclaimed him instead of betraying him and surrendering both him and the people who remained true to him to violence.

Well, if you start with the **real** proposition about the Book of Abraham, that's **really** where we ought to go first. And that is: Is Joseph Smith the kind of man that would be capable of receiving a revelation to outline for us something going back to the era of Abraham and give us insight by restoring a text? Is Joseph Smith capable of doing that? Or is he a craven manipulator who's dishonest and inventive and fanciful, egomaniacal, and in it for his own self-gain? **That's** the real question that the "Book of Abraham translation issues" raise.

And for the answer to **that** question, I don't think you can parse your way through a relic of papyri—which is clearly only a fragment of what he was working with and doesn't match at all the description of the text being "in a beautiful hand in both red and black ink" (from a letter Oliver Cowdery sent to William Frye, December 25, 1835; published in *Messenger and Advocate* of the same month). It's a rather sloppy hand (the fragment we have), and there's no red ink. It's black ink, and it's sloppily done.

I don't think we should let Joseph Smith off the hook for being accountable and responsible to **us** for being a virtuous man, for being a truthful man, for being a reliable man. But I don't think you answer those questions by an **appeal** to a fragment of papyri and what modern Egyptologists may be able to **divine** from a complex language that had migrated from hieroglyph to hieratic to demotic—and that, too, over millennia of time in which…

I mean, Abraham came along at the first intermediate period. These papyri? They were created in the Greco-Roman era. What? About eighteen dynasties later? After the influence of the Greco-Roman world? The *Book of Breathings* and the text from which this was drawn —the *Book of the Dead*—these are very, very Egyptologically late documents. There's nothing comparable to it in an existing culture. Maybe in China. Maybe if you go to Hong Kong, and you walk down the street in Hong Kong, and you take a look at all the advertisements that are on the billboards that are in both English and Mandarin (or Cantonese—I don't know what they're using on the road signs or their billboards there) and you take that as the measure of reconstructing something from one of the earliest Chinese dynasties. And you say, "There was no McDonalds back then; it doesn't work." You're literally trying to bridge a gulf that is almost unimaginably foreign.

So, the earliest pictographic representations were done alongside a **story**. So, you get a pictographic representation, and you get a story that tells you what this picture is about. Can the picture be replicated to tell yet another story by making a few minor changes and then telling a different story? The answer to that is (obviously), Yes, you could. It's not until later that you begin to insert into the text (in addition to the pictographic representation) additional commentary that's designed to explain what this particular one is telling you in this particular setting. But that doesn't mean that the representation hasn't been borrowed from another account or an earlier account or a different account and been slightly modified and adapted in order to tell another story, based upon the same kind of pictographic representation.

The fact that I have concluded that Joseph Smith was a restrained man —in many respects, a very modest man—whose defense of what he believed to be the truth was fierce but who recognized that there were a lot of people (including his own wife, Emma Smith) who had a better education than did he—

Joseph was like a sponge when he thought he could get truth or help from others, and he was meek and humble in that respect. But if God had revealed something to him, he was an iron-fisted, immovable man for the truth, personally and privately—just as the Scriptures say concerning Moses. Moses was the meekest of all men. If you just read the dialogue from Moses (in Exodus), you'll see nothing but meekness in that man. If you'll read Joseph Smith's three documents in *A Man Without Doubt,* you'll see a meek man—**unbelievably frustrated** by some of the circumstances into which he was put, **searching** to find the right way out of the dilemma, **trying** to get God aroused to anger in the same way that the circumstances aroused Joseph to anger, but **submitting always** to whatever the will of God was for him. Ultimately, Joseph Smith left to go to be imprisoned in Carthage knowing he would not come back from there (or at least expecting that he would not) and commenting about how his life was no value to his friends as he returned, and he went back for the slaying.

Say what you want about those final moments in the life of Joseph Smith. He put himself in harm's way to prove his fidelity to his friends. He would not forsake **them** (as they claimed he was doing in **their** hour of need) and ultimately gave his life up. That's not the conduct of a conman. That's not the way in which someone who's going to lie and cheat and steal and behave as an immoral exploiter of others would conduct their lives. Joseph, in my view, was not just a virtuous man, but he qualified as one of those who hath no greater love, because he went back and surrendered at the behest of his brethren—in part, with the hope that by losing **his** life, Nauvoo would be spared the slaughter that had gone on at Far West and Haun's Mill and elsewhere.

And so, when you ask about the translation issues and the controversy over the Book of Abraham, the bottom line/the real issue is: However the mind of Joseph was set on fire with the restoration text of Father Abraham's account of his search, you have to decide that the content either is from heaven, or it's a lie.

There was a series (it's now been abandoned, but it's a series that was begun at Brigham Young University), the first volume of it—the Book of Abraham series—the first volume of it was pretty good. What they did was take concepts that are included in the text of the Book of Abraham which were completely unknown in the Christian world at the time that the Book of Abraham was put into print. They had to be **unique** concepts. If you could already find them in the Bible or if you could already find them in what was available to the Christian world generally, then those weren't included. They had to be **unique** ideas. They took and gathered the unique ideas that come out in the Book of Abraham (about which Joseph Smith would have known nothing), and then they looked into other material that exists (from diverse places) about legends or stories concerning the life of Abraham. And what they found is that there were **Hindu** traditions that talked about Abraham, that preserved some of the very same incidents that are only found in the Book of Abraham (at the time Joseph published the Book of Abraham). They found there were **Islamic** texts that were similarly describing the same kind of event, the same incident that's unique to the Book of Abraham. They found sources that were in **Coptic Egyptian** texts. They amalgamated into one volume (it's a pretty big volume) all of the parallel accounts from the life of Abraham (in cultures from around the world or religious traditions from around the world) that Joseph Smith nailed on the head in his account of the Book of Abraham.

That approach does not defend Joseph Smith as a translator of Egyptian, because it has nothing to do with the papyri. But it does a pretty good job of defending Joseph Smith as a **revelator**, as someone to whom God could reveal light and truth, and he could accurately record it—because echoes of the unique material in the Book of Abraham show up in the ancient world and in other cultures that date back nearly to the time of Abraham. So, the real question is: Do you trust Joseph?

Question 3: Okay. Oh, here's one. This was from a kid, and I like this question. "Why are there angels?"

Answer: That's a great question.

> *[Angels] are subject [to God], to minister according to the word of his command, shewing themselves unto them of strong faith and a firm mind in every form of godliness. And the office of their ministry is to call men unto repentance, and to fulfill and to do the work of the covenants of the Father which he hath made unto the children of men, …declaring the word of Christ unto the chosen vessels of the Lord, that they may bear testimony of him; and by so doing, the Lord…prepareth the way that the residue of men may have faith in Christ.* (Moroni 7:6 RE)

There's a system that was adopted before the foundation of the world that was designed to bring to pass the salvation/the resurrection of all mankind after we fall into the grave. That system requires a lot of things to come together in order to achieve the purposes of God. You might think that the purpose of angels (in some of the online extravagant claims that we read that people make) is to appeal to the vanity and the pride of those to whom they come.

But my experience teaches me that the purpose of angels is to: first, cry repentance to the individual—because every individual before God is in need of repentance. There are none of us who have gone through life or who go through life daily without giving offense—however unintended and however slight—we, nevertheless, give offense to our fellow man and to God. We excuse ourselves. We just don't measure up. The office of the angelic ministrant is to snap you back out of the fog of indifference to the casualness in which you discharge your daily obligations and to awaken you to the **peril** that each of us face if we don't repent and return to God. It's to make us soberly assess our own personal inadequacies.

But their office isn't to get someone, somewhere, to pay attention to them and to try and be a better boy or girl. Their office is to invoke the salvation process itself, for the benefit of mankind.

Those to whom angelic ministrants have come from Heaven are given assignments to labor for the salvation of others. They use their own resources, and they wear out their lives and their time in pursuing the obligations imposed upon them, which include:

- The salvation of others.
- The crying of repentance to others.
- The bringing to pass the fulfillment of the covenants that God made with the Fathers.

If they're not laboring on an errand such as that but they claim to be receiving "God and Jesus in their living room who came and told them all about this or that," I don't know who they're entertaining, but it certainly doesn't fit the model, and it certainly doesn't fulfill the covenants of the Father nor **do** the work that's necessary in order to prepare the people for the coming of the ~~world~~ [Lord] so that the whole Earth is not utterly wasted at His coming.

Salvation for the souls of men is something that no one ought to be trifling with, least of all those who are vain and proud. And I don't care if that vanity comes because they think they're somehow specially chosen by some imagined encounter with the Great Beyond, or if they think they've been so careful in their study of Scripture that they know better than all others because they can clearly see a pattern through their own study, labor, and effort. I don't care what you think the correct interpretation of the Scriptures are or will be. It's fair game to look at 'em in whatever fashion you want to look at them. But when an angel from Heaven **tells** you what God is doing—or when the Lord Himself declares **what and how** He intends to go about vindicating the covenants that **He** made with the Fathers—then there's no room to come up with a contrary interpretation. The fact is your interpretation, then, is wrong. And the humble man and the searcher for light and truth will adapt what they understand from their learning and study to what it is that the Lord has declared. And what they will find is that if they'll conform to the word of the Lord, that their study and their learning is still of great benefit because it helps them to see things more clearly.

Scriptures are sometimes written deliberately in a way that conceals how the Lord intends to fulfill them—in order to let those who may mean mischief never arrive at the correct formula. And the proud and the haughty and all those that do wickedly are not necessarily irreligious or not necessarily unpersuaded that there's a restoration that is taking place through Joseph—they simply will not **yield** to what it is that God says they mean; they will not **yield** to the work that God says He now has underway.

So, angels align with the work of God, and they help bring about the repentance of **all** mankind.

Question 4: "If Christ is the prototype of the saved man, is Mary the prototype of the saved woman?"

Answer: Yes.

Question 4 (continued): "How did She earn Her place on the Throne without having atoned?"

Answer: Because She sacrificed and led the Lamb to the slaughter. She had a Lamb whose "fleece was white as snow," and She led that Lamb everywhere She wanted it to go. And She gave up Her Son and attained to the resurrection and laid claim upon Her body because She condescended to come here and to fulfill that work. Read *Our Divine Parents* (Denver C. Snuffer, Jr., Gilbert, Arizona, March 25, 2018). I don't know if that question was asked by someone that hasn't read *Our Divine Parents*, but that talk addresses that issue.

Question 5: [Chuckle] This is a **great** question. It's probably one of the more important questions that someone came up with: "The 'name of the Lord,' 'believe in His name,' 'believe **on** His name,' 'do things **in** His name,' and in the Testimony of St. John [they lift the quote] 'what name is now yours.' No one asked, 'What name is now yours?' Can you help us understand the importance of the name of the Lord?"

Answer: Yeah, uh, okay— Okay, let's put it into a bigger context. Hebrew (in the Old Testament form) lacked vowels. As a consequence of the lack of vowels, the name for the Lord had four Hebrew characters—the tetragram[maton]—which, lacking vowels, became unpronounceable. The pronunciation of that name was the **property** of the High Priest. And the correct pronunciation went from High Priest to High Priest who would use that name in the Holy of Holies in order to participate in the ordinances that were required there.

Because the name (we know the consonants, but we don't know the vowels [YHWH]) lacked the ability to pronounce it, when Jerome was working on the Latin Vulgate version and came to the letters, he rendered it "Jehovah." And there are a lot of people who, today, have supplied different vowels, and they render it "Yahweh." (I think the "Yahweh" pronunciation was the creation of a Germanic theological movement in the 1940s, and Yahweh came out of that—although the Germans may have borrowed it earlier from Yittish or from Hebrew sources.) But the truth of the matter is that the name of God, like **many** Hebrew words, are late-in-time reconstructions of probable pronunciations of the Hebrew lettering, and they've gained common acceptance at this point. But if you were to take someone who is absolutely fluent in speaking modern Hebrew and you were to take them back and put them in a setting with/contemporaneous with Moses, even though they may be relying upon the same basic language, they may not even be able to communicate with one another because the pronunciations are so incredibly strange.

"Strange."

"StrănGeh."

"StrānGee."

The word "strange"—how are you gonna pronounce that?

"Străn Jee." If someone were to say "străn jee" to you, would you know they intended to be saying strange? You'd think it was gibberish.

The modern convention of how we reconstruct pronunciations is— across the board, and I don't care if you're appealing to the most learned Rabbi breathing today—is **wrong**. It's not correct. And I **know** that to be the case. So, having said that…

Jerome supplied us with "Jehovah." It was early; and so subsequent additions of Christian literature accepted the convention and used that term as a nomenclature where anyone who's reading the Bible knows the Personage that we are attempting to assign this identity to or this name to. We know Who we're talking about. But what the correct pronunciation may be, notwithstanding, we're **calling** Him, "Jehovah." And so, King James' translators, Wycliffe, others who rendered the… Martin Luther in his German Bible, they all adopted the pronunciation that had been suggested. So it's just an agreed-upon convention. We know Who we're talking about. We're gonna use this as the Person about whom we're talking.

Then others come along and think, "Well, this is the vulgar, on the street, common, ill-informed, uneducated name for the Almighty. But, surely, the Almighty deserves the dignity and the benefit of higher learning, and our higher learning suggests after we lay 'four years prostrate to the higher mind [and] got [our] paper [which set us] free' (see *Closer to Fine*, Indigo Girls)—we now can say with authority should be 'Yahweh.' It's Yahweh; that's His name—ohmmmm— because only the uninitiated in the mysteries of our theological schools use the common and vulgar term 'Jehovah.' So, when you say, 'Jehovah,' I know (from my vantage point atop the ivory tower) that I'm really talking to a Plebeian and a pedestrian and the ignorant who has not yet been initiated into correct pronunciations."

Well, it's not Yahweh, either.

The name in Greek of Joshua (or Yeshua)—in Greek is Jesus. And the New Testament was either originally composed (or in its first translations composed) in Greek. And so the name that we inherited, as a consequence of running all the stories about Yeshua (or Joshua) through Greek, is Jesus. And the status of being "anointed"—which is what Messiah (or Mashiach) means: "anointed." I mean, it could have been "Joshua, the Anointed," but it turned into "Jesus." And the word in Greek for "anointing" is "Christ" or "Christos." And so Jesus became Jesus Christ, and that became the common vernacular by which the identity of that Person who came and taught the Sermon on the Mount, who lived and died as a Jewish teacher, crucified on a Roman cross, and raised the third day from the dead is in our common language referred to as Jesus Christ.

Now, you can say, "I would like to be more pure and use 'Yeshua.'" Or, "I would like to be at least more Hebraic and call Him 'Joshua.'" And, "I don't like 'Christ'—I like 'Messiah' or 'Mashiach.' I like that better."

And as long as what you're talking about is the same person (the identity of Whom is fixed by Scripture), I'm not gonna quibble over how you want to pronounce it.

But the fact of the matter is that in the restoration process, God (who condescends and who is humble enough to speak with men plainly, in plain humility, as one man talks to another) took absolutely no offense to the Book of Mormon and the modern revelations calling Him by the name "Jesus Christ." **I use** the name Jesus Christ because **He** took no offense in that name.

When John the Baptist came and visited with Oliver and Joseph and conferred upon them authority to baptize, the only name he mentioned was "Messiah." *Upon you, my fellow servants, in the name of Messiah I confer the priesthood of Aaron* (Joseph Smith History 14:1 RE). John's a good Jewish boy, and so, he uses a Hebrew-based term rather than a Greek-based term. But it's still not the original Hebrew, pronounced correctly, because that's been lost. The idea…

(Well, I'm not gonna go there. That's a-whole-nother subject, and that's minutes that I don't wanna take.) The correct pronunciation of God belongs in the **last** dispensation as it belonged in the beginning: in the temple. And if there were ever a full Restoration, that would be one of the things about which information would be granted, and we'd finally clear that up.

But for the present, so far as **I** am concerned, "Jesus Christ" is a perfectly-fitting name to be used in prayer, in addressing the Almighty, or in referring to Him. And if someone else wants to call Him "Yeshua," it's not gonna trouble me—because I know Who they're talking about. If they want to call Him "Messiah" rather than "Christ," that doesn't trouble me, either. If they want to call Him "Yahweh," I'm fine with that, too. But that doesn't mean I agree that they're correctly nailing the ancient pronunciation of the name (that they're going to some trouble to pretend they possess great knowledge about).

Question 6: "What does it mean when the Answer to the Covenant states to not forsake the house of Israel?" (See T&C 158:11.)

Answer: You know, the house of Israel occupies a very unique place in history. That is true not only of the Native American remnant of the house of Israel but also of the Jewish house of Israel. We are not to forsake them by ignoring them, by forgetting them, by failing to pray concerning them—people who believe strongly enough in the preservation of their culture... In the Native American sense, their culture was ravaged by apostasy before the arrival of European conquerors, devastated by disease that was imported, defeated in war waged against them, and then consigned to reservation property; and yet, despite all that, there are Native Americans who hold on to a culture that reaches back and has within it echoes of the very truths that we also find in the Book of Mormon.

Their highest and holy teachings resound with the same themes of light and darkness, creation by God, power in the heavens, accountability for the good deeds you do. They reach more closely and correctly into an understanding that nature itself is an extension of God and the mind of God and that harmony between man and nature is something that is part of their religion and should be also part of ours.

The Jews have persisted through centuries of persecution and slaughter. My own family line (when you get back far enough) includes a series of Rabbis. My last name is actually an Americanization of a German... It's an **old** German word, because the transition occurred in the 1400s. In German, the word meant "breath" or "spirit." There's a Hebrew word that means "breath" or "spirit" that is the probable original family-name that got converted into the Germanic (old Germanic) name or the old Germanic word for "breath," which is, well, it's spelled "S-c-h-n-a-u-f-e-r," which, when they migrated to America (that happened before there was a United States—my ancestors were here long before —more than a century and a half before—this country was founded), it was too hard to pronounce, and so it got converted into something that they can pronounce here. At the same time, there were others who came over with the same last name, and their names got altered into other various forms, but the original name goes back to that *ru'ach,* the word for "breath." It's what animated Adam when he was given breath; it's what the Holy Spirit of God is called in their language.

I don't think that how we decide to pronounce matters when we have language in Scripture that... I don't think you improve or show greater respect or show greater homage or honor to God by adopting a different form. I think you show greater respect for God—no matter by what name you choose to call Him—by your heed and your diligence to what it is that He asks of you. It is in the **doing** of what's requested that we show the respect that He asks of us.

Question 7: Here's another one: "Christ said that the gifts of the spirit would follow those who believe. The gifts are far too **un**common, even among us. Your ideas, please."

Answer: Well, one of the things that we are cautioned about is boasting about the gifts of the spirit that we experience. There have been a lot of spiritual/divine encounters, miraculous encounters, vindicated blessings that I have either witnessed or participated in or I know about. And I say very, very little about them.

One of the problems with significant signs is that when **that** is the focus—and not obedience and laboring to achieve what the Lord would have done—when the focus is upon signs and we boast about 'em, you attract sign-seekers, including the adulterers who lust after such things and run from sign-giver to sign-giver. Christ constantly told those to whom He performed some miraculous work, "See that you tell no man," and they would go out, and they would brag about it, and they would shout about it, and they... And then the net result of that was that a lot of followers were attracted who were not attracted to the **work**. A lot of people were excited to hear some new titillating thing, but they weren't willing to roll up their sleeves and sacrifice. They were not willing to sell all that they have, give to the poor, and "Come, follow [him]," as he asked the rich young man on the road that he was traveling toward Jerusalem—even though, had the rich young man done that, we would probably all be talking about him today in a name and not in a category. He relegated himself to merely a category because he was unwilling to step out of that category, have his name known to God and to us by the sacrifice that he made in order to follow the Lord.

The fact is that however appealing you may believe the things of God to be from what you read in Scripture, when you begin to live them, you realize every single one of them lived under a strain—a burden:

- Those words of Moses in early Exodus help illustrate it.

- Nephi's lamentation about all the trouble that they had (and all the suffering that they did and what they had to endure) was so significant that he can't even explain all the troubles that they passed through.

- Joseph Smith's life was filled with compromise by his friends, treachery by those that should have stood by him, betrayal, loss after loss, economic circumstance that brought about trouble after trouble, advisers that told him if he would do this that they would do that, who then failed to keep their obligation to him.

So, there are signs. They do exist. I have witnessed many of them, but I find no value in talking about or appealing to the minds and hearts of those to whom signs are appealing. I would rather keep them and ponder them in my own heart to try to understand—and then to arrive at the point where it is possible, using the Scriptures, to teach the truths—just as Nephi (who would not reveal what he'd encountered in a heavenly vision) used Isaiah in order to testify of the things that had been revealed to him. That's a good pattern. And so I speak very little about some of the most important things, but I take them into account as I try to teach things that will bring us all to the **labor** of keeping the covenants of the Father.

Question 8: Okay, so now I'm just gonna do something entertaining that reaches far and wide, and you can do with this as you see fit. Okay, "Who were the three Wisemen who visited Jesus after He was born? Where did they come from?"

Answer: Probably Magna [audience laughter]. I say that... I hope no one's from Magna! I say that because I use Magna in a lot of my personal humor. (I don't know... If I do this, someone's gonna be sorely offended.) But Magna's a small town; it's a mining town. And it's suffered a lot because of mine tailings. And so, you know, there's kind of a perception that if you live in Magna, you're probably gonna have buck-teeth and three legs because your genetic makeup has been altered by the chemicals from the mine out there (that is now bigger than the mountain that it's been carved in).

So, I will occasionally use Magna in a self-deprecating way. Someone pays you a compliment, and you say, "Well, that's the rough equivalent of being the homecoming queen at Magna." [Audience laughter.] And I really, I mean, I'm saying this stuff while I'm apologizing for saying it, but I have a perverse sense of humor in that way—and Magna suffers a lot at my expense.

So, the three Wisemen…

Okay, they didn't come from Magna. There's a lot of lore that got preserved that actually **can** be pieced together to tell a story. And I'm gonna tell one version of that story because **I like it**, and it appeals to me in ways that are evidence of God's mercy and caring and love for us. So, here is that story, piecing together a diverse group of legends and tales:

Before Adam was cast out of the Garden of Eden (into the world in which death would enter, and Adam would be obligated to succumb to that death), there was an anointing oil prepared in Eden itself that was designed to be used in order to help the Descendant of Adam who would come to crush the head of the serpent that—once He was anointed—would equip Him to come back from the grave and be resurrected. And that was entrusted into Adam's care (before he was cast out of the Garden) as something to be preserved and handed down until the time that the Messiah comes. And as circumstances would have it, that got passed from those that had the responsibility, down through the generations until, finally, Melchizedek turned it over to father Abraham who, in turn, handed it down through his lineage. And subsequently, there was a line entrusted not only with possession of the anointing oil that came from Eden but also knowledge about the signs that would be given when the moment came for the oil to be delivered.

And so it was that the sign was given. They recognized and interpreted it correctly. They went to the place where it had been stored by their ancestors. They retrieved it, and then they traveled to find Him who was born the King of the Jews. And upon finding the family (with a sign that signified—from above, according to their understanding and interpretation of the signs—that this was the child, this was the family), they delivered the gifts, which were, in turn, used. But the oil for anointing was kept. And that oil was handed down until, finally, the moment came when the Savior intended to go up and to provoke His crucifixion.

And preliminary to that moment, Mary (the mother) instructed Mary (the consort of Christ) in the manner by which this was to be done. And so, He was anointed—in preparation for His death and His burial and His rising again—with what had been set out and kept (originating in Eden) to be used in order to complete the process of qualifying Him to return again, to have strength in the loins and in the sinews, and the power to rise again from the dead and to lay hold upon all of the faculties of the immortal, physical body.

And so, He was anointed—at the end—with the oil that had been entrusted, originally, to Adam and handed down with an obscure and small body of believers (who were dying out and who were older and the last of their tradition, it seemed). But the Messiah came, and they discharged the obligation, and the blessing was able to be given, and the Savior was able to rise from the dead. And so, He opened the way, then, for the return from the grave of **everyone** who has faith on His name and accepts (on condition of repentance) the terms to have His atonement applied to us.

Now, I know we're a little bit early, but I'm tired of talking, and I'm really looking forward to the closing hymn, which I understand is going to be as good as the musical number in the interlude, which was absolutely wonderful. So, Tausha, if you wanna come up, then I'll get outta here and return to…

You can't see anyone; these lights, they blind you. So, as far as you know, you're just talking to an empty group.

Thanks.

Appendix: Personal Revelation

Paper based upon a Lecture delivered in Sandy, UT
September 16, 2008

Jesus Christ had to be willing to receive the light and truth. Believe it or not, today we're just talking about the same thing. This is just about personal revelation. All of it is. And it's about how you receive light and truth.

All right, one problem with treating you as if you were a jury is the mandatory statement in the Doctrine and Covenants—much ignored by us but nevertheless the case—which says, *If ye receive not the Spirit ye shall not teach* (D&C 42:14). I view that as mandatory. *If ye receive not the Spirit **ye shall not**...* is one of the prohibitions on what we ought to be doing. (I'm always amazed at those who are eager to do this kind of thing. I am a reluctant draftee. I don't want to do this. I don't think I will ever do this again. Doug Mendenhall nags me to these things. I'm telling you that if he tells you I'm coming again, don't believe him, because I view this as a terrible responsibility.) Anytime you're going to take up the subject of truth and you're going to speak, I think you have an obligation to do so by the spirit, and if you don't, then the requirement is: Shut up. Just don't do it.

We have this erroneous reading of the description given in section 138 about those that were called to be rulers.[80] There is a parallel to be drawn between the statement in section 138 and the description given by Abraham in the pre-existence. That's about how Abraham was chosen: "You were one of them; you were one of them that were chosen before the world began to be a ruler."[81]

In the Book of Mormon, the equation is *ruler* and *teacher*. It has nothing to do with position or rank or authority. Being a ruler[82] has everything to do with whether or not you teach. Nephi says in the Book of Mormon that my brothers are always angry at me because I'm going to be a teacher and a ruler over them.[83] Teacher and ruler are an equivalent.

Abraham presided over a family, but Abraham learned great truths, he taught great truths, and he is distinguished as a consequence of the things which he learned and he taught. You can occupy a position of authority and never say one thing worth anyone remembering, and therefore, you are not (by definition, using the Book of Mormon) a *ruler*.

On the other hand, you can be one of the least of the Lord's. In fact, the most memorable statements I have heard in church meetings came from a stake president bearing testimony while talking about the David and Goliath conflict in the Old Testament. They came from an elderly woman, widowed and in ill health, bearing testimony in a fast and testimony meeting. When I think about those talks that have affected me, that have enlightened me, that have enlivened me, it is the rule that they come from odd places. It is the exception when I hear something like Hugh B. Brown's "Profile of a Prophet,"[84] which still resonates with me. There are talks, the greatness of which will endure forever. Paul talking on Mars Hill is still resonating in the world.[85]

(Well, I'll be quiet while they move the chalkboard. I surrender to the chaos. Just out of curiosity, do we have a marker and an eraser? Because it's a lot of trouble to go to. Oh, we do.)

If you read section 42 and what the Scriptures generally have to say about this subject, the obligation becomes that if you're going to say something, to say it by the spirit. (I'm hoping that the trip to and from the airport, the soccer game that I've had to go to, and the fact that when I leave here, I'm in a hurry to get my daughter and get her to the pet store to buy the frozen pinky mice for her pet corn snake and then get her to her babysitting appointment at 6 o'clock will all come together somehow happily—and that I can forget about that while I'm here. Have you seen her corn snake? It's pink, light-colored, and a pretty snake, as snakes go.) By the way, all of this bears on a subject that we'll get to, but it is necessary to triangulate in if you're really going to say something meaningful.

One of the latest offerings about our greatest controversy, we now have in publication, *Massacre at Mountain Meadows*.[86] Everyone has referred to it as "Turley's book" when it was coming out, but listed, in order of priority, the authors are:

1. Ronald Walker, who is an independent historian and writer of Latter-day Saint history.

2. Richard Turley is listed second; he's an assistant church historian for The Church of Jesus Christ of Latter-day Saints, and then

3. Glen Leonard is listed as the third author, as the former director of the LDS Museum of Church History and Art.

It is published by Oxford University and carried by Deseret Book. It was the intention that it be published by Oxford Press to bear the imprimatur of independent scholarly approval on the book and not be something that is simply an apology.

But when you go back to the Acknowledgments portion of the book and you look at who all was involved in getting this into print, it references:

> ...Colleagues in the Family and Church History Department and other departments of The Church of Jesus Christ of Latter-day Saints and Brigham Young University traveled to many libraries, archives, and other historical institutions...[87]

...and then it listed all of the institutions that they went to, and it is formidable.[88]

They give a special thanks to all of those from those various church institutional sources who participated in this information gathering and give credit to them. Then they thank "the professionalism of several editors" and then list the editors, many of them inside the Church or Deseret Book, but then they also thank an editor from Oxford University Press. They thank:

> Others at church headquarters or Brigham Young University who gave countless hours of assistance with their various skills and knowledge includ[ing]...

...and they give a page-and-a-half list of names.[89] These are names that are involved in doing the review, and included among them is Dean C. Jessee, who is working on the *Joseph Smith Papers*.

They also thank "the skills and knowledge of archivists, librarians, historians" and who provided information and some "three dozen friends and scholars [who] read it and offer[ed] feedback" on the manuscript. Included among them are some very interesting names like:

> Lavina Fielding Anderson, Richard L. Anderson, Sharon Avery, …Lowell C. Bennion, …Ed Firmage, …John H. Groberg, … Stephen D. Robison, …John W. Welch….[90]

(Jack Welch is ubiquitous. You can't get anything into print without Jack Welch's name appearing somewhere, always printed as "John W. Welch.") There is thanks given to doctors who helped them[91] and to others who are scholars that looked into it and pages of names. Among the names that appear are:

> Richard L. Bushman, John K. Carmack, …Sheri L. Dew, Ronald K. Esplin, …Armaud L. Mauss, Cory H. and Karen Maxwell [my suspicion is Karen did more than Cory did, but that is just my suspicion, and] Jan Shipps.[92]

And then, they end all of these many pages of "Who's Who" with:

> We also express appreciation for the support and feedback of Russell M. Nelson and Dallin Oaks, advisors to the Family and Church History Department, and of Marlin K. Jensen, Church Historian.[93]

Therefore, from all of this, I assume that this is a very deliberate book. This is a very calculated and intentional book. The words that appear in this have been weighed carefully in the balance and chosen in order to have an effect. Let's accept that as a given for the moment. (Go read the "Acknowledgments" if you would like to check that and reach your own conclusion.)

There are precious few things which appear in this book, *Massacre at Mountain Meadows*, which touch upon the subject of revelation or visitations. I think I can read all of them to you. I may have missed some because I just finished the book a few hours ago and may not have been as deliberate as I went through it as they were in preparing it, but I think these are the relevant quotes.

This first quote is talking about the primary villain responsible—ultimately, the only one that will be executed for the crime of murder of over a hundred and twenty people at Mountain Meadows. This is Brother John D. Lee:

> During missionary tours to Illinois, Kentucky, and Tennessee, Lee said he beheld heavenly visions, contested with evil spirits, and defeated other Christian ministers with strong, inspired words. Although at first timid and inexperienced before a congregation, he soon believed he was transformed by a higher power. "My tongue was like the pen of a ready writer. I scarcely knew what I was saying," he reflected, after speaking to a congregation for an hour and a half.
>
> "I grew in grace from day to day," he said....[94]

That's from page 60: "...beheld heavenly visions, contested with evil spirits, [and] defeated other Christian ministers with strong, inspired words."

Beginning on page 65, there's another source they quote at some length, speaking also about John D. Lee on the subject of inspiration and the spirit:

> Thomas D. Brown...wrote an extended passage in his diary that accused Lee of having an "abundance of dreams, visions and revelations" that he used for his own purposes. Brown believed the actual source of Lee's information was more ordinary. "He listened behind a fence to Bros. P[eter] Shirts and W[illia]m Young who are talking of his immeasurable selfishness, and he repeated it next meeting as having read it from a sheet let down from the heavens before his eyes," Brown claimed.

Then on page 66, there is the incident in which Lee (thinking he was temporarily out of favor with his adopted father, Brigham Young) was troubled over whether he would get the appointment to be the U.S. Indian farmer to the Paiute people. This was a governmental position which Brigham Young could make an official appointment, as Young was at the time the governor and his adopted father. Lee was sweating over that because it meant an income for him. Brigham Young did make the appointment, which gratified Lee because now he knew he was not out of sync with his adopted father.

> When Lee learned of his appointment, he wept—not because it satisfied his ambition, he said, but because it allowed him to continue to serve. He later said that several days before Young's letter arrived, "an angel of the Lord…stood by [his] bedside and talked…about these and many other things."[95]

Now, are you picking up a pattern yet about how spiritual phenomenon are being dealt with in this deliberate book? We're confining it exclusively to Lee in this account, and since John Lee will ultimately turn out to be filled with all manner of wickedness and chicanery, revelation is made dubious.

Then an incident occurs (that is set out on page 172) after Lee led the early abortive attack and personally became involved in the surrounding of the emigrants' wagons (when they were dug-in) in the fracas that ensued. In the bullet fire that was going on, he got hit several times in his clothing, but he did not get injured. Then, a couple of Mormon communication bearers, Willden and Clewes, arrived. (By the way, you'll want this account in your own mind to juxtapose with the statement about Willard Richards—why he escaped Carthage Jail without any injury and what some people believe that possession of the temple rites do for you,[96] which is not mentioned in *Massacre at Mountain Meadows*, but keep that in mind.)

> At one point—perhaps after getting bullet holes in his clothing —

Undoubtedly, because that's the point: He has the bullet holes. But this is between dashes; it's just to remind you that we have got that background.

> At one point—perhaps after getting bullet holes in his clothing —Lee had told the Paiutes "that the bullets of the emigrants would not hurt the 'Mormons' the same as the Indians." Seeing Willden and Clewes, the Paiutes decided to test Lee's claim. They "demanded that Willden and Clewes should put on

Indian attire and run unarmed past the emigrant camp within easy range of the rifles, to a neighboring point about a hundred yards distant." It may have been the same route Jackson's brother took when he was shot. The two white men concluded that they would have to "take their chances" in doing what the Indians demanded "or risk being killed by them. So they ran, amid a shower of bullets from the emigrant camp and reached the opposite point in safety." The men then returned to the Paiute camp, where they "were heartily cheered for their bravery after their perilous run." Soon, said Clewes, "we were hailed from a ridge on our left; we looked around and there stood John D. Lee." Lee told the Indians to return to their camp— "pacif[ying] their feelings by making explanations to them"—then sat down and talked to Clewes and Willden.[97]

Well, we get that. In the context of this book and this treatment—and given the fact that the focus of the tale is upon the worst crime committed in the history of the Church—these are the first words; this is the Preface:

On September 11, 1857, Mormon settlers in southern Utah used a false flag of truce to lull a group of California-bound emigrants from their circled wagons and then slaughter them. When the killing was over, more than one hundred butchered bodies lay strewn across half-mile stretch of an upland meadow. Most of the victims were women and children. The perpetrators were members of the Church of Jesus Christ of Latter-day Saints aided by Indians.[98]

It makes no apology for the Church's involvement but instead exposes it. It limits the damage to those who were locally involved in perpetrating it and doesn't gloss it over. It's a very raw, candid description—including of the killings themselves.

I've read to you from this book essentially all of those deliberately-prepared statements in it with respect to the subject of visions, revelations, and visitations.

And so, if you are going to form an opinion about how we regard the subject of visitations, and this is the latest statement from all of the gathered "powers that be," blue-bloods, insiders, credentialed folks—all the good people that we rely upon—if that's what they had to say about it, you would have a hard time reconciling that with what our nineteen-year-old missionaries do.

The nineteen-year-old missionaries go out, they hand people the Book of Mormon, and they say, "Look! Look, here in Moroni 10:4, it says *Ask God*, and He's going to tell you. And oh, by the way, this whole thing began when Joseph Smith read in Scripture, *Ask of God*. Joseph read that *God…giveth to all men liberally and upbraideth not* (James 1:5 LE). And Moroni says if you *ask with a sincere heart,* God's going to answer you." Our missionaries go about saying to everyone, "You go get revelation."

In the *Massacre at Mountain Meadows*, we encounter Richard E. Turley, Jr., the Assistant LDS Church Historian, writing in a way that is reviewed by the LDS Church Historian, Marlin K. Jensen (who I knew when he was still practicing law). No one seems to have said, "Wait a minute—for a church whose bedrock indispensably remains the presence of the spirit, and in order to expand requires those that would like to join to go ask of God and get an answer to prayer, ought we not to do something more with the passing mention of revelation then to simply confine it to the guy who gets executed for the crime?"

John D. Lee is the guy who led the charge that created the problem and the guy who shot someone. We—the Church—had to cover it up because white men were involved in this incident, and if the emigrants got out, the emigrants were going to spread the word of that. Ought this book not put revelation in the hands of someone else and in some other context?

There is a little bit more—and to be fair, I probably ought to read that on page 181—because the sisters were involved. This is after the militia had set off from Cedar City to finish the deed and to kill the remaining emigrants under the direction of the stake president.

> At 2:00 that afternoon, leaders of the Cedar City Female Benevolent Society held their regular meeting. "Sister Haight" reported she had been visiting some of the Cedar women and "taught them the necessity of being obedient to their husbands"

and not to be fearful in these "troublesome" and "squally times." …They had advised the women they visited "to attend strictly to secret prayer in behalf of the brethren that are out acting in our defence."[99]

So, prayer creeps in here, too. There's also this comment on page 187 in the chapter "Decoyed Out and Destroyed," as they got ready for the final killings:

The men sat in a circle off by themselves and began by praying for "Divine guidance," a sacrilege that only the passions of the time could explain.[100]

So, we also have an example of prayer in the book.

Now, I find this troublesome. I find it more than troublesome. I find it troubling enough that it's worth commenting on as we get into the subject of revelation. Because there is a competition afoot. It is a competition that, if history should inform us of anything, it should inform us of this tension. This is always the case. There is always an effort to turn the gospel of Christ into religion and then to turn religion into something that is very different from its founding. You have to be on your guard, and the Church has to be on its guard. Every one of us have to wage war against this process because this process is foreseeable, predictable, and knowable. If you want to know how it happened in the past, all you have to do is study the past. But the present cannot be studied; it is only lived. And we do not always notice it as we live it.

I was surprised in reading…

(I watched the soccer game today; okay, I did. But there were timeouts. I don't know what they did to bring that little girl into that crumpled ball off the field. I mean, it didn't look like that, but the girl that kicked her was rather big. And then we had halftime, and so there [were] long periods when I was reading this just a few hours ago.)

The book I'm wading into at the moment is the latest in "The Collected Works of Hugh Nibley," *Eloquent Witness: Nibley on Himself, Others, and the Temple.* Some of this material struck me. This is a publication of "The Neal A. Maxwell Institute for Religious

Scholarship and Hugh Nibley and Associates, LLC."[101] (There didn't used to be a Hugh Nibley and Associates—the next generation after Brother Nibley's death LLC'd up.) The volume is printed by Deseret Book Company, so there's hope. There's happy news. This squeaked through. These two books (*Mountain Meadows Massacre* and *Eloquent Witness*) came out at virtually the same time. They were hot on the shelves when I walked in and picked them up a few days ago.

This is Nibley in an interview that they've published:

> And the two marks of the Church I see are and have been for a long time these: a reverence for wealth and a contempt for the scriptures. Naturally, the two go hand in hand. We should call attention to the fact that these things we are doing are against the work of the Lord. There is one saying of Joseph Smith I think of quite often. If the heavens seem silent at a time when we desperately need revelation, it is because of covetousness in the Church. "God had often sealed up the heavens because of covetousness in the Church." And now the Church isn't just shot through with covetousness, it is **saturated** with covetousness. And so the heavens are going to be closed. We're told we don't get revelation if we put our trust in money in the bank.[102]

Okay, what do you do? That's answered a little later in the same book, about how you seal the heavens up because you are covetous.[103]

One page 127 in *Eloquent Witness* is a description of what happened in the Christian church during the history of Christianity and the church fathers. At this point in the narrative, we are a couple of hundred years post-Christ, into the era when the apostles are gone, and we've got a limit on ongoing revelation. I'm reading Hugh Nibley's words:

> When the Church lost revelation it had to turn to another source for guidance and so it threw itself into the arms of the established schools of learning. The schoolmen, as one of them expresses it, took over the office and function once belonging to the prophets and once in power guarded their authority with jealous care, quickly and violently suppressing any suggestion of a recurrent inspiration.[104]

I shouldn't read this, but on the same page is a great comment by Nibley:

> While I was at Berkeley I was asked to speak to a student group on the subject, "Is the University of California anti-religious?" After considerable inquiry, I was forced to admit that the Berkeley institution is if anything less anti-religious than BYU, where religion is under more conscious and deliberate attack. But I do not for that reason hold my BYU colleagues culpable **—they cannot help themselves**. By its very nature the university is the rival of the Church; its historic mission has been to supply the guiding light which passed away with a loss of revelation, and it can make no concessions to its absolute authority without forfeiting that authority.[105]

Here's another quote a couple of pages later:

> The celebrations of the learned men and **not** the utterances of the prophets comprise the gospel [according to the university]. This has been the credo of the Christian schoolmen since the days of Clement of Alexandria: the universities—Christian, Moslem, Jewish, or pagan—has its own religion, and the basic tenet of that religion is the denial of revelation.[106]

(Then Nibley quotes from C.S. Lewis, but I'm not going to read that.) So, there's hope, because this Nibley volume is from some of the same folks as those involved with the *Massacre at Mountain Meadows* book. (I didn't look, but I'm sure Jack Welch has his name in here somewhere, too.[107] You can't get into print without him appearing here, as he does in the other.)

There is hope—perhaps some schizophrenia—but hope, nonetheless, in the way that these publications unfold.

So, what of it all? Our language is still permeated by words of usage and descriptors which presumed a whole different world than the one we live in now: words like "envision" or "light." We accept the idea of describing anything that is not in front of your face and using the word "envision" as the manner and the proper word to use when you're talking about it. For example:

- Can you **envision** what Utah will look like in 2050?
- Can you **envision** what the new temple in Draper will look like when it is completed?
- Can you **envision** this or that?

This word usage is a holdover from another period of time in which the visionary experience was so commonplace that it leaked into and permeated the vocabulary, and we all thought it perfectly appropriate.

- Can you give me further **light** on that subject?
- Can you shed some **light** on that?
- Are we **enlightened** on the subject yet?

You can be talking about anything from General Motors to solving the problem of sabermetrics. (Sabermetrics is a subject worthy of devotion. If anyone here wants to devote themselves to a Ph.D. effort, that's the study of mathematics and baseball and figuring out what really wins games. I think we owe a lot to Billy Beane, the general manager of the Oakland A's. If you have a resistance to reading obscenities in print, then you ought not to get it, but if you'd really like to know what playing baseball is all about, the book *Moneyball* [108] is just full of light and truth—and a number of obscenities at the same time.)

Joseph Smith brought a flood of light—literally, a flood of light. He defies categorization. (I appreciate the efforts of the scholars. I applaud the work that they do. But they don't give us the answers.) You have to find a revelator if you would like to get the answers. The preeminent one for our time was and is Joseph Smith. He covered the turf. What we're trying to do is catch up with him and to figure out what it was that he was talking about. Joseph repeatedly said, "Hey, I can't go any further than this. The Lord forbid me from saying any more."

> *And many other things did he say [reveal] unto me, which I cannot write at this time.* (JS-H 1:20 LE)

> *But great and marvelous are the works of the Lord, and the mysteries of his kingdom which he showed unto us, which surpass all understanding…which he commanded us we should not write while we were yet in the Spirit.* (D&C 76:114-115)

In the account of the First Vision, the account that we find in section 76, and (repeatedly) in the Book of Mormon, we get right up to the precipice, and then the curtain is closed. The Scriptures say, "Nah, we're not going to go there." And why aren't we going to go there? We're not going to go there because we would profane it. We would take and desecrate it if we put it on public view.

Doesn't the Lord want us to know this stuff? Well, of course, He does! In the proper setting, with the proper person, in the proper light, so that you know that it will not be profaned or desecrated, the Lord will show anything to anyone that anyone would like to see. He's told us that. Joseph said that repeatedly: "He didn't show me anything that he won't show unto the least of you."[109]

(Hey, Benjamin, can you come here? Make sure you lock it when you come back. In the middle of the car, I left the *Teachings of the Prophet Joseph Smith*. It's a small, leather-bound copy, and it's right in-between the seats. We need Joseph in more ways than one.)

Joseph Smith was way, way out ahead, and we still have not caught up. Plus, we display the least amount of curiosity about the things which are most enticing. He throws out a statement and just dangles it—and then no more. What was the reaction of Nephi to the dangling statements versus the reaction of Laman and Lemuel to the dangling statements? We know what Laman and Lemuel said. They said, *The Lord maketh no such thing known unto us* (1 Nephi 15:9 LE). And what did Nephi say? He said, *Have ye inquired of the Lord?* (Ibid. vs.8). Have you asked? Have you asked? Have you asked? "No, we have not asked; for the Lord maketh no such thing known unto us."

Now, you are warned to be careful—you must be very careful. In the *Encyclopedia of Mormonism* on the subject of "Revelation," one of the great precautionary statements there is that the devil is going to crop up and mislead you.[110]

On KSL this week, I noticed a news article on the 30th anniversary of a terrible August 1978 event.[111] The news again repeated how a woman threw her seven children off an 11th-floor hotel balcony thirty years ago, and after killing them, she jumped off and killed herself. Then the brother-in-law to the woman (the uncle to the children) was again quoted explaining how the husband—his brother—was Jesus Christ and God the Father and that because the husband had committed suicide back then, the family committed mass suicide to be with him again. The uncle was quoted:

> They couldn't live without him. Can you imagine what kind of faith it would take for a whole family to leap from the 11th floor of a hotel? Can you imagine what kind of faith that would take?[112]

That incident is another cautionary tale from the Church's newspaper: Be careful. Be afraid. Be very, very afraid. Revelation, you see, could turn you into John D. Lee. Revelation may lead you to throw people off a balcony. Be very afraid. These are not just random happenstances. This is the era in which we find ourselves. This is the times in which we live.

This is a comment that Joseph made, from page 51 of the *Teachings of the Prophet Joseph Smith*. (There is so much which I would canonize in the *Teachings* if I were given discretion to ask you to sustain things and add to Scripture. We'd have a bigger quad, and we'd all look like high priests.)

> We consider that God has created man with a mind capable of instruction, and a faculty which may be enlarged in proportion to the heed and diligence given to the light communicated from heaven to the intellect; and that the nearer man approaches perfection, the clearer are his views, and the greater his enjoyments….

This is Joseph Smith using prose to describe the process because, for Joseph, it was prosaic; it was poetry; it was a thing of beauty. "Light communicated from heaven to the intellect." "A mind capable of instruction…a faculty which may be enlarged in proportion to the heed and diligence [that's] given."[113] These aren't just idle words. These are Joseph trying to put into the English language a description of a process. And the process works.

Well, a couple of other Scriptures before we start on to something. This is from Doctrine and Covenants section 93, one of Joseph's most profound revelations, beginning in verse 27:

> *And no man receiveth a fulness unless he keepeth his commandments. He that keepeth his commandments receiveth truth and light, until he is glorified in truth and knoweth all things...*

Well, that's interesting: keeping commandments, receiving truth and light, glorified in truth, knows all things. Then he adds,

> *Man was also in the beginning with God. Intelligence, or the light of truth, was not created or made, neither indeed can be. All truth is independent in that sphere in which God has placed it, to act for itself, as all intelligence also; otherwise there is no existence.*
>
> *...The glory of God is intelligence, or, in other words, light and truth. Light and truth forsake that evil one.*
>
> *...And that wicked one cometh and taketh away light and truth, through disobedience, from the children of men, and because of the tradition of their fathers.* (D&C 93:27-30,36-37,39)

Well, we are trying to acquire light and truth, aren't we?

So, we've got these interesting statements. There's this notion that there is some relationship between keeping commandments, on the one hand, and receiving truth and light, on the other hand. Then, there is this statement about *intelligence, or the light of truth, was not created or made* (Ibid. vs. 29)—intelligence was not created or made. Intelligence or "the light of truth," and "the glory of God," then—it is redefined *glory of God...intelligence...light and truth* (Ibid. vs. 36). Okay, in two separate statements, in verses 29 and 36, it's reiterated for us twice that intelligence, that which can't be created or destroyed—and **can't** be created or destroyed—intelligence is light and truth. Light and truth, co-equal with God.

Now, that's an interesting statement because here we have the word "intelligence," and it appears in the **singular**. When you go back to Abraham chapter 3, beginning in verse 22, it says,

> *Now the Lord had shown unto me, Abraham, the **intelligences** that were organized...*

Now we've encountered something that has a **plural** to it. And in Abraham chapter 3, when it talks about the plural form of this,

> *...the intelligences that were organized before the world was; and among all these there were many of the noble and great ones; ...he stood among those that were...* (Abraham 3:22 LE, emphasis added)

From what then were your spirits organized? Light and truth. At your core, at your nub, at the very essence of what it is that constitutes you to be you, what is it that constitutes you to be you? Light and truth. There's another place where a description is given of the Christ—the Lord—in the pre-existence: *In the beginning was the Word* (John 1:1 LE). Now, that's an interesting thought, that word. What you have at your core is light and truth or intelligence, which is what? The glory of God. God the Father—you're derivative from Him. He is the Creator or the Organizer—but what He created or organized you from is light and truth.

This ought to become increasingly obvious as you look at what we were reading in section 93. Why is it necessary for you to keep His commandments in order for you to receive truth and light? Why? Why is that the way it works? Why must you keep the commandments if you want to get more of this? Because we're trying to harmonize ourselves with Him. We're trying to get back to Him. We're trying to get ourselves aligned correctly so that when we resonate in the same way that He resonates, we can pick up on things that are not pick-up-able in the absence of that resonance. We're trying to get in harmony with God.

Therefore, what are the commandments? What use are they? He's giving us a blueprint. Some portions of the blueprint may appear altogether ridiculous. We're supposed to do them anyway. And why are we supposed to do the things that may even seem ridiculous anyway? Because at your very core, you know if it comes from Him. You know when you're getting light and truth from Him. There is never a futile act. You know when you pay tithing that you are doing something He asked you to do. And you know what? If it involves a sacrifice, you know all the more by that sacrifice.

This is what Joseph was trying to get across in the Lectures on Faith. Would you like to know God? Then go inconvenience yourself by following what He asks of you, and you will unlock inside yourself resonance with the light and truth of God. It's an unfolding process. It grows.

You got to go back to section 50 for that. Let me find that (which is really also borrowed from the Proverbs):

> *That which is of God is light, and he that receiveth light, and continueth in God, receiveth more light; and that light groweth brighter and brighter until the perfect day.* (D&C 50:24)

Proverbs 4:18 is a similar thought.[114] It's a dynamic process. It involves your interface with God. (You know, we're victims of our time. Another 500 years and the gospel will be perverted by computer terminology.) The way you link up to God—there's computer lingo again—is by this mechanism of obeying the commandments that He's given you. It's never futile, and it's never superfluous. It is how you—as a being, at your core, made of light and truth—know that you're pleasing God.

In the Lectures on Faith, Joseph said you had to know that the sacrifice you are making was pleasing to God.[115] How can you know that? You can know that because, in your core, you have light and truth; that's why I read the quote a few minutes ago. The nearer you come to God and the more obedient you are—the more "heed and diligence" were the words he used in that statement—the more heed and diligence that you give, the more correct your understanding will be.[116] Why is that the case? Because you are enlightened, because you are enlivened, because you are drawing closer to Him.

(By the way, since we're not in church, you can actually get your Scriptures out and read along. I talk in a ward tomorrow as the High Council representative, and it is "prohibito" tomorrow,[117] but today you can get your Scriptures out. Can you hear that annoying rustling of the pages? Because these things aren't made of paper. These pages are made of fabric that's caught in your hearing. It's just annoying. It grieves the spirit and withdraws itself! You know, if we can't laugh at ourselves, there's something really, really wrong with us. If we take ourselves so seriously that we can't look and say that the most comedic thing on earth is a Mormon trying to live his religion, then we missed the point.)

We do not attain to perfection in this life. The visions that we read in Scripture all have a constant theme. The constant theme is: A wretch managed to make it into the presence of God, and then God fixes the wretch. What was the very first thing—not in our current version of the First Vision, but it is in the earlier versions that Joseph wrote—what is the very first thing God does when Joseph is in His presence? He forgives his sins and cleans the mess up. "Joseph, you know, you're a wretch; let's fix that. Okay, now you can endure My presence." Isaiah, in the temple, says,

> *Woe is me! for I am undone; because I am a man of unclean lips, and I dwell in the midst of a people of unclean lips.* (Isaiah 6:5 LE)

Fetch the coal, fix the guy. Coals from the altar, touch to the lips; there! Purged; you're okay.[118] Look, we really are comedic. Our religion promises the fantastic; it promises the perfection of us frail, messed up, insecure human souls. We get hungry; we get thirsty; we get tired. We're vulnerable; we're subject to pain. We're going to ultimately die, every one of us. We have infirmities, and they progress over time. What about us can possibly be perfected? And you look at it and say, "I can't detect a perfectible thing." Oh, wait, there is one thing. You can be perfect in your desire. You can hope for it. And for God, that's enough —as long as you make the kind of sacrifice that He would like to have you make preliminarily. And we're talking about that at this point.

One of the great descriptions of how Christ did what He did—in addition to D&C 93—is in section 20 of the Doctrine and Covenants, beginning at verse 21:

> *Wherefore, the Almighty God gave his Only Begotten Son, as it is written in those scriptures which have been given of him. He suffered temptations but **gave no heed unto them**. He was*

crucified, died, and rose again the third day; And ascended into heaven.... (D&C 20:21-24, emphasis added)

"**He** suffered temptations but gave no **heed** unto them." Turn back to D&C section 130, verse 19, which says,

> *And if a person gains more knowledge and intelligence in this life through his diligence and obedience than another, he will have so much the advantage in the world to come.*

That's what Christ did. Christ gave **no heed** to the things that were pulling him in the one direction, and He gave **strict** heed to the things that were enticing Him to the other direction. And as section 93 explains, He obtained a fullness of that.[119] Therefore, if there is an increasing flow of light and an increasing flow of truth that comes to someone by their heed and diligence in following the commandments, then that seems like a fairly simple formula for someone to follow if they're interested in obtaining further light and knowledge.

There was a time when all of these words crept into our language, and their usage in our common vernacular became popular when everyone simply assumed that we all were in contact with the mystic, with the mythic, and with the forces that were around you. Everyone simply assumed that was the case. There was a way of describing the phenomenon. The way that the ideal was reduced to words was by using the concept of a "third eye." Why that? It was because, physically, your eyes are the source that light gets into you. You perceive light through your eyes. Then, if you're going to collect light from somewhere else, two things are essential. The first thing is you have to realize that it's there, and then you have to be willing to see it. It was a fairly common thing because people weren't as well educated as they are now. They weren't schooled in naturalism and the philosophies of men—which we have so successfully co-mingled with Scripture that we have essentially supplanted, in all of Christendom, the gospel of Christ and replaced it with the doctrines, the precepts, and the creeds of men. (And we're beginning to develop our own set of creeds.)

Why? Well, it's hard to keep the commandments. It involves inconvenience and sacrifice. It's hard. For some folks, in a trial and error kind of way, it's like riding a bicycle. When you start riding a bicycle, you get bloodied elbows and bloodied knees, and you make mistakes, and it's unhappy. But you know what? You can write a Ph.D. thesis on riding a bicycle without ever getting on a bike or ever suffering an injury. Isn't that interesting? Because that's essentially the trade-off that we've made. That's the trade-off that Christendom made, and that's the trade-off that is rapidly, rapidly advancing right now for the Restoration.

Why would Satan ever change his agenda? Why would he ever invent a new tool if the old one works perfectly well? If I can use the sexual appetite of men to destroy a David, well, why not just bust that thing out all the time and aim it at whoever happens to promiscuously[120] get in front of me? In any event, why invent a new way of corrupting the truth when the old way has been so entirely serviceable?

When the Jews returned from the discipline of Babylon, they learned the wrong lesson. They became sophisticates in the Babylonian system of thought—which, as Lehi would tell us, was necessary because they were the only people that would kill their God,[121] and they had to be in the right frame of mind. That is, they had to be screwed up in order to be willing to kill their God, because no one else would do it.

It takes a lot of learning to really be in hell, because the gospel of Christ beckons people to become childlike and to become simple. That's not to say the gospel is simplistic. The gospel comprehends all truth, and it involves light, and it involves everything that was, everything that is, and everything that will be.[122] There are enormous surprises along the way. The gospel of Christ ought to be a delightful process of discovering new things all the time.

There was a time when people understood the idea that you could take in light. It was possible to tune in and to receive information. This information was so readily available that you just had to be sensitized to the awareness of its existence and the willingness to look into the matter for you to begin receiving it. This was whether you were Lutheran, Calvinist, or involved in folk magic. In fact, folk magic largely grew out of the idea that you can tune into these things.

This has been a war that has been waged (and waged successfully). Indeed, it's my own people that did it, my ancestors of the Scottish Enlightenment. They won—David Hume and the gang—and whether you know it or not, your minds are full of that crap. Joseph Smith was carefully selected at the time that he came (at the end of one epoch), and the American Revolution was a war fought against some of that emerging belief system. We wanted to preserve an island, a place where you could still be in touch with the deity and be free to accept and receive things from the deity. There were more things in play at the time of the American Revolution than simply a new form of representative government. It was trying to preserve an ideal that was rapidly fading, to allow an environment in which people could continue to be in touch with God—however you envisioned your God to be—because there were things available that, if you would let them in, would speak to you (if you were willing to see them).

Why does a mother suddenly know that her child is in danger at the edge of the camp, with her back turned, and drops everything and runs and catches her child before he or she falls in the creek? We've all read stories about intuition. (Or is it PMS? Somehow it's ovarian. We tend to reduce that to the biological function now.) But, there was a time when everyone accepted the fact that was sight, that was vision, and that was light. She saw it. She envisioned it.

You do fall down and scuff your elbows and your knees when you learn to ride a bike. But when you finally master it, it's the closest thing you will do to flight other than flying. I don't even think an airplane feels like flight as much as riding a bicycle does. (I'm so converted to the principle that I own four Harleys, and I fly about on them. That flight has cost me a few tickets.)

You can talk about bicycles, you can build them, you can repair them, and you can have discourses on them without ever having experienced a bike. What the schoolmen are trying to do is change the subject. The subject ceases to be that sensation, that wonderment, that childlike experience of getting in the seat and running down the road and leaning as you propel yourself under your own strength into something that nearly replicates flight itself. The schoolmen change that into something that can be controlled with "bona fides." We can credential it and give you a Bachelors of Bicycledom, and we can give you a Masters of Derailleurs (now we are getting even more specialized because it's not simply the bicycle as one component—at the Masters level, we're talking derailleurs). And if you'd like to go on to and graduate up to axles, well, that's a Ph.D.

And so, we never encounter the vision. We can fill libraries up with crap talking about it and never do it. And the gospel which Christ delivered (and the thing Joseph was trying to describe for us) was the **doing** of it.

There is another analogy which I like a lot. It's an analogy I borrow from John Larsen, and it's not original with me. He likens this process to the launchpad that's built down at Cape Canaveral, Florida, where we have this enormous infrastructure, and it's all kept and preserved and polished. But if you never fly anything out of it, then all you've got is a launchpad. The gospel of Christ was designed to be a launch pad. One of the unfortunate things about launching is you melt a bunch of stuff, and you make a mess. I mean, anytime you fire one off, it gets kind of ugly at that place of light and heat for a while.

Of all things we Mormons would like to be, it is orderly, punctual, and uniform. We would hate to have a mess, chaos, or a disaster. We all remember Hiram Page, right? We got a section in the Doctrine and Covenants about Page.[123] He's the guy with a peep stone (the seer stone) that got rebuked for having visions because they came from the wrong place. **We learned the wrong lesson from that!** The lesson from that is not that Hiram Page got misled and had a false revelation using a peep stone that gave him bad information. The message from that is spirits were afoot. Now, let's weed them out; let's figure out which ones are bad and which ones are good But let's stay in touch with them. Let's keep the dialogue going. Take that stone and take a hammer to it. Go find some others, because as far as I know, Hiram Page is the only one other than Joseph in this dispensation who claimed to have contemporaneous revelation using a seer stone (although I'm sure there were others, they aren't published). The whole idea of crystal-ball-gazing and the Urim and Thummim—these things are traditions. Their echoes are found everywhere, and they're based upon the truth.

Look at the last sentence of Ether chapter 4, verse 11:

For because of my Spirit he shall know that these things are true; for it persuadeth men to do good. And whatsoever thing persuadeth men to do good is of me; for good cometh of none save it be of me. I am the same that leadeth men to all good; he that will not believe my words will not believe me—that I am. (Ether 4:11-12 LE)

It's a real simple test: "…he that will not believe my words will not believe me." Did the words you heard originate from God? You should be able to tell that. You should be able to say, sitting and listening, "I hear God in that." Then whoever it is that is speaking—it doesn't matter if she's an elderly widow; it doesn't matter if he's the stake president; it doesn't matter—you have to hear **Him** in the words that come. Then it ceases to be the woman or the man who is standing in front of you, and it becomes the Lord. (As for the speaker, good for the person that they resonated with Him, and they caught on to something.)

Turn back to Moroni chapter 7, verse 16, and it's the same thing: *For behold, the Spirit of Christ is given to every man.* Wow, now there's another thought: the Spirit of Christ given to everyone. You have a link to Christ by virtue of the fact that you're here on Earth.

The Spirit of Christ is given to every man, [in this sense, "man" means mankind; it's not sexist] *that he may know good from evil; wherefore, I show unto you the way to judge; for every thing which inviteth to do good, and to persuade to believe in Christ, is sent forth by the power and gift of Christ; wherefore ye may know with a perfect knowledge it is of God. But whatsoever thing persuadeth men to do evil, and believe not in Christ, and deny him, and serve not God, then ye may know with a perfect knowledge it is of the devil; for after this manner doth the devil work, for he persuadeth no man to do good, no, not one; neither do his angels; neither do they who subject themselves unto him.* (Moroni 7:16-17 LE)

Satan is so committed to doing evil that he's treacherous even to those who will follow him. He won't support those who say, "I'll follow you Satan if you'll do something for me."

Satan will say, "I'll do it. Come, follow me." If you come follow him, he doesn't support you.

Then you say, "Wait a minute. You said you'd make that bargain?"

And he says, "I'm a liar from the beginning. I'll always tell you what you what to hear because I'm a liar." He is unreliable. He doesn't even support those who follow him. The Book of Mormon makes this point repeatedly with those who, after having followed him and succeeded in bringing others to apostatize, are not sustained by him.[124]

The thing to fear is not the existence of Satan or the fact that you may be deceived—that's a given. Turn on your TV. Do Toyota trucks really get that mileage? You're being deceived every time Wall Street has your attention. The glitter, the glitz, and the garbage they're trying to sell you. If you love your family, you'll buy some wretched piece of trinkery from someone somewhere, because they know you like families. If you love your wife, you'll do some hopelessly pathetic physical acquisition and make an offering to the goddess, and then she'll be pleased. It just doesn't work that way! Because if you come bearing rings and trinkets and you're a jerk, she's going to see right through the rings and the trinkets to the jerk. They're not fooled. Hollywood says, "Hey! Trick them this way, and you know, we've got Viagra for the elderly. It could work out."

It's not difficult—as Moroni points out both in his interlude in Ether, and then again in chapter 7 of Moroni[125]—it's not difficult to tell the difference. It's really not. "Satan deceived me! Well, why did he deceive me? Well, he deceived me primarily because I wanted to be deceived. I knew it was a crappy deal. I knew what I was up to was no good. I had this nagging feeling at my core (because I am, after all, made of light and truth) that something was wrong with this. But I did it anyway." How many times do the primary antagonists of the Book of Mormon —when they're caught, and they're not supported by Satan, and they collapse at the last day—how many times do they confess, "Yeah, I knew all along I was deceived. I knew all along it was wrong, but I did it. I taught it. I preached it, I participated in it, I urged it. I knew it was a lie, but I nearly believed it myself because I had success at it. It looked good, it felt good, it was fun."[126]

There is nothing more fun however than gathering light and truth. We're sent down here on a journey in which we are supposed to be getting "added upon."[127] Those are the words. That was the goal. We're going to send people down to the second estate, and what's the goal? The goal is to be added upon. But what are we adding? What are you adding to yourself that you didn't have before? You're adding light and truth. You came with a certain amount of it. You're supposed to leave with a greater quantity of it.

There is the description of Christ given in verse 11 of section 93: *And I, John, bear record that I beheld his glory, as the glory of the Only Begotten of the Father.*

You're just going to have to do your best with this. We've got this accepted and wrong idea that God the Father and his unnamed Consort—Mrs. God the Father—had a Son, and we know Him as Jesus or Jehovah. Then, They had another son (or sons) and some others, and we got a Lucifer, then some others—these are called sons of the morning. Then we assume there is this birth order, and eventually, we get down to the rabble that we were among. That picture is this linear development of the family of God.

If you read very carefully what we find in section 93, there's another picture. That picture is that you have this group (imagine all these are little stick figures because I don't have the time to draw them) you have them all, and...

Oh—I think I can read you something on this from Alma chapter 13:

> And this is the manner after which they were ordained—being called and prepared from the foundation of the world according to the foreknowledge of God, on account of their exceeding faith and good works; in the first place being left to choose good or evil; therefore they having chosen good, and exercising exceedingly great faith, are called with a holy calling....Or in fine, **in the first place** they were on the same standing with their brethren. (Alma 13:3,5 LE, emphasis added)

Let's change that picture, and let's say that instead of this [linear development], everyone "in the first place" was just alike. Everyone had the same potential. Everyone had the same light and truth; everyone was made of that. Everyone began just like one another.

Where did the birth order come from? Where did Christ come from? Let's read D&C 93, beginning at verse 11. This is John being quoted here in the revelation. (I'm starting at verse 11, but we'll back up in a minute.)

> *And I, John, bear record that I beheld his glory, as the glory of the Only Begotten of the Father, full of grace and truth, even the Spirit of truth, which came and dwelt in the flesh, and dwelt among us.*

This is Him. He came and dwelt here. But I'm talking about the pre-existence.

> *I...saw that he received not of the fulness at the first... And he received not of the fulness at first, but continued from grace to grace, until he received a fulness; And thus he was called the **Son of God**, because he received not of the fulness at the first.* (D&C 93:11-14, emphasis added)

What did He do? One of this group, one of this family, one of this assortment of equally placed people, one of them went from grace to grace until He received a fullness. **He proved** it could be done. **He showed** the way. **He** was called the Only Begotten of the Father. He was called that because **He** embodied the word of God. Would you like to know what God the Father's word was? Look at Him. Look at the "Only Begotten." Did you or I make it without Him? No, we didn't. We didn't make it here without Him. **Christ proved the word of the Father by the things which He did**. As a consequence of Christ doing it, some few others, in turn, were also able to rise up. And they became sons of the morning.

The picture that we get in D&C section 93, coupled with Alma chapter 13, is different than the picture that you sometimes pick out or get described for you. Look at verse 30 of section 93:

> *All truth is independent in that sphere in which God has placed it, to act for itself, as all intelligence also; otherwise there is no existence.*

Did Christ exist? If Christ existed, He had to be free to choose for Himself. This had to be a voluntary act on His part. He had to be willing to receive the light and truth.

Believe it or not, we are still just talking about the same thing. This is just about personal revelation. All of this talk is. And it's about how you receive light and truth—because we're acting out (again) here what we acted out once before, and the process is the same here as the process was there, although here it's coupled with a lot of illusions that are guaranteed to make you progress whether you want to or not. Being added upon is coming.

When you look at the **word of God**, what you're seeing in Christ is the embodiment or the fulfillment of what the Father **said**. When Christ defines Himself in Third Nephi chapter 11, and He tells you who He is in a very brief introduction, He can't tell you who He is without referring to the Father three times: *I have suffered the will of the Father in all things from the beginning* (3 Nephi 11:11 LE), He tells us. He is the word of the Father. He is the embodiment of the things that the Father would like to have for us. So, why do we obey the commandments? Why do we follow the process? Why do **we** want to go from grace to grace, and **how** do we open the third eye to be able to resonate with and receive light and truth into ourselves from the Being who is defined as light and truth?

I read another book just a few days ago. (I've heard that the author has actually written a good book.) I was challenged to read this one, and I was challenged **by** reading it. You can't pick up that title without.... Well, maybe you can. *Odds Are, You're Going to Be Exalted*. The author, Alonzo Gaskill, "…holds a master's degree in theology and a Ph.D. in biblical studies [and] he works as an assistant professor of Church history and doctrine at BYU."[128] He has credentials. I was actually going to leave him alone, but I heard him on the radio a couple of days ago. And it was the tone in his voice—it was the absolute, resolute, bitter, hostile conviction that "God wouldn't do that!" on the radio that just struck me, that convinced me I don't want to talk to the man. But in any event, here's a quote from his book:

> The thought that God would promote something that would ensure that the vast majority of His children would never again be able to dwell in His presence is **incomprehensible**. And the assumption that our mother in heaven would idly sit back and allow such a guaranteed flop to eternally strip her of any

interaction with her spirit offspring is equally unfathomable. Such could not—and did not—happen![129]

I couldn't contain myself, and I wrote, **Why?** Nature tells us that of all the male turtles that are born, precious few of them are ever going to survive long enough to reproduce. Of all the bull elk that are born, precious few of them are going to survive long enough to ever reproduce.

Gaskill's made the cataclysmic leap of presuming that all children who die under the age of eight are promised something other than the Celestial kingdom,[130] which is what the Scriptures say that they are promised (they inherit the Celestial kingdom).[131] He's leapt to exaltation, which is a different kind of life within the Celestial kingdom. He does some math calculations based upon the Millennium, based upon the number of children which infant mortality rates tells us will die before the age of eight, the city of Enoch, and people who are unaccountable because they are mentally impaired—which I presume would include most of the faculty of many of our learned universities—and this all equals, in his computation,[132] that the odds are you're going to be exalted. The problem is none of us fit in the category of those who Gaskill is exalting:

- You've lived beyond the age of eight (except the kids that aren't listening).

- I was going to say you're not retarded—I need to at least hesitate on that point. I don't think you're mentally-impaired, although some of us are.

- You don't live during the Millennium

- You weren't in the city of Enoch, and

- You're not part of the Nephite centuries and the post-visitation by Christ.

Odds are you're going to be exalted: Peddle that to children under eight, and peddle it during the Millennium, so then maybe you have a relevant audience. But the audience to which this is directed is you. And he's trying to tell you that this isn't hard when everything that the

Savior said implies very strongly that this is hard, and that few there be that make it,[133] and that it's designed just like nature is designed: to start with a lot and end up with a few.

The lessons of nature tell us that you will start with a lot, and you will end up with a few—just like this overly generous outpouring of priesthood ordinations to anyone who is twelve-years-old or older who happens to be baptized in the Church results in just the most promiscuous series of priesthood certificates of any dispensation ever. But then we read,

> *Behold, there are many called, but few are [then] chosen. And why are they not chosen? Because their hearts are set so much upon the things of this world, and aspire to the honors of men, that they do not learn this one lesson—That the rights of the priesthood are inseparably connected with the powers of heaven, and that the powers of heaven cannot be controlled nor handled only upon the principles of righteousness. That they may be conferred upon us, it is true; but when we undertake to cover our sins, or to gratify our pride, our vain ambition, or to exercise control or dominion or compulsion upon the souls of the children of men, in any degree of unrighteousness, behold, the heavens withdraw themselves; the Spirit of the Lord is grieved; and when it is withdrawn, Amen to the priesthood or the authority of that man.* (D&C 121:34-37)

Odds are you are going to be … a priest? "They may be conferred upon us, it is true." But I just read a bunch of limitations.

Odds are you're going to be exalted? You can go to the temple and fetch an ordinance, but unless it's sealed upon you by the Holy Spirit of Promise, all those things are conditional.

The call is to do this. The call is to come down here and be a gatherer of light. It doesn't matter if the process seems so ephemeral, it seems gossamer—that it seems like the web of a spider and so delicate that the blowing of the wind can tear it apart—that's exactly how it's supposed to be. Because you're trying to get in harmony with God. You are trying to gather a substance that proves your existence by your free will choice to accept light and truth. When you do, Joseph said, you could taste the truth.[134] When you do, you can feel the truth. You can sense its presence, you can let it into you, you can resonate with it.

(Boy, we're not going to have the time to get through this stuff. And I have to go buy frozen pinky mice.)

When you go back to D&C 93 and Abraham 3, you learn in the description that's given in Abraham that Christ, acting in the role of the Father, shows all

> ...the [organized] intelligences...that [existed] before the world was; and among all these there were [a subset called] many [that were] noble and great...; And God saw these souls that they were good, and he stood in the midst of them, and he said: These I will make my rulers. (Abraham 3:22-23 LE)

These are the people that are going to teach truth and light. These are the ones that are going to come down and bring to you revelation. These are the ones that are going to shed forth light and truth. They're not administrators.

> These I will make my rulers; for he stood among those that were spirits, and he saw that they were good; and he said unto me: Abraham...

So, we know one of them is like the Son of God, but another one is Abraham.

> Abraham, thou art one of them; thou wast chosen before thou wast born. And there stood one among them that was like unto God...

And that's Christ. Christ stood among them.

> ...and he [Christ] said unto those who were with him:

Christ, talking to "noble and great," He says to them, "We,"

> We will go down [this group], for there is space there, and we will take of these materials, and we will make an earth whereon these may dwell; And we will prove them...to see if they will do all things whatsoever the Lord their God shall command them; And they who keep their first estate... (Ibid. vs. 23-26)

...and so on.

This is from the *Teachings of the Prophet Joseph Smith*, page 375:

> "Now," says God, when He visited Moses in the bush, (Moses was a stammering sort of a boy like me) God said, "Thou shalt be a God unto the children of Israel." God said, "Thou shalt be a God unto Aaron, and he shall be thy spokesman."
>
> I [this is Joseph] believe those Gods that God reveals as Gods to be sons of God, and all can cry, "Abba, Father!" Sons of God who exalt themselves to be Gods, even from before the foundation of the world, and are the only Gods I have a reverence for.

This is Joseph, just in the middle of a talk, saying that there is a group who exalted themselves to be gods even before they were born, and all of them can cry, "Abba, Father!"

Abraham served as the prophet-leader of a little, tiny family. We read about him now and think him a big cheese, but at the time, he led a badly-fractured family and presided over a small group. His apparent one public ministry in Jerusalem resulted in him getting run out of town. From then on, he ministered only inside his own family. Abraham had a fairly interesting career, in a varied climate, and managed to get to sit on Pharaoh's throne because he taught some things about the heavens (and ingratiated himself to Pharaoh, not the least of reason was his wife and her beauty). Abraham went on to lead a relatively private life in a family. And we all call him the father of the righteous.

Christ's largest audience was, in all likelihood, the group He spoke to at the temple in Bountiful **after** His resurrection. In all probability, even in the temple, during His mortal ministry, He didn't have as big an audience as He did at the temple in Bountiful. Perhaps as He hung on the cross, as the crowds were gathering to attend the festivities at the Passover in Jerusalem, more people passed by Him and wagged their tongue at Him in His final state of making the sacrifice, but we don't know that.

The folks who the Scriptures identify as being most clearly "noble and great" are people that really didn't have much more responsibility in life than every one of you have inside your own family. We get filled with covetousness because celebrity-dom has come to Zion. And I mean this in all sincerity—I do not intend to be a celebrity. This is one of the reasons why I don't like talking at these things. Because I think to the extent that you attract attention for yourself, you are missing the mark. The best of us are horribly flawed—the **best** of us are. Anyone that would attract light or distract people for themselves (and take it off of the perfect example that you find in Christ) is a fool. They practice the wrong sort of religion.

We're down here to gather light. Whether you recognize it or not, **you** are a son or a daughter of light. That's what you are. You are down here to gather more of it. The place where you're primarily responsible for presiding and conducting is inside the confines of your own family. That's why Abraham is remembered. That's why Lehi is remembered. For the most part, the public ministry of ancient prophets was met with almost universal failure. Noah saved his own family. You rarely find a prophet or prophetess (and they are in Scripture, as well) who succeeds in their own lifetime.

Christ got it right when He was saying the only words of the prophets that you really respect are the dead ones.[135] And why do you respect the dead ones? Because then the professors of religion can take over, and they can package them and parse them and explain them—or explain them away—without the living oracle there to be able to say, "Not so fast!"

You can take the words of any of them and parlay them into whatever you want them to become. Hence, Joseph's insistence that every one of us become a prophet and prophetess, every one of us get in touch with the things of the spirit, every one of us receive what is out there in the way of light, and welcome it into yourself. Vessels of light—that's what you're supposed to be.

It is very basic, and I think it is, in all likelihood, the case that the first principles and ordinances of the gospel are not the first principles meaning, "the beginning," but they are the first principles meaning, "the primary, the essentials, the ones that must be kept, and the ones that are always in front of you."

- Faith: You have to have faith in the existence of that light and that truth.

- Repentance: Why? Because you're made of light and truth, and if you won't reconcile and resonate with it, you won't welcome it in. You create a barrier to it; it can't be shed into you.

- Faith, repentance, baptism: You're supposed to be doing that every week when you partake of the sacrament—that ordinance which Christ celebrated repeatedly with the Nephites, over and over. He's taking the time to do the sacrament, and we are also supposed to be taking the time to be doing that.

- And then after you have had faith, and after you've repented, and after you've partaken of the sacrament or received baptism, then what happens? You receive the Holy Ghost.

Go to D&C section 130, verse 22:

> *The Father has a body of flesh and bones as tangible as man's; the Son also; but the Holy Ghost has not a body of flesh and bones, but is a personage of Spirit. Were it not so, the Holy Ghost could not **dwell in us**.* (Emphasis added)

Receive the Holy Ghost and let it **dwell** in you. I don't know if the odds are you're going to be exalted or not, but I can tell you that the way in which that will happen—if it does happen—is going to be through your connection with the spirit. It will be unlike the way in which revelation is portrayed in this (the latest offering by the powers that be), as something perverse and something that only the nutcases engage in.

Moroni chapter 7 is a dissertation on all of those things of the spirit, and it says, Hey, *if these things have ceased, then [there is no] faith* (Moroni 7:38 LE), and no one's being saved. And it's just that simple. If it doesn't happen, no one's being saved. You're a child of light; you're a son or a daughter of light; you proceed from the glory of God or the intelligence of God which is light and truth. At your core, what is there is light and truth—but it has been made independent; it gets to choose for itself. Otherwise, there is no existence.

Each of you need to receive the Holy Ghost and to permit it to dwell in you. There are a lot of symbols that get employed in the Scriptures. One of the words that gets employed to describe the Holy Ghost (which should dwell in you) is the third member of the godhead. Would you like to be like your Father in Heaven? Then, receive ye the Holy Ghost. He is as close, He is as intimate, and He is as in connection with you as the very substance out of which you were originally organized. If you would like to be in touch with Him, keep His commandments.

Follow Him. Even if you do your best, you're not going to do a very good job. But the Scriptures talk in terms of your sincerity: those who keep all His commandments or seek earnestly to do so. Even the best of us are doing things wrong that we don't even know are wrong yet because we haven't got that much light and truth yet. We proceed to blunder around in the china shop, breaking the furniture and damaging all of the things that we ought to be holding sacred, and we do it with reckless abandon. And God doesn't care about that, because He hasn't brought us that far up the ladder yet to respect the furniture. He's just trying to get us to stop messing our pants and stop putting graffiti on the walls—if we'll just settle down enough to do that.

The atonement of Christ is a work in progress. He's trying to fix us, and He does that by giving us a little light, and a little more light, and a little more yet—until finally you look back upon yourself from two decades earlier, and you say, "What a wretch was I!" It's a progression in light and truth. You're still a wretch, you're just 20 years away from recognizing it still. Start obeying further and getting more light and truth, and you will be astonished at what it is you're going to become.

Let me end by bearing testimony to you that, in my view, the LDS Church is exactly what it ought to be, staffed exactly as it should be, filled with all you good people, with all of the things that you bring with you to the party. And that this is a perfect environment in which each one of you get the opportunity to work out your own salvation with fear and trembling before the Lord. (And you ought to be afraid. You ought to be fearful because the things that you hold onto in your secret sins are the very things that you ought to be abandoning. The fact that you're holding onto them means you have not yet chosen the light and the truth. You ought to be abandoning that junk, whatever it is.)

We all have our shortcomings. We all have our temptations. We all have our failings. Despite the bundle of insecurities (and there were many in the prophet Joseph Smith), the prophet Joseph Smith met the Lord. Despite the fact that Isaiah was a self-confessed man of unclean lips in the presence of the Lord didn't stop him from entering into the presence of the Lord. The fact that Peter is... Peter is not even a personality. He's a syndrome. He's got pathologies. This Peter, the chief apostle, the rock, the one that the Lord relied upon, the one that He put first and preeminent... And Paul? You have to trust Paul to someone with authority to write prescriptions to deal with him, as a psychologist is insufficient. These people met with the Lord. It is not a distant mountain It is not an insurmountable problem.

Have faith, repent, go and partake of the sacrament. Do so—and I use the word advisedly—do so worthily.

By the way, do you know how to determine if you are worthy or not? You ask the Lord. You don't do as brother Gaskill suggests and simply presume it. You do as Joseph said: After thinking about his native cheery temperament and his inclination towards irreverence, he decided to inquire of the Lord to find out what his standing was. It had been four years since the First Vision, and Joseph wanted to know. Joseph didn't presume. In fact, if he were presuming, he would have presumed to the contrary that he was worthy. "How am I doing, Lord?" And the Lord answered in the form of the angel Moroni.[136]

Don't settle for a book about riding the bike. Don't settle for polishing up the launch pad. It was designed to be set in motion. It was designed to engage you. You're supposed to be part of this. The prophetic history of all that we read needs to come down to and be embodied in you and your life.

You have whole generations of people that went before you, and you have people that are coming after, whose faith—just like our faith in the pre-existence—was stimulated by the word of God embodied in the life of Christ. You have people looking upon you and having faith as a consequence of what you're doing. You're called saviors on Mount Zion not simply because you trek to the temple and you fall asleep during the endowment. You're called that because all of those that went before and all who come after have an investment in your life, in you. **You** are the source of faith. **You** are the source of light for many.

Live your life as if you're on stage because, believe me, you are. There are people who are being redeemed as a consequence of the investment that they have in you. A failing, flagging, despondent ancestor is being buoyed up by the example you set. You have no private moments, and you have no private sins, so stop holding onto them. For goodness sake, they're not only being shouted on the rooftops in the day of judgment, they're being shouted on the rooftops right now. This is only the illusion of privacy. Everything you do is on display, which is why it is so important that you be one who gathers light and truth. You be one who is open to receiving these things, which God offers liberally. (Liberally—however perverse that may be in political terms in Utah— that's a descriptor of God. He spends money like a Democrat with the federal budget when it comes to giving you light and truth. God giveth liberally. Deficit spending does not matter.)

He gives liberally, so where's the impediment? The impediment is we lack the faith to bring ourselves into harmony with perfect perpendicularity to the Earth (because as long as you're in sympathy with the Earth, you're out of sync with Heaven). You have to get perpendicular to it. You have to draw a line between you and it. That's one of the reasons why we have gravity. That's one of the symbols that God gave us in this life. If you can walk, you're walking around teaching a lesson (about getting in harmony with God) to yourself. All things testify of Christ. They all do.

And I bear testimony of Him in His name, Amen.

---

80   See D&C 138:55-56.
81   See Abraham 3:22-23 LE.
82   Think of the meaning of "guide," as in a "ruler" is a guide to follow— like a 12-inch ruler lets you measure length or draw a straight line up to 12 inches in length.
83   See 1 Nephi 2:22, 16:37, and 2 Nephi 5:19, all LE.

84   Hugh B. Brown, "The Profile of a Prophet," reprinted in *"Praise to the Man": Fifteen Classic BYU Devotionals about the Prophet Joseph Smith* (Provo: Brigham Young University, 2005), 59-69; also excerpt reprinted in *Ensign*, June 2006 (speech given at Brigham Young University, October 4, 1955).

85   See Acts 17:16-34 LE.

86   Ronald W. Walker, Richard E. Turley, Jr., & Glen M. Leonard, *Massacre at Mountain Meadows* (New York: Oxford University Press, 2008).

87   *Ibid.* p. 233.

88   *Ibid.* pp. 233-241.

89   *Ibid.* pp. 234-235.

90   *Ibid.* pp. 235-236.

91   *Ibid.* p. 234.

92   *Ibid.* p. 236.

93   *Ibid.* p. 237.

94   *Ibid.* p. 60.

95   *Ibid.* p. 66.

96   "Willard Richards' Remarkable Escape. Dr. Richards' escape was miraculous; he being a very large man, and in the midst of a shower of balls, yet he stood unscathed, with the exception of a ball which grazed the tip end of the lower part of his left ear. His escape fulfilled literally a prophecy which Joseph made over a year previously, that the time would come that the balls would fly around him like hail, and he should see his friends fall on the right and on the left, but that there should not be a hole in his garment" (*History of the Church*, vol. 6, p. 619). "Elder John Taylor confirmed the saying that Joseph and Hyrum and himself were without their robes in the jail at Carthage, while Doctor Richards had his on, but corrected the idea that some had, that they had taken them off through fear. W. W. Phelps said Joseph told him one day about that time, that he had laid aside his garment on account of the hot weather" (William Clayton, *An Intimate Chronicle: The Journals of William Clayton* [Salt Lake City: Signature Books, 1995], p. 222). "This garment protects from disease, and even death, for the bullet of an enemy will not penetrate it. The Prophet Joseph carelessly left off this garment on the day of his death, and had he not done so, he would have escaped unharmed" (Hubert Howe Bancroft, *History of Utah* [San Francisco: History Company, 1890], p. 357 fn.17).

97   *Massacre at Mountain Meadows*, p. 172.

98   *Ibid.* p. ix.

99   *Ibid.* p. 181, see also p. 135.

100   *Ibid.* pp. 187, 189.

101   Hugh Nibley, *Eloquent Witness: Nibley on Himself, Others, and the Temple* (Salt Lake City: Deseret Book, 2008), p. iv.

102   *Ibid.* p. 87, emphasis in original. From an interview on November 11, 1983.

103   *Ibid.* pp. 115-116, 250-251, 370-372.

104   *Ibid.* p. 127. From an open letter addressed to a BYU graduate student, dated July 29, 1960.

105   *Ibid.*, emphasis in original.
106   *Ibid.* p. 129, emphasis in original.
107   "John W. Welch" is acknowledged twice: *Ibid.* p. ii ("general editor") and p. xvi (Foreword).
108   Michael Lewis, *Moneyball: The Art of Winning an Unfair Game* (New York: Norton, 2003).
109   "God hath not revealed anything to Joseph, but what He will make known unto the Twelve, and even the least Saint may know all things as fast as he is able to bear them" (*TPJS*, p. 149).
110   "Revelation" in *Encyclopedia of Mormonism* (1992), vol. 3, pp. 1225-1228.
111   John Hollenhorst, "Religious Cult That Inspired Tragedy Re-emerging in Salt Lake," *KSL.com*, Aug. 15, 2008, https://www.ksl.com/article/4017237/religious-cult-that-inspired-tragedy-re-emerging-in-salt-lake
112   Ibid.
113   *TPJS*, p. 51.
114   "But the path of the just is as the shining light, that shineth more and more unto the perfect day" (Proverbs 4:18 LE).
115   See Lectures on Faith 6.
116   See Alma 12:9-11 LE.
117   Shortly before this talk, a letter from the LDS First Presidency discouraged the faithful from opening Scriptures during sacrament meetings because of the distracting noise it made.
118   See Isaiah 6:6-7 LE.
119   See D&C 93:2-6,12-14,16-17,26.
120   In that context, the word means "randomly," and it was a pun. But if you have to explain humor, it isn't really funny.
121   See 2 Nephi 10:3 LE.
122   See D&C 93:24.
123   See D&C 28.
124   See Alma 30:60 LE.
125   See Ether 12:6-41; Moroni 7:15-19 LE.
126   See Alma 30:52-53 LE.
127   See Abraham 3:26 LE.
128   Alonzo L. Gaskill, *Odds Are, You're Going to Be Exalted* (Salt Lake City: Deseret Book, 2008), book jacket back flap.
129   *Ibid.* p. 17, emphasis added.
130   *Ibid.* pp. 25-32.
131   See D&C 137:10.
132   *Odds Are, You're Going to Be Exalted*, pp. 15-40.
133   See Matthew 7:14; 3 Nephi 14:4; 27:33; D&C 132:22, all LE.
134   See *TPJS*, p. 355.
135   See Matthew 23:29-35 LE.
136   See Joseph Smith-History 1:28-30 LE.

Milton Keynes UK
Ingram Content Group UK Ltd.
UKHW021955111023
430424UK00006B/89